ABOUT THIS PUBLICATION

FOR SERVICE ASSISTANCE

Customer Service
1.704.898.0770

North Carolina General Statues is published by The Muliti-Media Group of Greater Charlotte in Charlotte, North Carolina. Copyright 2015 by the Multi-Media Group of Greater Charlotte. This book or parts thereof may not be reproduced in any form, stored in a retrieval system, or transmitted in any form by any means—electronic, mechanical, photocopy, recording or otherwise—without prior written permission of the publisher, except as provided by United States of America copyright law.

The records required by U.S. Code 2257(a) through (c) and the pertinent regulations 28 C.F.R. Cli. 1, Part 75 with respect to this publication and all materials associated with such records are maintained by The Multi-Media Group of Greater Charlotte, Publisher and available for review by Attorney General.

www.visionbooks.org

Copyright © 2015 by MMGGC
All rights reserved!

TID: 5061697
ISBN (10) digit: 1502915146
ISBN (13) digit: 978-1502915146

123-4-56789-01239-Paperback
123-4-56789-01239-Hardback

First Edition

090520140547

Printed in the United States of America

2015 EDITION

North Carolina Criminal Law And Procedure-Pamphlet # 47

Printed In conjunction with the Administration of the Courts

North Carolina Criminal Law and Procedure
Pamphlet Reference Guide

Chapters	Pamphlet
Chapter 1 Civil Procedure	1
Chapter 1 Civil Procedure (Continue)	2
Chapter 1A Rules of Civil Procedure	2
Chapter 1B Contribution.	2
Chapter 1C Enforcement of Judgments.	2
Chapter 1D Punitive Damages.	2
Chapter 1E Eastern Band of Cherokee Indians.	2
Chapter 1F North Carolina Uniform Interstate Depositions and Discovery Act.	2
Chapter 2 - Clerk of Superior Court [Repealed and Transferred.]	3
Chapter 3 - Commissioners of Affidavits and Deeds [Repealed.]	3
Chapter 4 - Common Law	3
Chapter 5 - Contempt [Repealed.]	3
Chapter 5A - Contempt	3
Chapter 6 - Liability for Court Costs	3
Chapter 7 - Courts [Repealed and Transferred.]	3
Chapter 7A – Judicial Department	3
Chapter 7A – Continuation (Judicial Department)	4
Chapter 7A – Continuation (Judicial Department)	5
Chapter 7B - Juvenile Code	5
Chapter 8 - Evidence	6
Chapter 8A - Interpreters for Deaf Persons [Recodified.]	6
Chapter 8B - Interpreters for Deaf Persons	6
Chapter 8C - Evidence Code	6
Chapter 9 - Jurors	6
Chapter 10 - Notaries [Repealed.]	6
Chapter 10A - Notaries [Recodified.]	6
Chapter 10B - Notaries	6
Chapter 11 - Oaths	6
Chapter 12 - Statutory Construction	6
Chapter 13 - Citizenship Restored	6
Chapter 14 - Criminal Law	7
Chapter 14 –Criminal Law (Continuation)	8
Chapter 15 - Criminal Procedure	9
Chapter 15A - Criminal Procedure Act (Continuation)	10
Chapter 15A - Criminal Procedure Act (Continuation)	11
Chapter 15B - Victims Compensation	11
Chapter 15C - Address Confidentiality Program	11
Chapter 16 - Gaming Contracts and Futures	11
Chapter 17 - Habeas Corpus	11

Chapter 17A - Law-Enforcement Officers [Recodified.]	11
Chapter 17B - North Carolina Criminal Justice Education and Training System [Recodified.] Chapter 17C - North Carolina Criminal Justice Education and Training Standards Commission	11
	11
Chapter 17D - North Carolina Justice Academy	11
Chapter 17E - North Carolina Sheriffs' Education and Training Standards Commission	11
Chapter 18 - Regulation of Intoxicating Liquors [Repealed.]	12
Chapter 18A - Regulation of Intoxicating Liquors [Repealed.]	12
Chapter 18B - Regulation of Alcoholic Beverages	12
Chapter 18C - North Carolina State Lottery	12
Chapter 19 - Offenses against Public Morals	12
Chapter 19A - Protection of Animals	12
Chapter 20 - Motor Vehicles	13
Chapter 20 - Motor Vehicles (Continuation)	14
Chapter 20 - Motor Vehicles (Continuation)	15
Chapter 20 - Motor Vehicles (Continuation)	16
Chapter 21 - Bills of Lading	17
Chapter 22 - Contracts Requiring Writing	17
Chapter 22A - Signatures	17
Chapter 22B - Contracts Against Public Policy	17
Chapter 22C - Payments to Subcontractors	17
Chapter 23 - Debtor and Creditor	17
Chapter 24 – Interest	17
Chapter 25 – Uniform Commercial Code	18
Chapter 25 – Uniform Commercial Code (Continuation)	19
Chapter 25A – Retail Installment Sales Act	20
Chapter 25B - Credit	20
Chapter 25C - Sales of Artwork	20
Chapter 26 - Suretyship	20
Chapter 27 - Warehouse Receipts [Repealed.]	20
Chapter 28 - Administration [Repealed.]	20
Chapter 28A - Administration of Decedents' Estates	20
Chapter 28B - Estates of Absentees in Military Service	20
Chapter 28C - Estates of Missing Persons	20
Chapter 29 - Intestate Succession	21
Chapter 30 - Surviving Spouses	21
Chapter 31 - Wills	21
Chapter 31A - Acts Barring Property Rights	21
Chapter 31B - Renunciation of Property and Renunciation of Fiduciary Powers Act	21
Chapter 31C - Uniform Disposition of Community Property Rights at Death Act	21
Chapter 32 - Fiduciaries	21
Chapter 32A - Powers of Attorney	21
Chapter 33 - Guardian and Ward [Repealed and Recodified.]	21

Chapter 33A - North Carolina Uniform Transfers to Minors Act	21
Chapter 33B - North Carolina Uniform Custodial Trust Act	21
Chapter 34 - Veterans' Guardianship Act	22
Chapter 35 - Sterilization Procedures	22
Chapter 35A - Incompetency and Guardianship	22
Chapter 36 - Trusts and Trustees [Repealed.]	22
Chapter 36A - Trusts and Trustees	22
Chapter 36B - Uniform Management of Institutional Funds Act [Repealed.]	22
Chapter 36C - North Carolina Uniform Trust Code	22
Chapter 36D - North Carolina Community Third Party Trusts, Pooled Trusts	23
Chapter 36E - Uniform Prudent Management of Institutional Funds Act	23
Chapter 37 - Allocation of Principal and Income [Repealed.]	23
Chapter 37A - Uniform Principal and Income Act	23
Chapter 38 - Boundaries	23
Chapter 38A - Landowner Liability	23
Chapter 39 - Conveyances	23
Chapter 39A - Transfer Fee Covenants Prohibited	23
Chapter 40 - Eminent Domain [Repealed.]	23
Chapter 40A - Eminent Domain	23
Chapter 41 - Estates	23
Chapter 41A - State Fair Housing Act	23
Chapter 42 - Landlord and Tenant	23
Chapter 42A - Vacation Rental Act	23
Chapter 43 - Land Registration	23
Chapter 44 - Liens	24
Chapter 44A - Statutory Liens and Charges	24
Chapter 45 - Mortgages and Deeds of Trust	24
Chapter 45A - Good Funds Settlement Act	24
Chapter 46 - Partition	24
Chapter 47 - Probate and Registration	25
Chapter 47A - Unit Ownership	25
Chapter 47B - Real Property Marketable Title Act	25
Chapter 47C - North Carolina Condominium Act	25
Chapter 47D - Notice of Settlement Act [Expired.]	25
Chapter 47E - Residential Property Disclosure Act	25
Chapter 47F - North Carolina Planned Community Act	25
Chapter 47G - Option to Purchase Contracts	25
Chapter 47H - Contracts for Deed	25
Chapter 48 - Adoptions +	26
Chapter 48A - Minors	26
Chapter 49 - Bastardy	26
Chapter 49A - Rights of Children	26
Chapter 50 - Divorce and Alimony	26
Chapter 50A - Uniform Child-Custody Jurisdiction and	

Enforcement Act	26
Chapter 50B - Domestic Violence	26
Chapter 50C - Civil No-Contact Orders	26
Chapter 51 - Marriage	26
Chapter 52 - Powers and Liabilities of Married Persons	27
Chapter 52A - Uniform Reciprocal Enforcement of Support Act [Repealed.]	27
Chapter 52B - Uniform Premarital Agreement Act	27
Chapter 52C - Uniform Interstate Family Support Act	27
Chapter 53 - Banks	27
Chapter 53A - Business Development Corporations and North Carolina Capital Resource Corporations	28
Chapter 53B - Financial Privacy Act	28
Chapter 54 - Cooperative Organizations	28
Chapter 54A - Capital Stock Savings and Loan Associations [Repealed.]	28
Chapter 54B - Savings and Loan Associations	29
Chapter 54C - Savings Banks	29
Chapter 55 - North Carolina Business Corporation Act	30
Chapter 55A - North Carolina Nonprofit Corporation Act	31
Chapter 55B - Professional Corporation Act	31
Chapter 55C - Foreign Trade Zones	31
Chapter 55D - Filings, Names, and Registered Agents for Corporations, Nonprofit Corporations, and Partnerships	31
Chapter 56 - Electric, Telegraph and Power Companies [Repealed.]	31
Chapter 57 - Hospital, Medical and Dental Service Corporations [Recodified.]	31
Chapter 57A - Health Maintenance Organization Act [Recodified.]	31
Chapter 57B - Health Maintenance Organization Act [Recodified.]	31
Chapter 57C - North Carolina Limited Liability Company Act.	31
Chapter 58 - Insurance.	32
Chapter 58 - Insurance (Continuation)	33
Chapter 58 - Insurance (Continuation)	34
Chapter 58 - Insurance (Continuation)	35
Chapter 58 - Insurance (Continuation)	36
Chapter 58 - Insurance (Continuation)	37
Chapter 58 - Insurance (Continuation)	38
Chapter 58A - North Carolina Health Insurance Trust Commission [Recodified.]	38
Chapter 59 - Partnership.	39
Chapter 59B - Uniform Unincorporated Nonprofit Association Act.	39
Chapter 60 - Railroads and Other Carriers [Repealed and Transferred.]	39
Chapter 61 - Religious Societies	39
Chapter 62 - Public Utilities	39

Chapter 62 - Public Utilities (Continuation)	40
Chapter 62A - Public Safety Telephone Service And Wireless Telephone Service	40
Chapter 63 - Aeronautics	40
Chapter 63A - North Carolina Global TransPark Authority	40
Chapter 64 - Aliens	40
Chapter 65 – Cemeteries	40
Chapter 66 - Commerce and Business	41
Chapter 67 - Dogs	41
Chapter 68 - Fences and Stock Law	41
Chapter 69 - Fire Protection	41
Chapter 70 - Indian Antiquities, Archaeological Resources and Unmarked Human Skeletal Remains Protection	42
Chapter 71 - Indians [Repealed.]	42
Chapter 71A - Indians	42
Chapter 72 - Inns, Hotels and Restaurants	42
Chapter 73 - Mills	42
Chapter 74 - Mines and Quarries	42
Chapter 74A - Company Police [Repealed.]	42
Chapter 74B - Private Protective Services Act [Repealed.]	42
Chapter 74C - Private Protective Services	42
Chapter 74D - Alarm Systems	42
Chapter 74E - Company Police Act	42
Chapter 74F - Locksmith Licensing Act	42
Chapter 74G - Campus Police Act	42
Chapter 75 - Monopolies, Trusts and Consumer Protection	42
Chapter 75A - Boating and Water Safety	43
Chapter 75B - Discrimination in Business	43
Chapter 75C - Motion Picture Fair Competition Act	43
Chapter 75D - Racketeer Influenced and Corrupt Organizations	43
Chapter 75E - Unlawful Activities in Connection With Certain Corporate Transactions	43
Chapter 76 - Navigation	43
Chapter 76A - Navigation and Pilotage Commissions	43
Chapter 77 - Rivers, Creeks, and Coastal Waters	43
Chapter 78 - Securities Law [Repealed.]	43
Chapter 78A - North Carolina Securities Act	43
Chapter 78B - Tender Offer Disclosure Act [Repealed.]	43
Chapter 78C - Investment Advisers	43
Chapter 78D - Commodities Act	43
Chapter 79 - Strays [Repealed.]	43
Chapter 80 - Trademarks, Brands, etc.	44
Chapter 81 - Weights and Measures [Recodified.]	44
Chapter 81A - Weights and Measures Act of 1975.	44
Chapter 82 - Wrecks [Repealed.]	44
Chapter 83 - Architects [Recodified.]	44

Chapter 83A - Architects	44
Chapter 84 - Attorneys-at-Law	44
Chapter 84A - Foreign Legal Consultants	44
Chapter 85 - Auctions and Auctioneers [Repealed.]	44
Chapter 85A - Bail Bondsmen and Runners [Recodified.]	44
Chapter 85B - Auctions and Auctioneers	44
Chapter 85C - Bail Bondsmen and Runners [Recodified.]	44
Chapter 86 - Barbers [Recodified.]	44
Chapter 86A - Barbers	44
Chapter 87 - Contractors	44
Chapter 88 - Cosmetic Art [Repealed.]	44
Chapter 88A - Electrolysis Practice Act	44
Chapter 88B - Cosmetic Art	45
Chapter 89 - Engineering and Land Surveying [Recodified.]	45
Chapter 89A - Landscape Architects	45
Chapter 89B - Foresters	45
Chapter 89C - Engineering and Land Surveying	45
Chapter 89D - Landscape Contractors	45
Chapter 89E - Geologists Licensing Act	45
Chapter 89F - North Carolina Soil Scientist Licensing Act	45
Chapter 89G - Irrigation Contractors	45
Chapter 90 - Medicine and Allied Occupations	45
Chapter 90 - Medicine and Allied Occupations (Continuation)	46
Chapter 90 - Medicine and Allied Occupations (Continuation)	47
Chapter 90 - Medicine and Allied Occupations (Continuation)	48
Chapter 90A - Sanitarians and Water and Wastewater Treatment Facility Operators	48
Chapter 90B - Social Worker Certification and Licensure Act	48
Chapter 90C - North Carolina Recreational Therapy Licensure Act	48
Chapter 90D - Interpreters and Transliterators	48
Chapter 91 - Pawnbrokers [Repealed.]	48
Chapter 91A - Pawnbrokers Modernization Act of 1989	48
Chapter 92 - Photographers [Deleted.]	48
Chapter 93 - Certified Public Accountants	48
Chapter 93A - Real Estate License Law	49
Chapter 93B - Occupational Licensing Boards	49
Chapter 93C - Watchmakers [Repealed.]	49
Chapter 93D - North Carolina State Hearing Aid Dealers and Fitters Board.	49
Chapter 93E - North Carolina Appraisers Act	49
Chapter 94 - Apprenticeship	49
Chapter 95 - Department of Labor and Labor Regulations	49
Chapter 95 - Department of Labor and Labor Regulations (Continuation)	50
Chapter 96 - Employment Security	50
Chapter 97 - Workers' Compensation Act	50
Chapter 97 - Workers' Compensation Act (Continuation)	51

Chapter 98 - Burnt and Lost Records	51
Chapter 99 - Libel and Slander	51
Chapter 99A - Civil Remedies for Criminal Actions	51
Chapter 99B - Products Liability	51
Chapter 99C - Actions Relating to Winter Sports Safety and Accidents	51
Chapter 99D - Civil Rights	51
Chapter 99E - Special Liability Provisions	51
Chapter 100 - Monuments, Memorials and Parks	51
Chapter 101 - Names of Persons	51
Chapter 102 - Official Survey Base	51
Chapter 103 - Sundays, Holidays and Special Days	51
Chapter 104 - United States Lands	51
Chapter 104A - Degrees of Kinship	51
Chapter 104B - Hurricanes or Other Acts of Nature	51
Chapter 104C - Atomic Energy, Radioactivity and Ionizing Radiation [Repealed and Recodified.]	51
Chapter 104D - Southern States Energy Compact	51
Chapter 104E - North Carolina Radiation Protection Act	51
Chapter 104F - Southeast Interstate Low-Level Radioactive Waste Management Compact [Repealed]	51
Chapter 104G - North Carolina Low-Level Radioactive Waste Management Authority Act of 1987 [Repealed]	51
Chapter 105 - Taxation	51
Chapter 105 - Taxation (Continuation)	52
Chapter 105 - Taxation (Continuation)	53
Chapter 105 - Taxation (Continuation)	54
Chapter 105A - Setoff Debt Collection Act	55
Chapter 105B - Defaulted Student Loan Recovery Act	55
Chapter 106 - Agriculture	55
Chapter 106 - Agriculture (Continue)	56
Chapter 106 - Agriculture (Continue)	57
Chapter 107 - Agricultural Development Districts [Repealed.]	57
Chapter 108 - Social Services [Repealed and Recodified.]	57
Chapter 108A - Social Services	57
Chapter 108B - Community Action Programs	58
Chapter 108C Medicaid and Health Choice Provider Requirements.	58
Chapter 108D Medicaid Managed Care for Behavioral Health Services.	58
Chapter 109 - Bonds [Recodified.]	58
Chapter 110 - Child Welfare	58
Chapter 111 - Aid to the Blind	58
Chapter 112 - Confederate Homes and Pensions [Repealed.]	58
Chapter 113 - Conservation and Development	58
Chapter 113 - Conservation and Development (Continuation)	59

Chapter 113A - Pollution Control and Environment	59
Chapter 113A - Pollution Control and Environment (Continuation)	60
Chapter 113B - North Carolina Energy Policy Act of 1975	60
Chapter 114 - Department of Justice	60
Chapter 115 - Elementary and Secondary Education [Repealed.]	60
Chapter 115A - Community Colleges, Technical Institutes, and Industrial Education Centers [Repealed.]	60
Chapter 115B - Tuition and Fee Waivers	60
Chapter 115C - Elementary and Secondary Education	60
Chapter 115C - Elementary and Secondary Education (Continuation)	61
Chapter 115C - Elementary and Secondary Education (Continuation)	62
Chapter 115C - Elementary and Secondary Education (Continuation)	63
Chapter 115D - Community Colleges	63
Chapter 115E - Private Educational Facilities Finance Act [Recodified]	63
Chapter 116 - Higher Education	63
Chapter 116 - Higher Education (Continuation)	63
Chapter 116A - Escheats and Abandoned Property [Repealed.]	64
Chapter 116B - Escheats and Abandoned Property	64
Chapter 116C - Continuum of Education Programs	64
Chapter 116D - Higher Education Bonds	64
Chapter 117 - Electrification	64
Chapter 118 - Firemen's and Rescue Squad Workers' Relief and Pension Funds [Recodified.]	64
Chapter 118A - Firemen's Death Benefit Act [Repealed.]	64
Chapter 118B - Members of a Rescue Squad Death Benefit Act [Repealed.]	64
Chapter 119 - Gasoline and Oil Inspection and Regulation	64
Chapter 120 - General Assembly	65
Chapter 120 - General Assembly (Continuation)	66
Chapter 120 - General Assembly (Continuation)	67
Chapter 120C - Lobbying	67
Chapter 121 - Archives and History	67
Chapter 122 - Hospitals for the Mentally Disordered [Repealed.]	67
Chapter 122A - North Carolina Housing Finance Agency	67
Chapter 122B - North Carolina Agricultural Facilities Finance Act [Repealed.]	67
Chapter 122C - Mental Health, Developmental Disabilities, and Substance Abuse Act of 1985	67
Chapter 122C - Mental Health, Developmental Disabilities, and Substance Abuse Act of 1985 (Continuation)	68
Chapter 122D - North Carolina Agricultural Finance Act	68

Chapter 122E - North Carolina Housing Trust and Oil Overcharge Act	68
Chapter 123 - Impeachment	69
Chapter 123A - Industrial Development [Repealed.]	69
Chapter 124 - Internal Improvements	69
Chapter 125 - Libraries	69
Chapter 126 - State Personnel System	69
Chapter 127 - Militia [Repealed.]	69
Chapter 127A - Militia	69
Chapter 127B - Military Affairs	69
Chapter 127C - Advisory Commission on Military Affairs	69
Chapter 128 - Offices and Public Officers	69
Chapter 128 - Offices and Public Officers (Continuation)	70
Chapter 129 - Public Buildings and Grounds	70
Chapter 130 - Public Health [Repealed.]	70
Chapter 130A - Public Health	70
Chapter 130A - Public Health (Continuation)	71
Chapter 130A - Public Health (Continuation)	72
Chapter 130B - Hazardous Waste Management Commission [Repealed.]	72
Chapter 131 - Public Hospitals [Repealed.]	72
Chapter 131A - Health Care Facilities Finance Act	72
Chapter 131B - Licensing of Ambulatory Surgical Facilities [Repealed.]	72
Chapter 131C - Charitable Solicitation Licensure Act [Repealed.]	72
Chapter 131D - Inspection and Licensing of Facilities	72
Chapter 131E - Health Care Facilities and Services	72
Chapter 131E - Health Care Facilities and Services (Continuation)	73
Chapter 131F - Solicitation of Contributions	73
Chapter 132 - Public Records	73
Chapter 133 - Public Works	74
Chapter 134 - Youth Development [Recodified.]	74
Chapter 134A - Youth Services [Repealed.]	74
Chapter 135 - Retirement System for Teachers and State Employees; Social Security; Health Insurance Program for Children	74
Chapter 135 - Retirement System for Teachers and State Employees; Social Security; Health Insurance Program for Children	75
Chapter 136 - Transportation	75
Chapter 136 - Transportation (Continuation)	76
Chapter 137 - Rural Rehabilitation [Repealed.]	76
Chapter 138 - Salaries, Fees and Allowances	76
Chapter 138A - State Government Ethics Act	76
Chapter 139 - Soil and Water Conservation Districts	76

Chapter 140 - State Art Museum; Symphony and Art Societies	76
Chapter 140A - State Awards System	76
Chapter 141 - State Boundaries	76
Chapter 142 - State Debt	76
Chapter 143 - State Departments, Institutions, and Commissions	77
Chapter 143 - State Departments, Institutions, and Commissions (Continuation)	78
Chapter 143 - State Departments, Institutions, and Commissions (Continuation)	79
Chapter 143 - State Departments, Institutions, and Commissions (Continuation)	80
Chapter 143A - State Government Reorganization	80
Chapter 143B - Executive Organization Act of 1973	80
Chapter 143B - Executive Organization Act of 1973 (Continuation)	81
Chapter 143B - Executive Organization Act of 1973 (Continuation)	82
Chapter 143C - State Budget Act	83
Chapter 143D - The State Governmental Accountability and Internal Control Act	83
Chapter 144 - State Flag, Official Governmental Flags, Motto, and Colors	83
Chapter 145 - State Symbols and Other Official Adoptions.	83
Chapter 146 - State Lands	83
Chapter 147 - State Officers	83
Chapter 148 - State Prison System	84
Chapter 149 - State Song and Toast	84
Chapter 150 - Uniform Revocation of Licenses [Repealed.]	84
Chapter 150A - Administrative Procedure Act [Recodified.]	84
Chapter 150B - Administrative Procedure Act	84
Chapter 151 - Constables [Repealed.]	84
Chapter 152 - Coroners	84
Chapter 152A - County Medical Examiner [Repealed.]	84
Chapter 152A - County Medical Examiner [Repealed.] (Continuation)	85
Chapter 153 - Counties and County Commissioners [Repealed.]	85
Chapter 153A - Counties	85
Chapter 153B - Mountain Resources Planning Act	85
Chapter 153C - Uwharrie Regional Resources Act	85
Chapter 154 - County Surveyor [Repealed.]	85
Chapter 155 - County Treasurer [Repealed.]	85
Chapter 156 - Drainage	85
Chapter 156 – Drainage (Continuation)	86

Chapter 157 - Housing Authorities and Projects	86
Chapter 157A - Historic Properties Commissions [Transferred.]	86
Chapter 158 - Local Development	86
Chapter 159 - Local Government Finance	86
Chapter 159 - Local Government Finance (Continuation)	87
Chapter 159A - Pollution Abatement and Industrial Facilities Financing Act [Unconstitutional.]	87
Chapter 159B - Joint Municipal Electric Power and Energy Act	87
Chapter 159C - Industrial and Pollution Control Facilities Financing Act	87
Chapter 159D - The North Carolina Capital Facilities Financing Act	87
Chapter 159E - Registered Public Obligations Act	87
Chapter 159F - North Carolina Energy Development Authority [Repealed.]	87
Chapter 159G - Water Infrastructure	87
Chapter 159H - [Reserved.]	87
Chapter 159I - Solid Waste Management Loan Program and Local Government Special Obligation Bonds	87
Chapter 160 - Municipal Corporations [Repealed And Transferred.]	87
Chapter 160A - Cities and Towns	88
Chapter 160A - Cities and Towns (Continuation)	89
Chapter 160B - Consolidated City-County Act	89
Chapter 160C - Baseball Park Districts [Repealed.]	90
Chapter 161 - Register of Deeds	90
Chapter 162 - Sheriff	90
Chapter 162A - Water and Sewer Systems	90
Chapter 162B Continuity of Local Government in Emergency.	90
Chapter 163 Elections and Election Laws.	90
Chapter 163 Elections and Election Laws. (Continuation)	91
Chapter 164 Concerning the General Statutes of North Carolina.	92
Chapter 165 Veterans.	92
Chapter 166 Civil Preparedness Agencies [Repealed.]	92
Chapter 166A North Carolina Emergency Management Act.	92
Chapter 167 State Civil Air Patrol [Repealed.]	92
Chapter 168 Persons with Disabilities.	92
Chapter 168A Persons With Disabilities Protection Act.	92

§ 90-171.48. Criminal history record checks of applicants for licensure.

(a) Definitions. - The following definitions shall apply in this section:

(1) Applicant. - A person applying for initial licensure as a registered nurse or licensed practical nurse either by examination pursuant to G.S. 90-171.29 or G.S. 90-171.30 or without examination pursuant to G.S. 90-171.32. The term "applicant" shall also include a person applying for reinstatement of licensure pursuant to G.S. 90-171.35 or returning to active status pursuant to G.S. 90-171.36 as a registered nurse or licensed practical nurse.

(2) Criminal history. - A history of conviction of a State crime, whether a misdemeanor or felony, that bears on an applicant's fitness for licensure to practice nursing. The crimes include the criminal offenses set forth in any of the following Articles of Chapter 14 of the General Statutes: Article 5, Counterfeiting and Issuing Monetary Substitutes; Article 5A, Endangering Executive and Legislative Officers; Article 6, Homicide; Article 7A, Rape and Other Sex Offenses; Article 8, Assaults; Article 10, Kidnapping and Abduction; Article 13, Malicious Injury or Damage by Use of Explosive or Incendiary Device or Material; Article 14, Burglary and Other Housebreakings; Article 15, Arson and Other Burnings; Article 16, Larceny; Article 17, Robbery; Article 18, Embezzlement; Article 19, False Pretenses and Cheats; Article 19A, Obtaining Property or Services by False or Fraudulent Use of Credit Device or Other Means; Article 19B, Financial Transaction Card Crime Act; Article 20, Frauds; Article 21, Forgery; Article 26, Offenses Against Public Morality and Decency; Article 26A, Adult Establishments; Article 27, Prostitution; Article 28, Perjury; Article 29, Bribery; Article 31, Misconduct in Public Office; Article 35, Offenses Against the Public Peace; Article 36A, Riots, Civil Disorders, and Emergencies; Article 39, Protection of Minors; Article 40, Protection of the Family; Article 59, Public Intoxication; and Article 60, Computer-Related Crime. The crimes also include possession or sale of drugs in violation of the North Carolina Controlled Substances Act in Article 5 of Chapter 90 of the General Statutes and alcohol-related offenses including sale to underage persons in violation of G.S. 18B-302 or driving while impaired in violation of G.S. 20-138.1 through G.S. 20-138.5.

(b) All applicants for licensure shall consent to a criminal history record check. Refusal to consent to a criminal history record check may constitute grounds for the Board to deny licensure to an applicant. The Board shall ensure that the State and national criminal history of an applicant applying for initial licensure as a registered nurse or licensed practical nurse either by examination pursuant to G.S. 90-171.29 or G.S. 90-171.30 or without examination pursuant to G.S. 90-171.32 is checked. The Board may request a criminal history record check for applicants applying for reinstatement of licensure pursuant to G.S.90-171.35 or returning to active status pursuant to G.S. 90-171.36 as a registered nurse or licensed practical nurse.

The Board shall be responsible for providing to the North Carolina Department of Justice the fingerprints of the applicant to be checked, a form signed by the applicant consenting to the criminal record check and the use of fingerprints and other identifying information required by the State or National Repositories, and any additional information required by the Department of Justice. The Board shall keep all information obtained pursuant to this section confidential.

(c)   If an applicant's criminal history record check reveals one or more convictions listed under subsection (a)(2) of this section, the conviction shall not automatically bar licensure. The Board shall consider all of the following factors regarding the conviction:

(1)   The level of seriousness of the crime.

(2)   The date of the crime.

(3)   The age of the person at the time of the conviction.

(4)   The circumstances surrounding the commission of the crime, if known.

(5)   The nexus between the criminal conduct of the person and the job duties of the position to be filled.

(6)   The person's prison, jail, probation, parole, rehabilitation, and employment records since the date the crime was committed.

(7)   The subsequent commission by the person of a crime listed in subsection (a) of this section.

If, after reviewing the factors, the Board determines that the grounds set forth in subsections (1), (2), (3), (4), (5), or (6) of G.S. 90-171.37 exist, the Board may deny licensure of the applicant. The Board may disclose to the applicant information contained in the criminal history record check that is relevant to the denial. The Board shall not provide a copy of the criminal history record check to the applicant. The applicant shall have the right to appear before the Board to appeal the Board's decision. However, an appearance before the full Board shall constitute an exhaustion of administrative remedies in accordance with Chapter 150B of the General Statutes.

(d) Limited immunity. - The Board, its officers and employees, acting in good faith and in compliance with this section, shall be immune from civil liability for denying licensure to an applicant based on information provided in the applicant's criminal history record check. (2001-371, s. 2; 2009-133, s. 6; 2012-12, s. 2(ii).)

§ 90-171.49. Reserved for future codification purposes.

Article 9B.

Information and Financial Assistance for Nursing Students and Inactive Nurses.

§ 90-171.50. Existing scholarship and loan information to be consolidated and published.

The State Education Assistance Authority of the Board of Governors of The University of North Carolina shall consolidate information on existing scholarships and loan programs available for nursing education. The information shall be published in a brochure and made available to high schools, colleges, Area Health Education Centers, and other facilities. (1987 (Reg. Sess., 1988), c. 1049, s. 1(a).)

§ 90-171.51. Emergency Financial Assistance Fund.

There is established an Emergency Financial Assistance Fund for students in State educational nursing and licensed practical nursing programs, to be administered by each campus. Emergency need is defined as acute financial need caused by a particular event which immediately and severely impacts a particular student's ability to continue his or her educational program in nursing on that student's current schedule. Allowable expenses, for emergency assistance, shall include funds for child care, transportation, housing, and medical care; and shall not be considered as an ongoing source of income for those expenses. Emergency assistance shall be limited to four hundred dollars ($400.00) per academic year for any individual. The local Board of Trustees at each campus shall review quarterly the expenditures under this Fund, and the Department of Community Colleges and the Board of Governors of The University of North Carolina shall assess the Fund's impact on completion rates in these programs, and report their assessment to the General Assembly. (1987 (Reg. Sess., 1988), c. 1049, s. 2(a).)

§ 90-171.52. Nursing licensing exam follow-up assistance.

The Board of Governors of The University of North Carolina shall direct the constituent institutions and the State Board of Community Colleges shall direct the Community Colleges to provide follow-up assistance for their students who fail the nursing licensing exam for the first time. This follow-up assistance shall include consultation with the Board of Nursing on areas needing improvement and shall include providing additional appropriate preparation assistance before the next exam date. (1987 (Reg. Sess., 1988), c. 1049, s. 3.)

§ 90-171.53. Area Health Education Centers publicity programs.

The Area Health Education Centers of The University of North Carolina and the Board of Nursing shall cooperate in developing publicity on:

(1)   New salary levels and job opportunities in nursing;

(2)   The availability of refresher courses; and

(3)   License renewal requirements for registered nurses whose licenses are not currently active.

This information shall be provided to nurses without a current license in an effort to attract them back into nursing practice. (1987 (Reg. Sess., 1988), c. 1049, s. 5.)

§ 90-171.54. Reserved for future codification purposes.

Article 9C.

Nurses Aides Registry Act.

§ 90-171.55. Nurses Aides Registry.

(a)   The Board of Nursing, established pursuant to G.S. 90-171.21, shall establish a Nurses Aides Registry for persons functioning as nurses aides regardless of title. The Board shall consider those Level I nurses aides employed in State licensed or Medicare/Medicaid certified nursing facilities who meet applicable State and federal registry requirements as adopted by the North Carolina Medical Care Commission as having fulfilled the training and registry requirements of the Board. The Board may not charge an annual fee to a nurse aide I registry applicant. The Board may charge an annual fee of twelve dollars ($12.00) for each nurse aide II registry applicant. The Board shall adopt rules to ensure that whenever possible, the fee is collected through the employer or prospective employer of the registry applicant. Fees collected may be used by the Board in administering the registry. The Board's authority granted by this Article shall not conflict with the authority of the Medical Care Commission.

(b)   (1)   Each nurses aide training program, except for those operated by (i) institutions under the Board of Governors of The University of North Carolina, (ii) institutions of the North Carolina Community College System, (iii) public high schools, and (iv) hospital authorities acting pursuant to G.S. 131E-23(31), shall provide a guaranty bond unless the program has already provided a bond or an alternative to a bond under G.S. 115D-95. The Board of Nursing may revoke the approval of a program that fails to maintain a bond or an alternative to a bond pursuant to this subsection or G.S. 115D-95.

(2)   When application is made for approval or renewal of approval, the applicant shall file a guaranty bond with the clerk of the superior court of the county in which the program will be located. The bond shall be in favor of the students. The bond shall be executed by the applicant as principal and by a bonding company authorized to do business in this State. The bond shall be

conditioned to provide indemnification to any student, or his parent or guardian, who has suffered a loss of tuition or any fees by reason of the failure of the program to offer or complete student instruction, academic services, or other goods and services related to course enrollment for any reason, including the suspension, revocation, or nonrenewal of a program's approval, bankruptcy, foreclosure, or the program ceasing to operate.

The bond shall be in an amount determined by the Board to be adequate to provide indemnification to any student, or his parent or guardian, under the terms of the bond. The bond amount for a program shall be at least equal to the maximum amount of prepaid tuition held at any time during the last fiscal year by the program. The bond amount shall also be at least ten thousand dollars ($10,000).

Each application for a license shall include a letter signed by an authorized representative of the program showing in detail the calculations made and the method of computing the amount of the bond pursuant to this subdivision and the rules of the Board. If the Board finds that the calculations made and the method of computing the amount of the bond are inaccurate or that the amount of the bond is otherwise inadequate to provide indemnification under the terms of the bond, the Board may require the applicant to provide an additional bond.

The bond shall remain in force and effect until cancelled by the guarantor. The guarantor may cancel the bond upon 30 days notice to the Board. Cancellation of the bond shall not affect any liability incurred or accrued prior to the termination of the notice period.

(3) An applicant that is unable to secure a bond may seek a waiver of the guaranty bond from the Board and approval of one of the guaranty bond alternatives set forth in this subdivision. With the approval of the Board, an applicant may file with the clerk of the superior court of the county in which the program will be located, in lieu of a bond:

a. An assignment of a savings account in an amount equal to the bond required (i) which is in a form acceptable to the Board; (ii) which is executed by the applicant; and (iii) which is executed by a state or federal savings and loan association, state bank, or national bank, that is doing business in North Carolina and whose accounts are insured by a federal depositors corporation; and (iv) for which access to the account in favor of the State of North Carolina is subject to the same conditions as for a bond in subdivision (2) of this subsection.

b. A certificate of deposit (i) which is executed by a state or federal savings and loan association, state bank, or national bank, which is doing business in North Carolina and whose accounts are insured by a federal depositors corporation; and (ii) which is either payable to the State of North Carolina, unrestrictively endorsed to the Board; in the case of a negotiable certificate of deposit, is unrestrictively endorsed to the Board; or in the case of a nonnegotiable certificate of deposit, is assigned to the Board in a form satisfactory to the Board; and (iii) for which access to the certificate of deposit in favor of the State of North Carolina is subject to the same conditions as for a bond in subdivision (2) of this subsection. (1989, c. 323, s. 1; 1989 (Reg. Sess., 1990), c. 824, s. 5; 1999-254, s. 1.)

§ 90-171.56. Medication aide requirements.

The Board of Nursing shall do the following:

(1) Establish standards for faculty and applicant requirements for medication aide training.

(2) Provide ongoing review and evaluation, and recommend changes, for faculty and medication aide training requirements to support safe medication administration and improve client, resident, and patient outcomes. (2005-276, s. 10.40C(b); 2007-148, s. 3.)

§ 90-171.57. Reserved for future codification purposes.

§ 90-171.58. Reserved for future codification purposes.

§ 90-171.59. Reserved for future codification purposes.

Article 9D.

Nursing Scholars Program.

§ 90-171.60: Repealed by Session Laws 2011-74, s. 3(a), effective July 1, 2012.

§ 90-171.61: Repealed by Session Laws 2011-74, s. 3(a), effective July 1, 2012.

§ 90-171.62: Repealed by Session Laws 2011-74, s. 3(a), effective July 1, 2012.

§§ 90-171.63 through 90-171.64. Reserved for future codification purposes.

Article 9E.

Need-Based Nursing Scholarships.

§ 90-171.65: Repealed by Session Laws 2011-74, s. 4(a), effective July 1, 2012.

§§ 90-171.66 through 90-171.69. Reserved for future codification purposes.

Article 9F.

North Carolina Center for Nursing.

§ 90-171.70. North Carolina Center for Nursing; establishment; goals.

There is established the North Carolina Center for Nursing to address issues of supply and demand for nursing, including issues of recruitment, retention, and utilization of nurse manpower resources. The General Assembly finds that the Center will repay the State's investment by providing an ongoing strategy for the allocation of the State's resources directed towards nursing. The primary goals for the Center shall be:

(1) To develop a strategic statewide plan for nursing manpower in North Carolina by:

a. Establishing and maintaining a database on nursing supply and demand in North Carolina, to include (i) current supply and demand, and (ii) future projections; and

b. Selecting priorities from the plan to be addressed.

(2) To convene various groups representative of nurses, other health care providers, business and industry, consumers, legislators, and educators to:

a. Review and comment on data analysis prepared for the Center;

b. Recommend systemic changes, including strategies for implementation of recommended changes; and

c. To evaluate and report the results of these efforts to the General Assembly and others.

(3) To enhance and promote recognition, reward, and renewal activities for nurses in North Carolina by:

a. Promoting continuation of Institutes for Nursing Excellence programs as piloted by the Area Health Education Centers in 1989-90 or similar options;

b. Proposing and creating additional reward, recognition, and renewal activities for nurses; and

c. Promoting media and positive image-building efforts for nursing. (1991, c. 550, s. 3.)

§ 90-171.71. North Carolina Center for Nursing; governing board.

(a) The North Carolina Center for Nursing shall be governed by a policy-setting board of directors. The Board shall consist of 16 members, with a simple majority of the Board being nurses representative of various practice areas. Other members shall include representatives of other health care professions, business and industry, health care providers, and consumers. The Board shall be appointed as follows:

(1) Four members appointed by the General Assembly upon recommendation of the President Pro Tempore of the Senate, at least one of whom shall be a registered nurse and at least one other a representative of the hospital industry;

(2) Four members appointed by the General Assembly upon the recommendation of the Speaker of the House of Representatives, at least one of whom shall be a registered nurse and at least one other a representative of the long-term care industry;

(3) Four members appointed by the Governor, two of whom shall be registered nurses; and

(4) Four nurse educators, one of whom shall be appointed by the Board of Governors of The University of North Carolina, one other by the State Board of Community Colleges, one other by the North Carolina Association of Independent Colleges and Universities, and one by the Area Health Education Centers Program.

(b) The initial terms of the members shall be as follows:

(1)   Of the members appointed pursuant to subdivision (1) of subsection (a) of this section, two shall be appointed for terms expiring June 30, 1994, one for a term expiring June 30, 1993, and one for a term expiring June 30, 1992;

(2)   Of the members appointed pursuant to subdivision (2) of subsection (a) of this section, one shall be appointed for a term expiring June 30, 1994, two for terms expiring June 30, 1993, and one for a term expiring June 30, 1992;

(3)   Of the members appointed pursuant to subdivision (3) of subsection (a) of this section, one shall be appointed for a term expiring June 30, 1994, one for a term expiring June 30, 1993, and two for terms expiring June 30, 1992; and

(4)   Of the members appointed pursuant to subdivision (4) of subsection (a) of this section, the terms of the members appointed by the Board of Governors of The University of North Carolina and the State Board of Community Colleges shall expire June 30, 1994; the term of the member appointed by the North Carolina Association of Independent Colleges shall expire June 30, 1993; and the term of the member appointed by the Area Health Education Centers Program shall expire June 30, 1992.

After the initial appointments expire, the terms of all of the members shall be three years, with no member serving more than two consecutive terms.

(c)   The Board of Directors shall have the following powers and duties:

(1)   To employ the executive director;

(2)   To determine operational policy;

(3)   To elect a chairperson and officers, to serve two-year terms. The chairperson and officers may not succeed themselves;

(4)   To establish committees of the Board as needed;

(5)   To appoint a multidisciplinary advisory council for input and advice on policy matters;

(6)   To implement the major functions of the Center for Nursing as established in the goals set out in subsection (a) of this section; and

(7)   To seek and accept non-State funds for carrying out Center policy.

(d) The Board shall receive the per diem and allowances prescribed by G.S. 138-5 for State boards and commissions.

(e) The North Carolina Center for Nursing shall be administered by The University of North Carolina through the Center's Board of Directors established under this section. (1991, c. 550, s. 3; 1991 (Reg. Sess., 1992), c. 879, s. 4.)

§ 90-171.72. North Carolina Center for Nursing; State support.

The General Assembly finds that it is imperative that the State protect its investment and progress made in its nursing efforts to date. The General Assembly further finds that the North Carolina Center for Nursing is the appropriate means to do so. The Center shall have State budget support for its operations so that it may have adequate resources for the tasks the General Assembly has set out in this Article. (1991, c. 550, s. 3.)

§§ 90-171.73 through 90-171.79. Reserved for future codification purposes.

Article 9G.

Nurse Licensure Compact.

§ 90-171.80. Entering into Compact.

The Nurse Licensure Compact is hereby enacted into law and entered into by this State with all other states legally joining therein, in the form substantially as set forth in this Article. (1999-245, s. 1.)

§ 90-171.81. Findings and declaration of purpose.

(a) The General Assembly of North Carolina makes the following findings:

(1) The health and safety of the public are affected by the degree of compliance with and the effectiveness of enforcement activities related to states' nurse licensure laws.

(2) Violations of nurse licensure and other laws regulating the practice of nursing may result in injury or harm to the public.

(3) The expanded mobility of nurses and the use of advanced communication technologies as part of our nation's health care delivery system require greater coordination and cooperation among states in the areas of nurse licensure and regulation.

(4) New practice modalities and technology make compliance with individual states' nurse licensure laws difficult and complex.

(5) The current system of duplicative licensure for nurses practicing in multiple states is cumbersome and redundant to both nurses and states.

(b) The purposes of this Compact are to:

(1) Facilitate the states' responsibility to protect the public's health and safety.

(2) Ensure and encourage the cooperation of party states in the areas of nurse licensure and regulation.

(3) Facilitate the exchange of information between party states in the areas of nurse regulation, investigation, and adverse actions.

(4) Promote compliance with the laws governing the practice of nursing in each jurisdiction.

(5) Through the mutual recognition of party state licenses, grant all party states the authority to hold nurses accountable for meeting all state practice laws in the states in which their patients are located at the time care is rendered. (1999-245, s. 1.)

§ 90-171.82. Definitions.

The following definitions apply in this Article:

(1)   Adverse action. - A home or remote state action.

(2)   Alternative program. - A voluntary, nondisciplinary monitoring program approved by a nurse licensing board.

(3)   Compact. - This Article.

(4)   Coordinated licensure information system. - An integrated process for collecting, storing, and sharing information on nurse licensure and enforcement activities related to nurse licensure laws that is administered by a nonprofit organization composed of and controlled by state nurse licensing boards.

(5)   Current significant investigative information. -

a.   Investigative information that indicates a licensee has committed more than a minor infraction.

b.   Investigative information that indicates a licensee represents an immediate threat to public health and safety.

(6)   Home state. - The party state that is the nurse's primary state of residence.

(7)   Home state action. - Any administrative, civil, equitable, or criminal action permitted by the home state's laws that is imposed on a nurse by the home state's licensing board or another authority. The term includes the revocation, suspension, or probation of a nurse's license or any other action that affects a nurse's authorization to practice.

(8)   Licensee. - A person licensed by the North Carolina Board of Nursing or the nurse licensing board of a party state.

(9)   Licensing board. - A party state's regulatory agency that is responsible for licensing nurses.

(10)   Multistate licensure privilege. - Current official authority from a remote state permitting the practice of nursing as either a registered nurse or a licensed practical or vocational nurse in that state.

(11) Nurse. - A registered nurse or licensed practical or vocational nurse as those terms are defined by each party state's practice laws.

(12) Party state. - Any state that has adopted this Compact.

(13) Remote state. - A party state, other than the home state, where the patient is located at the time nursing care is provided. In the case of the practice of nursing not involving a patient, the term means the party state where the recipient of nursing practice is located.

(14) Remote state action. - Any administrative, civil, equitable, or criminal action permitted by the laws of a remote state that are imposed on a nurse by the remote state's nurse licensing board or other authority, including actions against a nurse's multistate licensure privilege to practice in the remote state. The term also includes cease and desist and other injunctive or equitable orders issued by remote states or their nurse licensing boards.

(15) State. - A state, territory, or possession of the United States, the District of Columbia, or the Commonwealth of Puerto Rico.

(16) State practice laws. - The laws and regulations of individual party states that govern the practice of nursing, define the scope of nursing practice, and create the methods and grounds for disciplining nurses. The term does not include the initial qualifications for licensure or the requirements necessary to obtain and retain a license, except for qualifications or requirements of the home state. (1999-245, s. 1.)

§ 90-171.83. General provisions and jurisdiction.

(a) A license to practice registered nursing that is issued by a home state to a resident in that state shall be recognized by each party state as authorizing a multistate licensure privilege to practice as a registered nurse in each party state. A license to practice practical or vocational nursing that is issued by a home state to a resident in that state shall be recognized by each party state as authorizing a multistate licensure privilege to practice as a licensed practical or vocational nurse in each party state. In order to obtain or retain a license, an applicant must meet the home state's qualifications for licensure and license renewal as well as all other applicable state laws.

(b) Party states may, in accordance with each state's due process laws, revoke, suspend, or limit the multistate licensure privilege of any licensee to practice in their state and may take any other actions under their applicable state laws that are necessary to protect the health and safety of their citizens. If a party state takes an action authorized in this subsection, it shall promptly notify the administrator of the coordinated licensure information system. The administrator shall promptly notify the home state of any actions taken by remote states.

(c) Every licensee practicing in a party state shall comply with the state practice laws of the state in which the patient is located at the time care is rendered. The practice of nursing is not limited to patient care, but shall include all nursing practice as defined by the state practice laws of a party state. The practice of nursing in a party state shall subject a nurse to the jurisdiction of the nurse licensing board and the laws and the courts in that party state.

(d) The Compact does not affect additional requirements imposed by states for advanced-practice registered nursing. A multistate licensure privilege to practice registered nursing granted by a party state shall be recognized by other party states as a license to practice registered nursing if a license to practice registered nursing is required by state law as a precondition for qualifying for advanced-practice registered nurse authorization.

(e) Persons not residing in a party state may continue to apply for nurse licensure in party states as provided for under the laws of each party state. The license granted to such persons shall not be recognized as granting the privilege to practice nursing in any other party state unless explicitly agreed to by that party state. (1999-245, s. 1.)

§ 90-171.84. Application for licensure in a party state.

(a) Upon receiving an application for a license, the licensing board in a party state shall ascertain through the coordinated licensure information system whether the applicant holds or has ever held a license issued by any other state, whether there are any restrictions on the applicant's multistate licensure privilege, and whether any other adverse action by any state has been taken against the applicant's license.

(b) A licensee in a party state shall hold licensure in only one party state at a time. The license shall be issued by the home state.

(c) A licensee who intends to change his or her primary state of residence may apply for licensure in the new home state in advance of the change. However, a new license shall not be issued by a party state until after the licensee provides evidence of a change in his or her primary state of residence that is satisfactory to the new home state's licensing board.

(d) When a licensee changes his or her primary state of residence by moving between two party states and obtaining a license from the new home state, the license from the former home state is no longer valid.

(e) When a licensee changes his or her primary state of residence by moving from a nonparty state to a party state and obtaining a license from the new home state, the license issued by the nonparty state shall not be affected and shall remain in full force if the laws of the nonparty state so provide.

(f) When a licensee changes his or her primary state of residence by moving from a party state to a nonparty state, the license issued by the former home state converts to an individual state license that is valid only in the former home state. The license does not grant the multistate licensure privilege to practice in other party states. (1999-245, s. 1.)

§ 90-171.85. Adverse actions.

(a) The licensing board of a remote state shall promptly report to the administrator of the coordinated licensure information system any remote state actions, including the factual and legal basis for the actions, if known. The licensing board of a remote state shall also promptly report any current significant investigative information yet to result in a remote state action. The administrator of the coordinated licensure information system shall promptly notify the home state of any such reports.

(b) The licensing board of a party state may complete any pending investigation of a licensee who changes his or her primary state of residence during the course of the investigation. It may also take appropriate action against a licensee and shall promptly report the conclusion of the investigation to the administrator of the coordinated licensure information system. The administrator of the coordinated licensure information system shall promptly notify the new home state of any action taken against a licensee.

(c)   A remote state may take adverse action that affects the multistate licensure privilege to practice within that party state. However, only the home state may take adverse action that affects a license that was issued by the home state.

(d)   For purposes of taking adverse action, the licensing board of the home state shall give to conduct reported by a remote state the same priority and effect that it would if the conduct had occurred within the home state. The board shall apply its own state laws to determine the appropriate action that should be taken against the licensee.

(e)   The home state may take adverse action based upon the factual findings of the remote state if each state follows its own procedures for imposing the adverse action.

(f)   This Compact does not prohibit a party state from allowing a licensee to participate in an alternative program instead of taking adverse action against the licensee. If required by the party state's laws, the licensee's participation in an alternative program shall be confidential information. Party states shall require licensees who enter alternative programs to agree not to practice in any other party state during the term of the alternative program without prior authorization from the other party state. (1999-245, s. 1.)

§ 90-171.86. Current significant investigative information.

(a)   If a licensing board finds current significant investigative information as defined in G.S. 90-171.82(5)a., the licensing board shall, after giving the licensee notice and an opportunity to respond if required by state law, conduct a hearing and decide what adverse action, if any, should be taken against the licensee.

(b)   If a licensing board finds current significant investigative information as defined in G.S. 90-171.82(5)b., the licensing board may take adverse action against the licensee without first providing the licensee notice or an opportunity to respond to the information. A hearing shall be promptly commenced and determined. (1999-245, s. 1.)

§ 90-171.87. Additional authority of party state nursing licensing boards.

Notwithstanding any other powers, party state nurse licensing boards may do any of the following:

(1) If otherwise permitted by state law, recover from licensees the costs of investigating and disposing of cases that result in adverse action.

(2) Issue subpoenas for both hearings and investigations that require the attendance and testimony of witnesses and the production of evidence. Subpoenas issued by a nurse licensing board in a party state for the attendance and testimony of witnesses or the production of evidence from another party state shall be enforced in the other party state by any court of competent jurisdiction according to the practice and procedure of that court. The issuing authority shall pay any witness fees, travel expenses, mileage, and other fees required by the laws of the party state where the witnesses or evidence are located.

(3) Issue cease and desist orders to limit or revoke a licensee's authority to practice in the board's state.

(4) Adopt uniform rules and regulations that are developed by the Compact administrators as provided in G.S. 90-171.89(c). (1999-245, s. 1.)

§ 90-171.88. Coordinated licensure information system.

(a) All party states shall participate in a cooperative effort to create a coordinated data base of all licensed registered nurses and licensed practical or vocational nurses. This system shall include information on the licensure and disciplinary history of each licensee, as contributed by party states, to assist in the coordination of nurse licensure and enforcement efforts.

(b) Notwithstanding any other provision of law, all party states' licensing boards shall promptly report to the coordinated licensure information system any adverse action taken against licensees, actions against multistate licensure privileges, any current significant investigative information yet to result in adverse action, and any denials of applications for licensure and the reasons for the denials.

(c)   Current significant investigative information shall be transmitted through the coordinated licensure information system only to party state licensing boards.

(d)   Notwithstanding any other provision of law, all party states' licensing boards contributing information to the coordinated licensure information system may designate information that shall not be shared with nonparty states or disclosed to other entities or individuals without the express permission of the contributing party state.

(e)   Any personally identifiable information obtained by a party state licensing board from the coordinated licensure information system shall not be shared with nonparty states or disclosed to other entities or individuals except to the extent permitted by the laws of the party state contributing the information.

(f)   Any information contributed to the coordinated licensure information system that is subsequently required to be expunged by the laws of the party state contributing the information shall be expunged from the coordinated licensure information system.

(g)   The Compact administrators, acting jointly and in consultation with the administrator of the coordinated licensure information system, shall formulate necessary and proper procedures for the identification, collection, and exchange of information under this Compact. (1999-245, s. 1.)

§ 90-171.89. Compact administration and interchange of information.

(a)   The executive director of the nurse licensing board of each party state or the executive director's designee shall be the administrator of this Compact for that state.

(b)   To facilitate the administration of this Compact, the Compact administrator of each party state shall furnish to the Compact administrators of all other party states information and documents concerning each licensee, including a uniform data set of investigations, identifying information, licensure data, and disclosable alternative program participation.

(c) Compact administrators shall develop uniform rules and regulations to facilitate and coordinate implementation of this Compact. These uniform rules shall be adopted by party states as authorized in G.S. 90-171.87(4). (1999-245, s. 1.)

§ 90-171.90. Immunity.

A party state or the officers, employees, or agents of a party state's nurse licensing board who act in accordance with this Compact shall not be liable for any good faith act or omission committed while they were engaged in the performance of their duties under this Compact. (1999-245, s. 1.)

§ 90-171.91. Effective date, withdrawal, and amendment.

(a) This Compact shall become effective as to any state when it has been enacted into the laws of that state. Any party state may withdraw from this Compact by enacting a statute repealing the Compact, but the withdrawal shall not take effect until six months after the withdrawing state has given notice of the withdrawal to the Compact administrators of all other party states.

(b) No withdrawal shall affect the validity or applicability of any report of adverse action taken by the licensing board of a state that remains a party to the Compact if the adverse action occurred prior to the withdrawal.

(c) This Compact does not invalidate or prevent any nurse licensure agreement or other cooperative arrangement between a party state and a nonparty state that is made in accordance with this Compact.

(d) This Compact may be amended by the party states. No amendment to this Compact shall become effective and binding upon the party states unless and until it is enacted into the laws of all party states. (1999-245, s. 1.)

§ 90-171.92. Dispute resolution.

If there is a dispute that cannot be resolved by the party states involved, the following procedure shall be used:

(1)   The party states shall submit the issues in dispute to an arbitration panel that shall consist of an individual appointed by the Compact administrator in the home state, an individual appointed by the Compact administrator in the remote states involved, and an individual appointed by the Compact administrators of all the party states involved in the dispute.

(2)   The decision of a majority of the arbitrators shall be final and binding. (1999-245, s. 1.)

§ 90-171.93. Construction and severability.

This Compact shall be liberally construed so as to effectuate the purposes as stated in G.S. 90-171.81(b). The provisions of this Compact shall be severable and if any phrase, clause, sentence, or provision of this Compact is declared to be contrary to the constitution of any party state or of the United States, or if the applicability thereof to any government, agency, person, or circumstance is held invalid, the validity of the remainder of this Compact and the applicability thereof to any government, agency, person, or circumstance shall not be affected. If this Compact shall be held contrary to the constitution of any party state, the Compact shall remain in full force and effect as to the remaining party states and in full force and effect as to the party state affected as to all severable matters. (1999-245, s. 1.)

§ 90-171.94. Applicability of compact.

This Article is applicable only to nurses whose home states are determined by the North Carolina Board of Nursing to have licensure requirements that are substantially equivalent or more stringent than those of North Carolina. (1999-456, s. 25.)

§ 90-171.95. Reserved for future codification purposes.

§ 90-171.96. Reserved for future codification purposes.

§ 90-171.97. Reserved for future codification purposes.

§ 90-171.98. Reserved for future codification purposes.

§ 90-171.99. Reserved for future codification purposes.

Article 9H.

Graduate Nurse Scholarship Program for Faculty Production.

§ 90-171.100: Repealed by Session Laws 2011-74, s. 2(a), effective July 1, 2012.

§ 90-171.101: Repealed by Session Laws 2011-74, s. 2(a), effective July 1, 2012.

Article 10.

Midwives.

§ 90-172. Repealed by Session Laws 1983, c. 897, s. 2, effective October 1, 1983.

§§ 90-173 through 90-178. Repealed by Session Laws 1957, c. 1357, s. 7.

Article 10A.

Practice of Midwifery.

§ 90-178.1. Title.

This Article shall be known and may be cited as the Midwifery Practice Act. (1983, c. 897, s. 1.)

§ 90-178.2. Definitions.

As used in this Article:

(1)   "Interconceptional care" includes but is not limited to:

a.   Family planning;

b.   Screening for cancer of the breast and reproductive tract; and

c.   Screening for and management of minor infections of the reproductive organs;

(2)   "Intrapartum care" includes but is not limited to:

a.   Attending women in uncomplicated labor;

b.   Assisting with spontaneous delivery of infants in vertex presentation from 37 to 42 weeks gestation;

c.   Performing amniotomy;

d.   Administering local anesthesia;

e. Performing episiotomy and repair; and

f. Repairing lacerations associated with childbirth.

(3) "Midwifery" means the act of providing prenatal, intrapartum, postpartum, newborn and interconceptional care. The term does not include the practice of medicine by a physician licensed to practice medicine when engaged in the practice of medicine as defined by law, the performance of medical acts by a physician assistant or nurse practitioner when performed in accordance with the rules of the North Carolina Medical Board, the practice of nursing by a registered nurse engaged in the practice of nursing as defined by law, or the rendering of childbirth assistance in an emergency situation.

(4) "Newborn care" includes but is not limited to:

a. Routine assistance to the newborn to establish respiration and maintain thermal stability;

b. Routine physical assessment including APGAR scoring;

c. Vitamin K administration; and

d. Eye prophylaxis for opthalmia neonatorum.

(5) "Postpartum care" includes but is not limited to:

a. Management of the normal third stage of labor;

b. Administration of pitocin and methergine after delivery of the infant when indicated; and

c. Six weeks postpartum evaluation exam and initiation of family planning.

(6) "Prenatal care" includes but is not limited to:

a. Historical and physical assessment;

b. Obtaining and assessing the results of routine laboratory tests; and

c. Supervising the use of prenatal vitamins, folic acid, iron, and nonprescription medicines. (1983, c. 897, s. 1; 1995, c. 94, s. 30.)

§ 90-178.3. Regulation of midwifery.

(a)   No person shall practice or offer to practice or hold oneself out to practice midwifery unless approved pursuant to this Article.

(b)   A person approved pursuant to this Article may practice midwifery in a hospital or non-hospital setting and shall practice under the supervision of a physician licensed to practice medicine who is actively engaged in the practice of obstetrics. A registered nurse approved pursuant to this Article is authorized to write prescriptions for drugs in accordance with the same conditions applicable to a nurse practitioner under G.S. 90-18.2(b).

(c)   Graduate nurse midwife applicant status may be granted by the joint subcommittee in accordance with G.S. 90-178.4. (1983, c. 897, s. 1; 2000-140, s. 60.)

§ 90-178.4. Administration.

(a)   The joint subcommittee of the North Carolina Medical Board and the Board of Nursing created pursuant to G.S. 90-18.2 shall administer the provisions of this Article and the rules adopted pursuant to this Article; Provided, however, that actions of the joint subcommittee pursuant to this Article shall not require approval by the North Carolina Medical Board and the Board of Nursing. For purposes of this Article, the joint subcommittee shall be enlarged by four additional members, including two certified midwives and two obstetricians who have had working experience with midwives.

(b)   The joint subcommittee shall adopt rules pursuant to this Article to establish:

(1)   A fee which shall cover application and initial approval up to a maximum of one hundred dollars ($100.00);

(2)   An annual renewal fee to be paid by January 1 of each year by persons approved pursuant to this Article up to a maximum of fifty dollars ($50.00);

(3) A reinstatement fee for a lapsed approval up to a maximum of five dollars ($5.00);

(4) The form and contents of the applications which shall include information related to the applicant's education and certification by the American College of Nurse-Midwives; and

(5) The procedure for establishing physician supervision as required by this Article.

(c) The joint subcommittee may solicit, employ, or contract for technical assistance and clerical assistance and may purchase or contract for the materials and services it needs.

(d) All fees collected on behalf of the joint subcommittee and all receipts of every kind and nature, as well as the compensation paid the members of the joint subcommittee and the necessary expenses incurred by them in the performance of the duties imposed upon them, shall be reported annually to the State Treasurer. All fees and other moneys received by the joint subcommittee pursuant to the provisions of the General Statutes shall be kept in a separate fund by the joint subcommittee, to be held and expended only for such purposes as are proper and necessary to the discharge of the duties of the joint subcommittee and to enforce the provisions of this Article. No expense incurred by the joint subcommittee shall be charged against the State.

(e) Members of the joint subcommittee who are not officers or employees of the State shall receive compensation and reimbursement for travel and subsistence expenses at the rates specified in G.S. 138-5. Members of the joint subcommittee who are officers or employees of the State shall receive reimbursement for travel and subsistence expenses at the rate set out in G.S. 138-6. (1983, c. 897, s. 1; 1995, c. 94, s. 31.)

§ 90-178.5. Qualifications for approval.

In order to be approved by the joint subcommittee pursuant to this Article, a person shall:

(1) Complete an application on a form furnished by the joint subcommittee;

(2)   Submit evidence of certification by the American College of Nurse-Midwives;

(3)   Submit evidence of arrangements for physician supervision; and

(4)   Pay the fee for application and approval. (1983, c. 897, s. 1.)

§ 90-178.6. Denial, revocation or suspension of approval.

(a)   In accordance with the provisions of Chapter 150B, the joint subcommittee may deny, revoke or suspend approval when a person has:

(1)   Failed to satisfy the qualifications for approval;

(2)   Failed to pay the annual renewal fee by January 1 of the current year;

(3)   Given false information or withheld material information in applying for approval;

(4)   Demonstrated incompetence in the practice of midwifery;

(5)   Violated any of the provisions of this Article;

(6)   A mental or physical disability or uses any drug to a degree that interferes with his or her fitness to practice midwifery;

(7)   Engaged in conduct that endangers the public health;

(8)   Engaged in conduct that deceives, defrauds, or harms the public in the course of professional activities or services; or

(9)   Been convicted of or pleaded guilty or nolo contendere to any felony under the laws of the United States or of any state of the United States indicating professional unfitness.

(b)   Revocation or suspension of a license to practice nursing pursuant to G.S. 90-171.37 shall automatically result in comparable action against the person's approval to practice midwifery under this Article. (1983, c. 897, s. 1; 1987, c. 827, s. 1.)

§ 90-178.7. Enforcement.

(a) The joint subcommittee may apply to the Superior Court of Wake County to restrain any violation of this Article.

(b) Any person who violates G.S. 90-178.3(a) shall be guilty of a Class 3 misdemeanor. (1983, c. 897, s. 1; 1993, c. 539, s. 633; 1994, Ex. Sess., c. 24, s. 14(c).)

Article 11.

Veterinarians.

§ 90-179. Purpose of Article.

In order to promote the public health, safety, and welfare by safeguarding the people of this State against unqualified or incompetent practitioners of veterinary medicine, it is hereby declared that the right to practice veterinary medicine is a privilege conferred by legislative grant to persons possessed of the personal and professional qualifications specified in this Article. (1973, c. 1106, s. 1.)

§ 90-180. Title.

This Article shall be known as the North Carolina Veterinary Practice Act. (1973, c. 1106, s. 1.)

§ 90-181. Definitions.

When used in this Article these words and phrases shall be defined as follows:

(1) "Accredited school of veterinary medicine" means any veterinary college or division of a university or college that offers the degree of doctor of veterinary medicine or its equivalent and that conforms to the standards required for accreditation by the American Veterinary Medical Association.

(2) "Animal" means any animal, mammal other than man and includes birds, fish, and reptiles, wild or domestic, living or dead.

(2a) "Animal dentistry" means the treatment, extraction, cleaning, adjustment, or "floating" (filing or smoothing) of an animal's teeth, and treatment of an animal's gums.

(3) "Board" means the North Carolina Veterinary Medical Board.

(3a) "Cruelty to animals" means to willfully overdrive, overload, wound, injure, torture, torment, deprive of necessary sustenance, cruelly beat, needlessly mutilate or kill any animal, or cause or procure any of these acts to be done to an animal; provided, that the words "torture," "torment," or "cruelty" include every act, omission, or neglect causing or permitting unjustifiable physical pain, suffering, or death.

(4) "Limited veterinary license" or "limited license" means a license issued by the Board under authority of this Article that specifically, by its terms, restricts the scope or areas of practice of veterinary medicine by the holder of the limited license; provided, that no limited license shall confer or denote an area of specialty of the holder of this limited veterinary license; and provided further, that unless otherwise provided by Board rule, the licensing requirements shall be identical to those specified for a veterinary license.

(5) "Person" means any individual, firm, partnership, association, joint venture, cooperative or corporation, or any other group or combination acting in concert; and whether or not acting as a principal, trustee, fiduciary, receiver, or as any kind of legal or personal representative, or as the successor in interest, assignee, agent, factor, servant, employee, director, officer, or any other representative of such person.

(6) "Practice of veterinary medicine" means:

a. To diagnose, treat, correct, change, relieve, or prevent animal disease, deformity, defect, injury, or other physical or mental conditions; including the prescription or administration of any drug, medicine, biologic, apparatus, application, anesthetic, or other therapeutic or diagnostic substance or technique on any animal.

b.   To represent, directly or indirectly, publicly or privately, an ability and willingness to do any act described in sub-subdivision a. of this subdivision.

c.   To use any title, words, abbreviation, or letters in a manner or under circumstances which induce the belief that the person using them is qualified to do any act described in sub-subdivision a. of this subdivision.

(7)   "Veterinarian" shall mean a person who has received a doctor's degree in veterinary medicine from an accredited school of veterinary medicine and who is licensed by the Board to practice veterinary medicine.

(7a)   "Veterinarian-client-patient relationship" means that:

a.   The veterinarian has assumed the responsibility for making medical judgments regarding the health of the animal and the need for medical treatment, and the client (owner or other caretaker) has agreed to follow the instruction of the veterinarian.

b.   There is sufficient knowledge of the animal by the veterinarian to initiate at least a general or preliminary diagnosis of the medical condition of the animal. This means that the veterinarian has recently seen and is personally acquainted with the keeping and care of the animal by virtue of an examination of the animal, or by medically appropriate and timely visits to the premises where the animal is kept.

c.   The practicing veterinarian is readily available or provides for follow-up in case of adverse reactions or failure of the regimen of therapy.

(7b)   "Veterinary license" or "license" means a license to practice veterinary medicine issued by the Board.

(8)   "Veterinary medicine" includes veterinary surgery, obstetrics, dentistry, and all other branches or specialties of veterinary medicine.

(9)   "Veterinary student intern" means a person who is enrolled in an accredited veterinary college, has satisfactorily completed the third year of veterinary college education, and is registered with the Board as a veterinary student intern.

(10) "Veterinary student preceptee" means a person who is pursuing a doctorate degree in an accredited school of veterinary medicine that has a preceptor or extern program, has completed the academic requirements of that program, and is registered with the Board as a veterinary student preceptee.

(11) "Veterinary technician" means either of the following persons:

a. A person who has successfully completed a post-high school course in the care and treatment of animals that conforms to the standards required for accreditation by the American Veterinary Medical Association and who is registered with the Board as a veterinary technician.

b. A person who holds a degree in veterinary medicine from a college of veterinary medicine recognized by the Board for licensure of veterinarians and who is registered with the Board as a veterinary technician. (1961, c. 353, s. 2; 1973, c. 1106, s. 1; 1993, c. 500 s. 1.)

§ 90-181.1. Practice facility names and levels of service.

(a) In order to accurately inform the public of the levels of service offered, a veterinary practice facility shall use in its name one of the descriptive terms defined in subsection (b) of this section. The name of a veterinary practice facility shall, at all times, accurately reflect the level of service being offered to the public. If a veterinary facility or practice offers on-call emergency service, that service must be as that term is defined in subsection (b) of this section.

(b) The following definitions are applicable to this section:

(1) "Animal health center" or "animal medical center" means a veterinary practice facility in which consultative, clinical, and hospital services are rendered and in which a large staff of basic and applied veterinary scientists perform significant research and conduct advanced professional educational programs.

(2) "Emergency facility" means a veterinary medical facility whose primary function is the receiving, treatment, and monitoring of emergency patients during its specified hours of operation. At this veterinary practice facility a veterinarian is in attendance at all hours of operation and sufficient staff is available to provide timely and appropriate emergency care. An emergency

facility may be an independent veterinary medical after-hours facility, an independent veterinary medical 24-hour facility, or part of a full-service hospital or large teaching institution.

(3) "Mobile facility" means a veterinary practice conducted from a vehicle with special medical or surgical facilities or from a vehicle suitable only for making house or farm calls; provided, the veterinary medical practice shall have a permanent base of operation with a published address and telephone facilities for making appointments or responding to emergency situations.

(4) "Office" means a veterinary practice facility where a limited or consultative practice is conducted and which provides no facilities for the housing of patients.

(5) "On-call emergency service" means a veterinary medical service at a practice facility, including a mobile facility, where veterinarians and staff are not on the premises during all hours of operation or where veterinarians leave after a patient is treated. A veterinarian shall be available to be reached by telephone for after-hours emergencies.

(6) "Veterinary clinic" or "animal clinic" means a veterinary practice facility in which the practice conducted is essentially an out-patient practice.

(7) "Veterinary hospital" or "animal hospital" means a veterinary practice facility in which the practice conducted includes the confinement as well as the treatment of patients.

(c) If a veterinary practice facility uses as its name the name of the veterinarian or veterinarians owning or operating the facility, the name of the veterinary practice facility shall also include a descriptive term from those listed in subsection (b) of this section to disclose the level of service being offered.

(d) Those facilities existing and approved by the Board as of December 31, 1993, may continue to use their approved name or designation until there is a partial or total change of ownership of the facility, at which time the name of the veterinary practice facility shall be changed, as necessary, to comply with this section. (1993, c. 500, s. 2.)

§ 90-182. North Carolina Veterinary Medical Board; appointment, membership, organization.

(a) In order to properly regulate the practice of veterinary medicine and surgery, there is established a Board to be known as the North Carolina Veterinary Medical Board which shall consist of eight members.

Five members shall be appointed by the Governor. Four of these members shall have been legal residents of and licensed to practice veterinary medicine in this State for not less than five years preceding their appointment. The other member shall not be licensed or registered under the Article and shall represent the interest of the public at large. Each member appointed by the Governor shall reside in a different congressional district.

The General Assembly, upon the recommendation of the President Pro Tempore of the Senate, shall appoint to the Board one member who shall have been a resident of and licensed to practice veterinary medicine in this State for not less than five years preceding the appointment. The General Assembly, upon the recommendation of the Speaker of the House of Representatives, shall appoint to the Board one member who shall have been a legal resident of and registered as a veterinary technician in this State for not less than five years preceding the appointment.

In addition to the seven members appointed as provided above, the Commissioner of Agriculture shall biennially appoint to the Board the State Veterinarian or another veterinarian from a staff of a North Carolina department or institution. This member shall have been a legal resident of and licensed to practice veterinary medicine in North Carolina for not less than five years preceding his appointment.

Every member shall, within 30 days after notice of appointment, appear before any person authorized to administer the oath of office and take an oath to faithfully discharge the duties of the office.

(b) No person who has been appointed to the Board shall continue his membership on the Board if during the term of his appointment he shall:

(1) Transfer his legal residence to another state; or

(2) Own or be employed by any wholesale or jobbing house dealing in supplies, equipment, or instruments used or useful in the practice of veterinary medicine; or

(3) Have his license to practice veterinary medicine revoked for any of the causes listed in G.S. 90-187.8.

(c) All members serving on the board on June 30, 1981, shall complete their respective terms. The Governor shall appoint the public member not later than July 1, 1981. No member appointed to the Board by the Governor, Lieutenant Governor, Speaker of the House of Representatives, or General Assembly on or after July 1, 1981, shall serve more than two complete consecutive five-year terms, except that each member shall serve until his successor is appointed and qualifies. The term of the veterinary technician appointed by the General Assembly upon the recommendation of the Speaker of the House of Representatives shall begin on June 30th of the year in which he or she is appointed.

(d) The appointing authority may remove his appointee for the reasons specified in subsection (b) or for any good cause shown and may appoint members to fill unexpired terms. (1903, c. 503, s. 2; Rev., s. 5432; C.S., s. 6755; 1961, c. 353, s. 3; 1973, c. 1106, s. 1; c. 1331, s. 3; 1981, c. 767, s. 1; 1993, c. 500, ss. 3, 4; 2001-281, ss. 1, 2; 2001-487, s. 104; 2012-120, s. 3.1.)

§ 90-183. Meeting of Board.

The Board shall meet at least four times per year at the time and place fixed by the Board. Other meetings may be called by the president of the Board by giving notice as may be required by rule. A majority of the Board shall constitute a quorum. Meetings shall be open and public except that the Board may meet in closed session to prepare, approve, administer, or grade examinations, or to deliberate the qualification of an applicant for license or the disposition of a proceeding to discipline a veterinarian.

At its last meeting of the fiscal year the Board shall organize by electing, for the following fiscal year, a president, a vice-president, a secretary-treasurer, and such other officers as may be prescribed by rule. Officers of the Board shall serve for terms of one year and until a successor is elected, without limitation on the number of terms an officer may serve. The president shall serve as chairman of Board meetings. (1903, c. 503, ss. 3, 4, 6, 7; Rev., s. 5433; C.S., s. 6756; 1973, c. 1106, s. 1; 1993, c. 500, s. 5.)

§ 90-184. Compensation of the Board.

In addition to such reimbursement for travel and other expenses as is normally allowed to State employees, each member of the Board, for each day or substantial portion thereof that the member is engaged in the work of the Board may receive a per diem allowance, as determined by the Board in accordance with G.S. 93B-5. None of the expenses of the Board or of the members shall be paid by the State. (1903, c. 503, s. 9; Rev., s. 5434; C.S., s. 6757; 1961, c. 353, s. 4; 1973, c. 1106, s. 1; 1981, c. 767, s. 2; 1991 (Reg. Sess., 1992), c. 1011, s. 4; 1993, c. 500, s. 6.)

§ 90-185. General powers of the Board.

The Board may:

(1)   Examine and determine the qualifications and fitness of applicants for a license to practice veterinary medicine in the State.

(2)   Issue, renew, deny, suspend, or revoke licenses and limited veterinary licenses, and issue, deny, or revoke temporary permits to practice veterinary medicine in the State or otherwise discipline veterinarians consistent with the provisions of Chapter 150B of the General Statutes and of this Article and the rules adopted under this Article.

(3)   Conduct investigations for the purpose of discovering violations of this Article or grounds for disciplining veterinarians.

(4)   Employ full-time or part-time personnel - professional, clerical, or special - necessary to effectuate the provisions of this Article, purchase or rent necessary office space, equipment, and supplies, and purchase liability or other insurance to cover the activities of the Board, its operations, or its employees.

(5) Appoint from its own membership one or more members to act as representatives of the Board at any meeting within or without the State where such representation is deemed desirable.

(6) Adopt, amend, or repeal all rules necessary for its government and all regulations necessary to carry into effect the provisions of this Article, including the establishment and publication of standards of professional conduct for the practice of veterinary medicine.

The powers enumerated above are granted for the purpose of enabling the Board effectively to supervise the practice of veterinary medicine and are to be construed liberally to accomplish this objective. (1973, c. 1106, s. 1; c. 1331, s. 3; 1981, c. 767, s. 3; 1987, c. 827, s. 1; 1993, c. 500, s. 7.)

§ 90-186. Special powers of the Board.

In addition to the powers set forth in G.S. 90-185 above, the Board may:

(1) Fix minimum standards for continuing veterinary medical education for veterinarians and technicians, which shall be a condition precedent to the renewal of a veterinary license, limited license, veterinary faculty certificate, zoo veterinary certificate, or veterinary technician registration, respectively, under this Article;

(2) Inspect any hospitals, clinics, mobile units or other facilities used by any practicing veterinarian, either by a member of the Board or its authorized representatives, for the purpose of reporting the results of the inspection to the Board on a form prescribed by the Board and seeking disciplinary action for violations of health, sanitary, and medical waste disposal rules of the Board affecting the practice of veterinary medicine, or violations of rules of any county, state, or federal department or agency having jurisdiction in these areas of health, sanitation, and medical waste disposal that relate to or affect the practice of veterinary medicine;

(3) Upon complaint or information received by the Board, prohibit through summary emergency order of the Board, prior to a hearing, the operation of any veterinary practice facility that the Board determines is endangering, or may endanger, the public health or safety or the welfare and safety of animals, and suspend the license of the veterinarian operating the veterinary practice facility,

provided that upon the issuance of any summary emergency order, the Board shall initiate, within 10 days, a notice of hearing under the administrative rules issued pursuant to this Article and Chapter 150B of the General Statutes for an administrative hearing on the alleged violation;

(4) Provide special registration for "veterinary technicians," "veterinary student interns" and "veterinary student preceptees" and adopt rules concerning the training, registration and service limits of such assistants while employed by and acting under the supervision and responsibility of veterinarians. The Board has exclusive jurisdiction in determining eligibility and qualification requirements for these assistants. Renewals of registrations for veterinary technicians shall be required at least every 24 months, provided that the certificate of registration for the veterinary technician is otherwise eligible for renewal;

(5) Provide, pursuant to administrative rules, requirements for the inactive status of licenses and limited veterinary licenses;

(6) Set and require fees pursuant to administrative rule for the following:

a. Issuance or renewal of a certificate of registration for a professional corporation, in an amount not to exceed one hundred fifty dollars ($150.00).

b. Administering a North Carolina license examination, in an amount not to exceed two hundred fifty dollars ($250.00).

c. Securing and administering national examinations, including the National Board Examination or the Clinical Competency Test, in amounts directly related to the costs to the Board.

d. Inspection of a veterinary practice facility in an amount not to exceed seventy-five dollars ($75.00).

e. Issuance or renewal of a license or a limited license in an amount not to exceed one hundred fifty dollars ($150.00).

f. Issuance or renewal of a veterinary faculty certificate, in an amount not to exceed one hundred fifty dollars ($150.00).

g. Issuance or renewal of a zoo veterinary certificate, in an amount not to exceed one hundred fifty dollars ($150.00).

h. Reinstatement of an expired license, a limited license, a veterinary faculty certificate, a zoo veterinary certificate, a veterinary technician registration, or a professional corporation registration in an amount not to exceed one hundred dollars ($100.00).

i. Issuance or renewal of a veterinary technician registration, in an amount not to exceed fifty dollars ($50.00).

j. Issuance of a veterinary student intern registration, in an amount not to exceed twenty-five dollars ($25.00).

k. Issuance of a veterinary student preceptee registration, in an amount not to exceed twenty-five dollars ($25.00).

l. Late fee for renewal of a license, a limited license, a veterinary technician registration, a veterinary faculty certificate, a zoo veterinary certificate, or a professional corporation registration, in an amount not to exceed fifty dollars ($50.00).

m. Issuance of a temporary permit to practice veterinary medicine in an amount not to exceed one hundred fifty dollars ($150.00).

n. Providing copies, upon request, of Board publications, rosters, or other materials available for distribution from the Board, in an amount determined by the Board that is reasonably related to the costs of providing those copies.

The fees set under this subdivision for the renewal of a license, a limited license, a registration, or a certificate apply to each year of the renewal period.

(7) Pursuant to administrative rule, to assess and recover against persons holding licenses, limited licenses, temporary permits, or any certificates issued by the Board, costs reasonably incurred by the Board in the investigation, prosecution, hearing, or other administrative action of the Board in final decisions or orders where those persons are found to have violated the Veterinary Practice Act or administrative rules of the Board issued pursuant to the Act; provided, that all costs shall be the property of the Board. (1973, c. 1106, s. 1; 1981, c. 767, s. 4; 1987, c. 827, s. 1; 1993, c. 500, s. 8.)

§ 90-187. Application for license; qualifications.

(a) Any person desiring a license to practice veterinary medicine in this State shall make written application to the Board.

(b) The application shall show that the applicant is a graduate of an accredited veterinary school, a person of good moral character, and such other information and proof as the Board may require by rule. The Board may receive applications from senior students at accredited veterinary schools but an application is not complete until the applicant furnishes proof of graduation and such other information required by this Article and Board rules. The application shall be accompanied by a fee in the amount established and published by the Board.

(c) An application from a graduate of a program not accredited by the American Veterinary Medical Association may not be considered by the Board until the applicant furnishes satisfactory proof of graduation from a college of veterinary medicine and of successful completion of a certification program developed and administered by (i) the Educational Commission for Foreign Veterinary Graduates of the American Veterinary Medical Association or (ii) the Program for the Assessment of Veterinary Education Equivalence (PAVE) of the American Association of Veterinary State Boards. The certification programs shall include examinations with respect to clinical proficiency and comprehension of and ability to communicate in the English language.

(d) If the Board determines that the applicant possesses the proper qualifications, it may admit the applicant to the next examination, or if the applicant is eligible for a license without examination under G.S. 90-187.3; the Board may grant the applicant a license. (1903, c. 503, ss. 3, 5, 8; Rev., s. 5435; C.S., s. 6758; 1951, c. 749; 1961, c. 353, s. 5; 1973, c. 1106, s. 1; 1981, c. 767, ss. 5, 6; 1993, c. 500, s. 9; 2013-356, s. 1.)

§ 90-187.1. Examinations.

The Board shall hold at least one examination during each year and may hold such additional examinations as may appear necessary. The executive director shall give public notice of the time and place for each examination at least 90 days in advance of the date set for the examination. A person desiring to take an examination shall make application at least 60 days before the date of the examination. The Board shall determine the passing score for the successful completion of an examination.

After each examination the executive director shall notify each examinee of the result of the examination. The Board shall issue licenses to the persons successfully completing the requirements for licensure required by this Article and by Board rule. (1903, c. 503, ss. 3, 5, 8; Rev., s. 5435; C.S., s. 6758; 1951, c. 749; 1961, c. 353, s. 5; 1973, c. 1106, s. 1; 1993, c. 500, s. 10.)

§ 90-187.2. Status of persons previously licensed.

Any person holding a valid license to practice veterinary medicine in this State on July 1, 1974, shall be recognized as a licensed veterinarian and shall be entitled to retain this status so long as he complies with the provisions of this Article, and Board rules adopted pursuant thereto. (1973, c. 1106, s. 1.)

§ 90-187.3. Applicants licensed in other states.

(a) The Board may issue a license without written examination, other than the written North Carolina license examination, to applicants already licensed in another state provided the applicant presents evidence satisfactory to the Board that:

(1) The applicant is currently an active, competent practitioner in good standing.

(2) The applicant has practiced at least three of the five years immediately preceding filing the application.

(3) The applicant currently holds an active license in another state.

(4) There is no disciplinary proceeding or unresolved complaint pending against the applicant at the time a license is to be issued by this State.

(4a) Any disciplinary actions taken against the applicant or his or her license by the other state in which he or she is licensed will not affect the applicant's competency to practice veterinary medicine as provided in this Article or any rules adopted by the Board.

(5) The licensure requirements in the other state are substantially equivalent to those required by this State.

(6) The applicant has achieved a passing score on the written North Carolina license examination.

(a1) Expired.

(b) The Board may issue a license without a written examination, other than the written North Carolina license examination, to an applicant who meets the requirements of G.S. 90-187(c).

(c) The Board may at its discretion orally or practically examine any person qualifying for licensure under this section, by administering a nationally recognized clinical competency test as well as the North Carolina license examination.

(d) The Board may issue a limited license to practice veterinary medicine to an applicant who is not otherwise eligible for a license to practice veterinary medicine under this Article, without examination, if the applicant meets the criteria established in subdivisions (1) through (6) of subsection (a) of this section. (1959, c. 744; 1973, c. 1106, s. 1; 1981, c. 767, s. 7; 1993, c. 500, s. 11; 1999-203, ss. 1, 2.)

§ 90-187.4. Temporary permit.

(a) The Board may issue, without examination, a temporary permit to practice veterinary medicine in this State:

(1) To a qualified applicant for license pending examination, provided that such temporary permit shall expire the day after the notice of results of the first examination given after the permit is issued.

(2) To a nonresident veterinarian validly licensed in another state, territory, or district of the United States or a foreign country, provided that such temporary permit shall be issued for a period of no more than 60 days.

(3) Temporary permits, as provided in (1) and (2) above, may contain any restrictions as to time, place, or supervision, that the Board deems appropriate. The State Veterinarian shall be notified as to the issuance of all temporary permits.

(b) A temporary permit may be summarily revoked by majority vote of the Board without a hearing. (1903, c. 503, ss. 3, 5, 8; Rev., s. 5435; C.S., s. 6758; 1951, c. 749; 1961, c. 353, s. 5; 1973, c. 1106, s. 1; 1993, c. 500, s. 12.)

§ 90-187.5. License renewal.

All licenses and limited licenses shall expire annually or biennially, as determined by the Board, on December 31 but may be renewed by application to the Board and payment of the renewal fee established and published by the Board. The executive director shall issue a new certificate of registration to all persons registering under this Article. Failure to apply for renewal within 60 days after expiration shall result in automatic revocation of the license or limited license and any person who shall practice veterinary medicine after such revocation shall be practicing in violation of this Article. Provided, that any person may renew an expired license or limited license at any time within two years following its expiration upon application and compliance with Board requirements and the payment of all applicable fees in amounts allowed by this Article or administrative rule of the Board; and further provided, that the applicant is otherwise eligible under this Article or administrative rules of the Board to have the license renewed. (1961, c. 353, s. 6; 1973, c. 1106, s. 1; 1993, c. 500, s. 13.)

§ 90-187.6. Veterinary technicians and veterinary employees.

(a) "Veterinary technicians," "veterinary student interns," and "veterinary student preceptees," before performing any services otherwise prohibited to persons not licensed or registered under this Article, shall be approved by and registered with the Board. The Board shall be responsible for all matters pertaining to the qualifications, registration, discipline, and revocation of registration of these persons, under this Article and rules issued by the Board.

(b) The services of a technician, intern, preceptee, or other veterinary employee shall be limited to services under the direction and supervision of a veterinarian. This employee shall receive no fee or compensation of any kind for services other than any salary or compensation paid to the employee by the veterinarian or veterinary facility by which the employee is employed. The employee may participate in the operation of a branch office, clinic, or allied establishment only to the extent allowable under and as defined by this Article or by rules issued by the Board.

(c) An employee under the supervision of a veterinarian may perform such duties as are required in the physical care of animals and in carrying out medical orders as prescribed by the veterinarian, requiring an understanding of animal science but not requiring the professional services as set forth in G.S. 90-181(6)a. In addition, a veterinary technician may assist veterinarians in diagnosis, laboratory analysis, anesthesia, and surgical procedures. Neither the employee nor the veterinary technician may perform any act producing an irreversible change in the animal. An employee, other than a veterinary technician, intern, or preceptee, may, under the direct supervision of a veterinarian, perform duties including collection of specimen; testing for intestinal parasites; collecting blood; testing for heartworms and conducting other laboratory tests; taking radiographs; and cleaning and polishing teeth, provided that the employee has had sufficient on-the-job training by a veterinarian to perform these specified duties in a competent manner. It shall be the responsibility of the veterinarian supervising the employee to ascertain that the employee performs these specified duties assigned to the employee in a competent manner. These specified duties shall be performed under the direct supervision of the veterinarian in charge of administering care to the patient.

(d) Veterinary student interns, in addition to all of the services permitted to veterinary technicians, may, under the direct personal supervision of a veterinarian, perform surgery and administer therapeutic or prophylactic drugs.

(e) Veterinary student preceptees, in addition to all of the services permitted to veterinary technicians and veterinary student interns, may, upon the direction of the employing veterinarian, make ambulatory calls and hospital and clinic diagnoses, prescriptions and treatments.

(f) Any person registered as a veterinary technician, veterinary student intern, or veterinary student preceptee, who shall practice veterinary medicine except as provided herein, shall be guilty of a Class 1 misdemeanor, and shall also be subject to revocation of registration. Any nonregistered veterinary employee employed under subsection (c) who practices veterinary medicine except as provided under that subsection shall be guilty of a Class 1 misdemeanor.

(g) Any veterinarian directing or permitting a veterinary technician, intern, preceptee or other employee to perform a task or procedure not specifically allowed under this Article and the rules of the Board shall be guilty of a Class 1 misdemeanor. (1973, c. 1106, s. 1; 1981, c. 767, ss. 8-11; 1993, c. 500, s. 14; c. 539, ss. 634, 635; 1995, c. 509, s. 42.)

§ 90-187.7. Abandonment of animals; notice to owner; relief from liability for disposal; "abandoned" defined.

(a) Any animal placed in the custody of a licensed veterinarian for treatment, boarding or other care, which shall be unclaimed by its owner or his agent for a period of more than 10 days after written notice by registered or certified mail, return receipt requested, to the owner or his agent at his last known address, shall be deemed to be abandoned and may be turned over to the nearest humane society, or dog pound or disposed of as such custodian may deem proper.

(b) The giving of notice to the owner, or the agent of the owner, of such animal by the licensed veterinarian, as provided in subsection (a) of this section, shall relieve the licensed veterinarian and any custodian to whom such animal may be given of any further liability for disposal.

(c) For the purpose of this Article the term "abandoned" shall mean to forsake entirely, or to neglect or refuse to provide or perform the legal obligations for care and support of an animal by its owner, or his agent. Such abandonment shall constitute the relinquishment of all rights and claims by the owner to such animal. (1973, c. 1106, s. 1.)

§ 90-187.8. Discipline of licensees.

(a) Upon complaint or information, and within the Board's discretion, the Board may revoke or suspend a license issued under this Article, may otherwise discipline a person licensed under this Article, or may deny a license required by this Article in accordance with the provisions of this Article, Board rules, and Chapter 150B of the General Statutes. As used in this section, the word "license" includes a license, a limited license, a veterinary faculty certificate, a zoo veterinary certificate, and a registration of a veterinary technician, a veterinary student intern, and a veterinary student preceptee.

(b) The Board may impose and collect from a licensee a civil monetary penalty of up to five thousand dollars ($5,000) for each violation of this Article or a rule adopted under this Article. The clear proceeds of these civil penalties shall be remitted to the Civil Penalty and Forfeiture Fund in accordance with G.S. 115C-457.2.

The amount of the civil penalty, up to the maximum, shall be determined upon a finding of one or more of the following factors:

(1) The degree and extent of harm to the public health or to the health of the animal under the licensee's care.

(2) The duration and gravity of the violation.

(3) Whether the violation was committed willfully or intentionally or reflects a continuing pattern.

(4) Whether the violation involved elements of fraud or deception either to the client or to the Board, or both.

(5) The prior disciplinary record with the Board of the licensee.

(6) Whether and the extent to which the licensee profited by the violation.

(c) Grounds for disciplinary action shall include but not be limited to the following:

(1) The employment of fraud, misrepresentation, or deception in obtaining a license.

(2) An adjudication of insanity or incompetency.

(3) The impairment of a person holding a license issued by the Board, when the impairment is caused by that person's use of alcohol, drugs, or controlled substances, and the impairment interferes with that person's ability to practice

within the scope of the license with reasonable skill and safety and in a manner not harmful to the public or to animals under the person's care.

(4) The use of advertising or solicitation which is false, misleading, or deceptive.

(5) Conviction of a felony or other public offense involving moral turpitude.

(6) Incompetence, gross negligence, or other malpractice in the practice of veterinary medicine.

(7) Having professional association with or knowingly employing any person practicing veterinary medicine unlawfully.

(8) Fraud or dishonesty in the application or reporting of any test for disease in animals.

(9) Failure to keep veterinary premises and equipment in a clean and sanitary condition, violating an administrative rule of the Board concerning the minimum sanitary requirements of veterinary hospitals, veterinary clinics, or other practice facilities, or violating other State or federal statutes, rules, or regulations concerning the disposal of medical waste.

(10) Failure to report, as required by the laws and regulations of the State, or making false report of, any contagious or infectious disease.

(11) Dishonesty or gross negligence in the inspection of foodstuffs or the issuance of health or inspection certificates.

(12) Conviction of a criminal offense involving cruelty to animals or the act of cruelty to animals.

(13) Revocation of a license to practice veterinary medicine by another state, territory or district of the United States only if the grounds for revocation in the other jurisdiction would also result in revocation of the practitioner's license in this State.

(14) Unprofessional conduct as defined in regulations adopted by the Board.

(15) Conviction of a federal or state criminal offense involving the illegal use, prescription, sale, or handling of controlled substances, other drugs, or medicines.

(16) The illegal use, dispensing, prescription, sale, or handling of controlled substances or other drugs and medicines.

(17) Failure to comply with regulations of the United States Food and Drug Administration regarding biologics, controlled substances, drugs, or medicines.

(18) Selling, dispensing, prescribing, or allowing the sale, dispensing, or prescription of biologics, controlled substances, drugs, or medicines without a veterinarian-client-patient relationship with respect to the sale, dispensing, or prescription.

(19) Acts or behavior constituting fraud, dishonesty, or misrepresentation in dealing with the Board or in the veterinarian-client-patient relationship. (1903, c. 503, s. 10; Rev., s. 5436; C.S., s. 6759; 1953, c. 1041, s. 16; 1961, c. 353, s. 7; 1973, c. 1106, s. 1; c. 1331, s. 3; 1981, c. 767, ss. 12, 13; 1987, c. 827, s. 1; 1993, c. 500, s. 15; 1998-215, s. 136.)

§ 90-187.9. Reinstatement.

Any person whose license is suspended or revoked may, at the discretion of the Board, be relicensed or reinstated at any time without an examination by majority vote of the Board on written application made to the Board showing cause justifying relicensing or reinstatement. (1961, c. 353, s. 8; 1973, c. 1106, s. 1.)

§ 90-187.10. Necessity for license; certain practices exempted.

No person shall engage in the practice of veterinary medicine or own all or part interest in a veterinary medical practice in this State or attempt to do so without having first applied for and obtained a license for such purpose from the North Carolina Veterinary Medical Board, or without having first obtained from the Board a certificate of renewal of license for the calendar year in which the person proposes to practice and until the person shall have been first licensed and registered for such practice in the manner provided in this Article and the rules and regulations of the Board.

Nothing in this Article shall be construed to prohibit:

(1)   Any person from administering to animals, the title to which is vested in the person or the person's employer, except when the title is so vested for the purpose of circumventing the provisions of this Article;

(2)   Any person who is a regular student or instructor in a legally chartered college from the performance of those duties and actions assigned as the person's responsibility in teaching or research;

(3)   Any veterinarian not licensed by the Board who is a member of the Armed Forces of the United States or who is an employee of the United States Department of Agriculture, the United States Public Health Service or other federal agency, or the State of North Carolina, or political subdivision thereof, from performing official duties while so commissioned or employed;

(4)   Any person from such practices as permitted under the provisions of G.S. 90-185, House Bill 659, Chapter 17, Public Laws 1937, or House Bill 358, Chapter 5, Private Laws 1941;

(5)   Any person from dehorning or castrating male food animals;

(6)   Any person from providing for or assisting in the practice of artificial insemination;

(7)   Any physician licensed to practice medicine in this State, or the physician's assistant, while engaged in medical research;

(8)   Any certified rabies vaccinator appointed, certified and acting within the provisions of G.S. 130A-186;

(9)   Any veterinarian licensed to practice in another state from examining livestock or acting as a consultant in North Carolina, provided the consulting veterinarian is directly supervised by a veterinarian licensed by the Board who must, at or prior to the first instance of consulting, notify the Board, in writing, that he or she is supervising the consulting veterinarian, give the Board the name, address, and licensure status of the consulting veterinarian, and also verify to the Board that the supervising veterinarian assumes responsibility for

the professional acts of the consulting veterinarian; and provided further, that the consultation by the veterinarian in North Carolina does not exceed 10 days or parts thereof per year, and further that all infectious or contagious diseases diagnosed are reported to the State Veterinarian within 48 hours; or

(10)   Any person employed by the North Carolina Department of Agriculture and Consumer Services as a livestock inspector or by the U.S. Department of Agriculture as an animal health technician from performing regular duties assigned to him or her during the course and scope of that person's employment. (1903, c. 503, s. 12; Rev., s. 5438; C.S., s. 6761; 1961, c. 353, s. 9; 1973, c. 1106, s. 1; 1983, c. 891, s. 11; 1993, c. 500, s. 16; 1995, c. 509, s. 43; 1997-261, s. 11; 2011-183, s. 62.)

§ 90-187.11. Partnership, corporate, or sole proprietorship practice.

A veterinary medical practice may be conducted as a sole proprietorship, by a partnership, or by a duly registered professional corporation.

Whenever the practice of veterinary medicine is carried on by a partnership, all partners must be licensed.

It shall be unlawful for any corporation to practice or offer to practice veterinary medicine as defined in this Article, except as provided for in Chapter 55B of the General Statutes of North Carolina. (1961, c. 353, s. 8; 1973, c. 1106, s. 1; 1993, c. 500, s. 17.)

§ 90-187.12. Unauthorized practice; penalty.

If any person shall

(1)   Practice or attempt to practice veterinary medicine in this State without first having obtained a license or temporary permit from the Board; or

(2)   Practice veterinary medicine without the renewal of his license, as provided in G.S. 90-187.5; or

(3) Practice or attempt to practice veterinary medicine while his license is revoked, or suspended, or when a certificate of license has been refused; or

(4) Violate any of the provisions of this Article,

said person shall be guilty of a Class 1 misdemeanor. Each act of such unlawful practice shall constitute a distinct and separate offense. (1913, c. 129, s. 2; C.S., s. 6762; 1961, c. 353, s. 10; c. 756; 1973, c. 1106, s. 1; 1993, c. 539, s. 636; 1994, Ex. Sess., c. 24, s. 14(c).)

§ 90-187.13. Injunctions.

The Board may appear in its own name in the superior courts in an action for injunctive relief to prevent violation of this Article and the superior courts shall have power to grant such injunctions regardless of whether criminal prosecution has been or may be instituted as a result of such violations. Actions under this section shall be commenced in the superior court district or set of districts as defined in G.S. 7A-41.1 in which the respondent resides or has his principal place of business or in which the alleged acts occurred. (1981, c. 767, s. 14; 1987 (Reg. Sess., 1988), c. 1037, s. 102.)

§ 90-187.14. Veterinary faculty certificates and zoo veterinary certificates.

(a) The Board may, upon application, issue veterinary faculty certificates in lieu of a license that otherwise would be required by this Article.

(b) The Board may, upon application, issue zoo veterinary certificates in lieu of a license that otherwise would be required by this Article, to veterinarians employed by the North Carolina State Zoo.

(c) The Board shall determine by administrative rule the application procedure, fees, criteria for the issuance, continuing education, renewal, suspension or revocation, and the scope of practice under the veterinary faculty certificate or the zoo veterinary certificate. There shall be an annual renewal of each certificate and all persons holding these certificates shall be subject to the jurisdiction of the Board in all respects under this Article. (1993, c. 500, s. 18.)

§ 90-187.15. Board agreement for programs for impaired veterinary personnel.

(a) The Board may enter into agreements with organizations that have developed programs for impaired veterinary personnel. Activities to be covered by these agreements may include investigation, review, and evaluation of records, reports, complaints, litigation, and other information about the practices or the practice patterns of veterinary personnel licensed or registered by the Board as these matters may relate to impaired veterinary personnel. Organizations having programs for impaired veterinary personnel may include a statewide supervisory committee or various regional or local components or subgroups.

(b) Agreements authorized under this section shall include provisions for the impaired veterinary personnel organizations to: (i) receive relevant information from the Board and other sources; (ii) conduct any investigation, review, or evaluation in an expeditious manner; (iii) provide assurance of confidentiality of nonpublic information and of the process; (iv) make reports of investigations and evaluations to the Board; and (v) implement any other related activities for operating and promoting a coordinated and effective process. The agreement shall include provisions assuring basic due process for veterinary personnel who become involved.

(c) Organizations entering into agreements with the Board shall establish and maintain a program for impaired veterinary personnel licensed or registered by the Board for the purpose of identifying, reviewing, and evaluating the ability of those veterinarians or veterinary technicians to function as veterinarians or veterinary technicians and provide programs for treatment and rehabilitation. The Board may provide funds for the administration of these impaired veterinary personnel peer review programs. The Board may adopt rules pursuant to Chapter 150B of the General Statutes to apply to the operation of impaired veterinary personnel programs, with provisions for: (i) definitions of impairment; (ii) guidelines for program elements; (iii) procedures for receipt and use of information of suspected impairment; (iv) procedures for intervention and referral; (v) arrangements for monitoring treatment, rehabilitation, posttreatment support, and performance; (vi) reports of individual cases to the Board; (vii) periodic reporting of statistical information; (viii) assurance of confidentiality of nonpublic information and of the process; and (ix) other necessary measures.

(d) Upon investigation and review of a veterinarian licensed by the Board or a veterinary technician registered with the Board, or upon receipt of a complaint or other information, an impaired veterinary personnel organization that enters into an agreement with the Board shall report to the Board detailed information about any veterinarian licensed or veterinary technician registered by the Board if:

(1) The veterinarian or veterinary technician constitutes an imminent danger to the public, to patients, or to himself or herself.

(2) The veterinarian or veterinary technician refuses to cooperate with the program, refuses to submit to treatment, or is still impaired after treatment and exhibits professional incompetence.

(3) It reasonably appears that there are other grounds for disciplinary action.

(e) Any confidential information or other nonpublic information acquired, created, or used in good faith by an impaired veterinary personnel organization or the Board regarding a participant pursuant to this section shall remain confidential and shall not be subject to discovery or subpoena in a civil case, nor subject to disclosure as a public document by the Board pursuant to Chapter 132 of the General Statutes. No person participating in good faith in an impaired veterinary personnel program developed under this section shall be required in a civil case to disclose any information, including opinions, recommendations, or evaluations, acquired or developed solely in the course of participating in the program.

(f) Impaired veterinary personnel activities conducted in good faith pursuant to any program developed under this section shall not be grounds for civil action under the laws of this State, and the activities are deemed to be State-directed and sanctioned and shall constitute "State action" for the purposes of application of antitrust laws. (2003-139, s. 1.)

§§ 90-188 through 90-202.1. Recodified as §§ 90-202.2 to 90-202.14.

Article 12A.

Podiatrists.

§ 90-202.2. "Podiatry" defined.

(a) Podiatry as defined by this Article is the surgical, medical, or mechanical treatment of all ailments of the human foot and ankle, and their related soft tissue structures to the level of the myotendinous junction. Excluded from the definition of podiatry is the amputation of the entire foot, the administration of an anesthetic other than local, and the surgical correction of clubfoot of an infant two years of age or less.

(b) Except for procedures for bone spurs and simple soft tissue procedures, any surgery on the ankle or on the soft tissue structures related to the ankle, any amputations, and any surgical correction of clubfoot shall be performed by a podiatrist only in a hospital licensed under Article 5 of Chapter 131E of the General Statutes or in a multispecialty ambulatory surgical facility that is not a licensed office setting, and that is licensed under Part D of Article 6 of Chapter 131E of the General Statutes. Before performing any of the surgeries referred to in this subsection in a multispecialty ambulatory surgical facility, the podiatrist shall have applied for and been granted privileges to perform this surgery in the multispecialty ambulatory surgical facility. The granting of these privileges shall be based upon the same criteria for granting hospital privileges under G.S. 131E-85.

(c) The North Carolina Board of Podiatry Examiners shall maintain a list of podiatrists qualified to perform the surgeries listed in subsection (b) of this section, along with specific information on the surgical training successfully completed by each licensee. (1919, c. 78, s. 2; C.S., s. 6763; 1945, c. 126; 1963, c. 1195, s. 2; 1971, c. 1211; 1975, c. 672, s. 1; 1995, c. 248, s. 1.)

§ 90-202.3. Unlawful to practice unless registered.

No person shall practice podiatry unless he shall have been first licensed and registered so to do in the manner provided in this Article, and if any person shall practice podiatry without being duly licensed and registered, as provided in this Article, he shall not be allowed to maintain any action to collect any fee for such services. Any person who engages in the practice of podiatry unless licensed and registered as hereinabove defined, or who attempts to do so, or who professes to do so, shall be guilty of a Class 1 misdemeanor. Each act of such unlawful practice shall constitute a separate offense. (1919, c. 78, s. 1; C.S., s. 6764; 1963, c. 1195, s. 2; 1967, c. 1217, s. 2; 1975, c. 672, s. 1; 1993, c. 539, s. 637; 1994, Ex. Sess., c. 24, s. 14(c).)

§ 90-202.4. Board of Podiatry Examiners; terms of office; powers; duties.

(a)   There shall be established a Board of Podiatry Examiners for the State of North Carolina. This Board shall consist of four members appointed by the Governor. Three of the members shall be licensed podiatrists who have practiced podiatry in North Carolina for not less than seven years immediately preceding their election and who are elected and nominated to the Governor as hereinafter provided. The other member shall be a person chosen by the Governor to represent the public at large. The public member shall not be a health care provider nor may he or she be the spouse of a health care provider. For purposes of Board membership, "health care provider" means any licensed health care professional and any agent or employee of any health care institution, health care insurer, health care professional school, or a member of any allied health profession. For purposes of this section, a person enrolled in a program to prepare him to be a licensed health care professional or an allied health professional shall be deemed a health care provider. For purposes of this section, any person with significant financial interest in a health service or profession is not a public member.

(b)   All Board members serving on June 30, 1981, shall be eligible to complete their respective terms. No member appointed to the Board on or after July 1, 1981, shall serve more than two complete consecutive three-year terms, except that each member shall serve until his successor is chosen and qualified.

(c)   Podiatrist members chosen as provided for in subsection (d) shall be selected upon the expiration of the respective terms of the members of the present Board of Podiatry Examiners. Membership on the Board resulting from appointment before July 1, 1981, shall not be considered in determining the permissible length of service under subsection (b). The Governor shall appoint the public member not later than July 1, 1981.

(d) The Governor shall appoint podiatrist members of the Board from a list provided by the Board of Podiatry Examiners. For each vacancy, the Board shall submit at least two names to the Governor. All nominations of podiatrist members of the Board shall be conducted by the Board of Podiatry Examiners, which is hereby constituted a Board of Podiatry Elections. Every podiatrist with a current North Carolina license residing in this State shall be eligible to vote in all elections. The list of licensed podiatrists shall constitute the registration list for elections. The Board of Podiatry Elections is authorized to make rules relative to the conduct of these elections, provided such rules are not in conflict with the provisions of this section and provided that notice shall be given to all licensed podiatrists residing in North Carolina. All such rules shall be adopted subject to the procedures of Chapter 150B of the General Statutes of North Carolina. From any decision of the Board of Podiatry Elections relative to the conduct of such elections, appeal may be taken to the courts in the manner provided by Chapter 150B of the General Statutes.

(e) Any initial or regular member of the Board may be removed from office by the Governor for good cause shown. Any vacancy in the initial or regular podiatrist membership of the Board shall be filled for the period of the unexpired term by the Governor from a list of at least two names submitted by the podiatrist members of the Board. Any vacancy in the public membership of the Board shall be filled by the Governor for the unexpired term.

(f) The Board is authorized to elect its own presiding and other officers.

(g) The Board, in carrying out its responsibilities, shall have authority to employ personnel, full-time or part-time, as shall be determined to be necessary in the work of the Board. The Board shall have authority to pay compensation to the member of the Board holding the position of secretary-treasurer on a basis to be determined by the Board; Provided that in the event the positions of secretary and treasurer are not combined but are held by different members of the Board, the Board shall have authority to pay compensation to the member holding the position of secretary and to the member holding the position of treasurer, if the Board so chooses, on a basis to be determined by the Board. The Board is required to keep proper and complete records with respect to all of its activities, financial and otherwise, and shall on or before January 30 of each year submit a written report to the Governor and to such other officials and/or agencies as other sections of the General Statutes may require, said report covering the activities of the Board during the previous calendar year, which report shall include a verified financial statement. The Board is authorized to adopt rules and regulations governing its proceedings and the practice of podiatry in this State, not inconsistent with the provisions of this Article. The Board shall maintain at all times an up-to-date list of the names and addresses of each licensed podiatrist in North Carolina, which list shall be available for inspection and which shall be included in the annual report referred to above. (1919, c. 78, s. 3; C.S., s. 6765; 1963, c. 1195, s. 2; 1967, c. 1217, s. 3; 1975, c. 672, s. 1; 1981, c. 659, s. 1; 1983, c. 217, ss. 1-4; 1987, c. 827, s. 1.)

§ 90-202.5. Applicants to be examined; examination fee; requirements; temporary licenses.

(a)   Any person not heretofore authorized to practice podiatry in this State shall file with the Board of Podiatry Examiners an application for examination accompanied by a fee not to exceed three hundred fifty dollars ($350.00), together with proof that the applicant is of good moral character, and has obtained a preliminary education equivalent to four years of instruction in a high school and three years of instruction in a college or university approved by the American Association of Colleges and Universities. Before taking the examination, the applicant must be a graduate of a college of podiatric medicine accredited by the National Council on Education of the American Podiatry Association.

Effective January 1, 1992, every applicant, as a prerequisite for licensure under this Article, shall complete one year of clinical residency or other equivalent postgraduate clinical program approved by the North Carolina Board of Podiatry Examiners and, before taking the North Carolina podiatry licensure examination, shall present evidence to the Board that he has passed the National Board Examination.

Any person licensed to practice podiatry on or before January 1, 1992, who is actively involved in a postgraduate clinical program approved by the Board shall be permitted to practice podiatry in the approved program pending its completion.

(b)   Effective January 1, 1992, the Board may issue a temporary license to practice podiatry to any applicant for licensure, for a period and under conditions established by the Board, while the person resides in North Carolina and is participating in a clinical residency or other equivalent postgraduate clinical program approved by the Board. A temporary license is valid only while the licensee is actively participating in the program and may not be extended beyond the determined length of training set by the Board. (1919, c. 78, s. 9; C.S., s. 6766; 1963, c. 1195, ss. 1, 2; 1967, c. 1217, s. 4; 1975, c. 672, s. 1; 1981, c. 659, s. 2; 1983, c. 217, s. 5; 1989, c. 214; 1991, c. 457, s. 1.)

§ 90-202.6. Examinations; subjects; certificates.

(a) The Board of Podiatry Examiners shall hold at least one examination annually for the purpose of examining applicants under this Article. The examination shall be at such time and place as the Board may see fit. The Board may make such rules and regulations as it may deem necessary to conduct its examinations and meetings. It shall provide, preserve and keep a complete record of all its transactions. Examinations for registration under this Article shall be in the English language and shall be written, oral, or clinical, or a combination of written, oral or clinical, as the Board may determine, and may include the following subjects: anatomy, physiology, bacteriology, chemistry, dermatology, podiatry, surgery, materia medica, pharmacology and pathology. No applicant shall be granted a license certificate by the Board unless he obtains a general average of 75 or over, and not less than fifty percent (50%) in any one subject. After such examination the Board shall without unnecessary delay, act on same and issue license certificates to the successful candidates signed by each member of the Board; and the Board of Podiatry Examiners shall report annually to each licensed podiatrist in the State of North Carolina.

(b) The Board may waive the administration of a written examination prepared by it for all initial applicants who have successfully completed the National Board of Podiatry Examination. The Board may administer to such applicants and require them to complete successfully an examination to test clinical competency in the practice of podiatry.

(c) Any applicant who fails to pass his examination shall within one year be entitled to reexamination upon the payment of an amount not to exceed three hundred fifty dollars ($350.00), but not more than two reexaminations shall be allowed any one applicant prior to filing a new application. Should he fail to pass his third examination, he shall file a new application before he can again be examined. (1919, c. 78, s. 4; C.S., s. 6767; 1963, c. 1195, s. 2; 1967, c. 1217, s. 5; 1975, c. 672, s. 1; 1981, c. 659, ss. 3, 4; 1983, c. 217, s. 6; 1991, c. 457, s. 2.)

§ 90-202.7. Applicants licensed in other states.

If an applicant for licensure is already licensed in another state to practice podiatry, the Board shall issue a license to practice podiatry to the applicant upon evidence that:

(1)   The applicant is currently an active, competent practitioner in good standing; and

(2)   The applicant has practiced at least five years immediately preceding his or her application with at least three of those five years being in a state that grants similar reciprocity to North Carolina podiatrists; and

(3)   The applicant currently holds a valid license in another state; and

(4)   No disciplinary proceeding or unresolved complaint is pending anywhere at the time a license is to be issued by this State; and

(5)   The licensure requirements in the other state are equivalent to or higher than those required by this State, and the licensure requirements of that other state grant similar reciprocity to podiatrists licensed in North Carolina.

Any license issued upon the application of any podiatrist from any other state shall be subject to all of the provisions of this Article with reference to the license issued by the North Carolina State Board of Podiatry Examiners upon examination of applicants, and the rights and privileges to practice the profession of podiatry under any license so issued shall be subject to the same duties, obligations, restrictions and conditions as imposed by this Article on podiatrists originally examined by the North Carolina State Board of Podiatry Examiners. (1919, c. 78, s. 6; C.S., s. 6768; 1967, c. 1217, s. 6; 1975, c. 672, s. 1; 1981, c. 659, s. 5; 1983, c. 217, s. 7; 1991, c. 457, s. 3.)

§ 90-202.8. Revocation of certificate; grounds for; suspension of certificate.

(a)   The North Carolina State Board of Podiatry Examiners, in accordance with Chapter 150B (Administrative Procedure Act) of the General Statutes, shall have the power and authority to: (i) refuse to issue a license to practice podiatry; (ii) refuse to issue a certificate of renewal of a license to practice podiatry; (iii) revoke or suspend a license to practice podiatry; and (iv) invoke such other disciplinary measures, censure, or probative terms against a licensee as it deems fit and proper;

in any instance or instances in which the Board is satisfied that such applicant or licensee:

(1) Has engaged in any act or acts of fraud, deceit or misrepresentation in obtaining or attempting to obtain a license or the renewal thereof;

(2) Is a chronic or persistent user of alcohol intoxicants or habit-forming drugs or narcotics to the extent that the same impairs his ability to practice podiatry;

(3) Has been convicted of any of the criminal provisions of this Article or has entered a plea of guilty or nolo contendere to any charge or charges arising therefrom;

(4) Has been convicted of or entered a plea of guilty or nolo contendere to any felony charge or to any misdemeanor charge involving moral turpitude;

(5) Has been convicted of or entered a plea of guilty or nolo contendere to any charge of violation of any state or federal narcotic or barbiturate law;

(6) Has engaged in any act or practice violative of any of the provisions of this Article or violative of any of the rules and regulations promulgated and adopted by the Board, or has aided, abetted or assisted any other person or entity in the violation of the same;

(7) Is mentally, emotionally, or physically unfit to practice podiatry or is afflicted with such a physical or mental disability as to be deemed dangerous to the health and welfare of his patients. An adjudication of mental incompetency in a court of competent jurisdiction or a determination thereof by other lawful means shall be conclusive proof of unfitness to practice podiatry unless or until such person shall have been subsequently lawfully declared to be mentally competent;

(8) Has advertised services in a false, deceptive, or misleading manner;

(9) Has permitted the use of his name, diploma or license by another person either in the illegal practice of podiatry or in attempting to fraudulently obtain a license to practice podiatry;

(10) Has engaged in such immoral conduct as to discredit the podiatry profession;

(11) Has obtained or collected or attempted to obtain or collect any fee through fraud, misrepresentation, or deceit;

(12) Has been negligent in the practice of podiatry;

(13) Is not professionally competent in the practice of podiatry;

(14) Has practiced any fraud, deceit or misrepresentation upon the public or upon any individual in an effort to acquire or retain any patient or patients;

(15) Has made fraudulent or misleading statements pertaining to his skill, knowledge, or method of treatment or practice;

(16) Has committed any fraudulent or misleading acts in the practice of podiatry;

(17), (18) Repealed by Session Laws 1981, c. 659, s. 7.

(19) Has wrongfully or fraudulently or falsely held himself out to be or represented himself to be qualified as a specialist in any branch of podiatry;

(20) Has persistently maintained, in the practice of podiatry, unsanitary offices, practices, or techniques;

(21) Is a menace to the public health by reason of having a serious communicable disease;

(22) Has distributed or caused to be distributed any intoxicant, drug, or narcotic for any other than a lawful purpose; or

(23) Has engaged in any unprofessional conduct as the same may be, from time to time, defined by the rules and regulations of the Board.

(a1) The Board shall establish a grievance committee to receive complaints concerning a practitioner's business or professional practices. The committee shall consider all complaints and determine whether there is probable cause. After its review, the committee may dismiss any complaint when it appears that probable cause of a violation cannot be established. Complaints which are not dismissed shall be referred to the Board.

(b) If any person engages in or attempts to engage in the practice of podiatry while his license is suspended, his license to practice podiatry in the State of North Carolina may be permanently revoked.

(c) Action of the Board shall be subject to judicial review as provided by Chapter 150B (Administrative Procedure Act). (1919, c. 78, ss. 12, 13; C.S., s. 6772; 1953, c. 1041, ss. 17, 18; 1963, c. 1195, s. 2; 1967, c. 691, s. 45; 1973, c. 1331, s. 3; 1975, c. 672, ss. 1, 2; 1981, c. 659, ss. 6-8; 1987, c. 827, s. 1; 1991, c. 636, s. 6; 1997-456, s. 27.)

§ 90-202.9. Fees for certificates and examinations; compensation of Board.

To provide a fund in order to carry out the provisions of this Article the Board shall charge not more than one hundred dollars ($100.00) for each license issued and one hundred dollars ($100.00) for each examination. From such funds the Board shall pay its members at the rate set out in G.S. 93B-5: Provided, that at no time shall the expenses exceed the cash balance on hand. (1919, c. 78, s. 14; C.S., s. 6773; 1967, c. 1217, s. 9; 1975, c. 672, s. 1.)

§ 90-202.10. Annual fee; cancellation or renewal of license.

On or before the first day of July of each year every podiatrist engaged in the practice of podiatry in this State shall transmit to the secretary-treasurer of the said North Carolina State Board of Podiatry Examiners his signature and post-office address, the date and year of his or her certificate, together with a fee to be set by the Board of Podiatry Examiners not to exceed two hundred dollars ($200.00) and receive therefor a renewal certificate. Any license or certificate granted by said Board under or by virtue of this section shall automatically be cancelled and annulled if the holder thereof fails to secure the renewal herein provided for within a period of 30 days after the first day of July of each year, and such delinquent podiatrist shall pay a penalty for reinstatement of twenty-five dollars ($25.00) for each succeeding month of delinquency until a six-month period of delinquency exists. After a six-month period of delinquency exists or after January 1 following the July 1 deadline, the said podiatrist must appear before the North Carolina Board of Podiatry Examiners and take a new examination before being allowed to practice podiatry in the State of North Carolina. (1931, c. 191; 1963, c. 1195, s. 2; 1967, c. 1217, s. 10; 1975, c. 672, s. 1; 1977, c. 621; 1991, c. 457, s. 4.)

§ 90-202.11. Continuing education courses required.

Beginning May 1, 1976, all registered podiatrists then or thereafter licensed in the State of North Carolina shall be required to take annual courses of study in subjects relating to the practice of the profession of podiatry to the end that the utilization and application of new techniques, scientific and clinical advances, and the achievements of research will assure expansive and comprehensive care to the public. The length of study shall be prescribed by the Board but shall not exceed 25 hours in any calendar year. Attendance must be at a course or courses approved by the Board. Attendance at any course or courses of study are to be certified to the Board upon a form provided by the Board and shall be submitted by each registered podiatrist at the time he makes application to the Board for the renewal of his license and payment of his renewal fee. The Board is authorized to treat funds set aside for the purpose of continuing education as State funds for the purpose of accepting any funds made available under federal law on a matching basis for the promulgation and maintenance of programs of continuing education. This requirement may be waived by the Board in cases of certified illness or undue hardship as provided in the rules and regulations of the Board. (1975, c. 672, s. 1.)

§ 90-202.12. Free choice by patient guaranteed.

No agency of the State, county or municipality, nor any commission or clinic, nor any board administering relief, social security, health insurance or health service under the laws of the State of North Carolina shall deny to the recipients or beneficiaries of their aid or services the freedom to choose the provider of care or service which are within the scope of practice of a duly licensed podiatrist or duly licensed physician as defined in this Chapter. (1967, c. 690, s. 3; 1975, c. 672, s. 1.)

§ 90-202.13. Injunctions.

The Board may appear in its own name in the superior courts in an action for injunctive relief to prevent violation of this Article and the superior courts shall have power to grant such injunctions regardless of whether criminal prosecution has been or may be instituted as a result of such violations. Actions under this section shall be commenced in the superior court district or set of districts as defined in G.S. 7A-41.1 in which the respondent resides or has his principal place of business or in which the alleged acts occurred. (1975, c. 672, s. 1; 1981, c. 659, s. 9; 1987 (Reg. Sess., 1988), c. 1037, s. 103.)

§ 90-202.14. Not applicable to physicians.

Nothing in this Article shall apply to a physician licensed to practice medicine or to a person acting under the supervision or at his direction in the course of such practice. (1975, c. 672, s. 1.)

Article 13.

Embalmers and Funeral Directors.

§§ 90-203 through 90-210.17: Recodified as §§ 90-210.18 to 90-210.25.

Article 13A.

Practice of Funeral Service.

§ 90-210.18: Repealed by Session Laws 2004-192, s. 1, effective January 1, 2005.

§ 90-210.18A. Board of Funeral Service created; qualifications; vacancies; removal.

(a) The General Assembly declares that the practice of funeral service affects the public health, safety, and welfare and is subject to regulation and control in the public interest. The public interest requires that only qualified persons be permitted to practice funeral service in North Carolina and that the profession merit the confidence of the public. This Article shall be liberally construed to accomplish these ends.

(b) The North Carolina Board of Funeral Service is created and shall regulate the practice of funeral service in this State. The Board shall have nine members as follows:

(1) Four members appointed by the Governor from nominees recommended by the North Carolina Funeral Directors Association, Inc. These members shall be persons licensed under this Article.

(2) Two members appointed by the Governor from nominees recommended by the Funeral Directors & Morticians Association of North Carolina, Inc. These members shall be persons licensed under this Article.

(3) One member appointed by the Governor who is licensed under this Article and who is not affiliated with any funeral service trade association.

(4) One member appointed by the General Assembly, upon the recommendation of the President Pro Tempore of the Senate. This member shall be a person who is not licensed under this Article or employed by a person who is licensed under this Article.

(5) One member appointed by the General Assembly, upon the recommendation of the Speaker of the House of Representatives. This member shall be a person who is not licensed under this Article or employed by a person who is licensed under this Article.

Members of the Board shall serve staggered three-year terms, ending on December 31 of the last year of the term or when a successor has been duly appointed, whichever is later. No member may serve more than two complete consecutive terms.

(c) Vacancies. - A vacancy shall be filled in the same manner as the original appointment, except that all unexpired terms of Board members appointed by the General Assembly shall be filled in accordance with G.S. 120-122. Appointees to fill vacancies shall serve the remainder of the unexpired term and until their successors have been duly appointed and qualified.

(d) Removal. - The Board may remove any of its members for neglect of duty, incompetence, or unprofessional conduct. A member subject to disciplinary proceedings as a licensee shall be disqualified from participating in the official business of the Board until the charges have been resolved. (2004-192, s. 2; 2007-531, s. 1.)

§ 90-210.19. Board members' oath of office.

The members of said Board, before entering upon their duties, shall take and subscribe to the oath of office prescribed for other State officers, which said oath shall be administered by a person qualified to administer such oath and shall be filed in the office of the Secretary of State. (1901, c. 338, ss. 3, 4; Rev., s. 4385; C.S., s. 6778; 1945, c. 98, s. 2; 1949, c. 951, s. 2; 1957, c. 1240, s. 2; 1969, c. 584, s. 1; 1973, c. 476, s. 128; 1975, c. 571.)

§ 90-210.20. Definitions.

(a) "Advertisement" means the publication, dissemination, circulation or placing before the public, or causing directly or indirectly to be made, published, disseminated or placed before the public, any announcement or statement in a newspaper, magazine, or other publication, or in the form of a book, notice, circular, pamphlet, letter, handbill, poster, bill, sign, placard, card, label or tag, or over any radio, television station, or electronic medium.

(b) "Board" means the North Carolina Board of Funeral Service.

(c) "Burial" includes interment in any form, cremation and the transportation of the dead human body as necessary therefor.

(c1) "Chapel" means a chapel or other facility separate from the funeral establishment premises for the primary purpose of reposing of dead human bodies, visitation or funeral ceremony that is owned, operated, or maintained by a funeral establishment under this Article, and that does not use the word "funeral" in its name, on a sign, in a directory, in advertising or in any other manner; in which or on the premises of which there is not displayed any caskets or other funeral merchandise; in which or on the premises of which there is not located any preparation room; and which no owner, operator, employee, or agent thereof represents the chapel to be a funeral establishment.

(c2) "Dead human bodies", as used in this Article includes fetuses beyond the second trimester and the ashes from cremated bodies.

(d) "Embalmer" means any person engaged in the practice of embalming.

(e) "Embalming" means the preservation and disinfection or attempted preservation and disinfection of dead human bodies by application of chemicals externally or internally or both and the practice of restorative art including the restoration or attempted restoration of the appearance of a dead human body. Embalming shall not include the washing or use of soap and water to cleanse or prepare a dead human body for disposition by the authorized agents, family, or friends of the deceased who do so privately without pay or as part of the ritual washing and preparation of dead human bodies prescribed by religious practices; provided, that no dead human body shall be handled in a manner inconsistent with G.S. 130A-395.

(f) "Funeral directing" means engaging in the practice of funeral service except embalming.

(g) "Funeral director" means any person engaged in the practice of funeral directing.

(h) "Funeral establishment" means every place or premises devoted to or used in the care, arrangement and preparation for the funeral and final disposition of dead human bodies and maintained for the convenience of the public in connection with dead human bodies or as the place for carrying on the practice of funeral service.

(i) "Funeral service licensee" means a person who is duly licensed and engaged in the practice of funeral service.

(j) "Funeral service" means the aggregate of all funeral service licensees and their duties and responsibilities in connection with the funeral as an organized, purposeful, time-limited, flexible, group-centered response to death.

(k) "Practice of funeral service" means engaging in the care or disposition of dead human bodies or in the practice of disinfecting and preparing by embalming or otherwise dead human bodies for the funeral service, transportation, burial or cremation, or in the practice of funeral directing or embalming as presently known, whether under these titles or designations or otherwise. "Practice of funeral service" also means engaging in making arrangements for funeral service, selling funeral supplies to the public or making financial arrangements for the rendering of such services or the sale of such supplies.

(l) "Resident trainee" means a person who is engaged in preparing to become licensed for the practice of funeral directing, embalming or funeral service under the personal supervision and instruction of a person duly licensed for the practice of funeral directing, embalming or funeral service in the State of North Carolina under the provisions of this Chapter, and who is duly registered as a resident trainee with the Board. (1957, c. 1240, s. 2; 1975, c. 571; 1979, c. 461, s. 6; 1987, c. 430, s. 2; c. 879, s. 6.2; 1997-399, s. 1; 2001-294, s. 2; 2003-420, ss. 1, 3; 2007-531, s. 2.)

§ 90-210.21. Repealed by Session Laws 1987, c. 430, s. 3.

§ 90-210.22. Required meetings of the Board.

The Board shall hold at least four meetings in each year. In addition, the Board may meet as often as the proper and efficient discharge of its duties shall require. Five members shall constitute a quorum. (1901, c. 338, ss. 5, 6, 7, 8; Rev., s. 4387; C.S., s. 6780; 1949, c. 951, s. 3; 1957, c. 1240, s. 2; 1969, c. 584, s. 2; 1973, c. 476, s. 128; 1975, c. 571; 1991 (Reg. Sess., 1992), c. 901, s. 4; 2003-420, s. 4.)

§ 90-210.23. Powers and duties of the Board.

(a) The Board is authorized to adopt and promulgate such rules and regulations for transaction of its business and for the carrying out and enforcement of the provisions of this Article as may be necessary and as are consistent with the laws of this State and of the United States.

(b) The Board shall elect from its members a president, a vice-president and a secretary, no two offices to be held by the same person. The president and vice-president and secretary shall serve for one year and until their successors shall be elected and qualified. The Board shall have authority to engage adequate staff as deemed necessary to perform its duties.

(c) The members of the Board shall serve without compensation provided that such members shall be reimbursed for their necessary traveling expenses and the necessary expenses incident to their attendance upon the business of the Board, and in addition thereto they shall receive per diem and expense reimbursement as provided in G.S. 93B-5 for every day actually spent by such member upon the business of the Board. All expenses, salaries and per diem provided for in this Article shall be paid from funds received under the provisions of this Article and shall in no manner be an expense to the State.

(d) Every person licensed by the Board and every resident trainee shall furnish all information required by the Board reasonably relevant to the practice of the profession or business for which the person is a licensee or resident trainee. Every funeral service establishment and its records and every place of business where the practice of funeral service or embalming is carried on and its records shall be subject to inspection by the Board during normal hours of operation and periods shortly before or after normal hours of operation and shall furnish all information required by the Board reasonably relevant to the business therein conducted. Every licensee, resident trainee, embalming facility, and funeral service establishment shall provide the Board with a current post-office address which shall be placed on the appropriate register and all notices required by law or by any rule or regulation of the Board to be mailed to any licensee, resident trainee, embalming facility, or funeral service establishment shall be validly given when mailed to the address so provided.

(d1) The Board is empowered to hold hearings in accordance with the provisions of this Article and of Chapter 150B to subpoena witnesses and to administer oaths to or receive the affirmation of witnesses before the Board.

In any show cause hearing before the Board held under the authority of Chapter 150B of the General Statutes where the Board imposes discipline against a licensee, the Board may recover the costs, other than attorneys' fees, of holding the hearing against all respondents jointly, not to exceed two thousand five hundred dollars ($2,500).

(e) The Board is empowered to regulate and inspect, according to law, funeral service establishments and embalming facilities, their operation, and the licenses under which they are operated, and to enforce as provided by law the rules, regulations, and requirements of the Division of Health Services and of the city, town, or county in which the funeral service establishment or embalming facility is maintained and operated. Any funeral establishment or embalming facility that, upon inspection, is found not to meet all of the requirements of this Article shall pay a reinspection fee to the Board for each additional inspection that is made to ascertain that the deficiency or other violation has been corrected. The Board is also empowered to enforce compliance with the standards set forth in Funeral Industry Practices, 16 C.F.R. 453 (1984), as amended from time to time.

(f) The Board may establish, supervise, regulate and control programs for the resident trainee. It may approve schools of mortuary science or funeral service, graduation from which is required by this Article as a qualification for the granting of any license, and may establish essential requirements and standards for such approval of mortuary science or funeral service schools.

(g) Schools for teaching mortuary science which are approved by the Board shall have extended to them the same privileges as to the use of bodies for dissecting while teaching as those granted in this State to medical colleges, but such bodies shall be obtained through the same agencies which provide bodies for medical colleges.

(h) The Board shall adopt a common seal.

(h1) The Board shall have the power to acquire, hold, rent, encumber, alienate, and otherwise deal with real property in the same manner as a private person or corporation, subject only to approval of the Governor and the Council of State. Collateral pledged by the Board for an encumbrance is limited to the assets, income, and revenues of the Board.

(h2) The Board may employ legal counsel and clerical and technical assistance, and fix the compensation therefor, and incur such other expenses as may be deemed necessary in the performance of its duties and the enforcement of the provisions of this Article or as otherwise required by law and as may be necessary to carry out the powers herein conferred.

(i)   The Board may perform such other acts and exercise such other powers and duties as may be provided elsewhere in this Article or otherwise by law and as may be necessary to carry out the powers herein conferred. (1901, c. 338, ss. 5, 6, 7, 8, 11; Rev., ss. 4386, 4387, 4389; C.S., ss. 6779, 6780, 6783; 1949, c. 951, s. 3; 1957, c. 1240, s. 2; 1969, c. 584, s. 2; 1973, c. 476, s. 128; 1975, c. 571; 1979, c. 461, ss. 8, 9; 1987, c. 827, s. 1; 1991, c. 528, s. 3; 1993, c. 164, s. 1; 1997-399, ss. 2, 3; 2003-420, s. 5(a), (b); 2007-531, s. 3.)

§ 90-210.24. Inspector.

(a)   The Board may appoint one or more agents who shall serve at the pleasure of the Board and who shall have the title "Inspector of the North Carolina Board of Funeral Service." No person is eligible for appointment as inspector unless at the time of the appointment the person is licensed under this Article as a funeral service licensee.

(b)   To determine compliance with the provisions of this Article and regulations promulgated under this Article, inspectors may

(1)   Enter the office, establishment or place of business of any funeral service licensee, funeral director or embalmer in North Carolina, and any office, establishment or place in North Carolina where the practice of funeral service or embalming is carried on, or where that practice is advertised as being carried on, or where a funeral is being conducted or a body is being embalmed, to inspect the records, office, establishment, or facility, or to inspect the practice being carried on or license or registration of any licensee and any resident trainee operating therein;

(2)   Enter any hospital, nursing home, or other institution from which a dead human body has been removed by any person licensed under this Article or their designated representative to inspect records pertaining to the removal and its authorization; and

(3)   May inspect criminal and probation records of licensees and applicants for licenses under this Article to obtain evidence of their character.

Inspectors may serve papers and subpoenas issued by the Board or any office or member thereof under authority of this Article, and shall perform other duties prescribed or ordered by the Board.

(c)   Upon request by the Board, the Attorney General of North Carolina shall provide the inspectors with appropriate identification cards, signed by the Attorney General or his designated agent.

(d)   The Board may prescribe an inspection form to be used by the inspectors in performing their duties. (1975, c. 571; 1979, c. 461, s. 10; 1993, c. 164, s. 2; 1997-399, s. 4; 2003-420, ss. 1, 6.)

§ 90-210.25. Licensing.

(a)   Qualifications, Examinations, Resident Traineeship and Licensure. -

(1)   To be licensed for the practice of funeral directing under this Article, a person must:

a.   Be at least 18 years of age.

b.   Be of good moral character.

c.   Be a graduate of a Funeral Director Program at a mortuary science college approved by the Board or a school of mortuary science accredited by the American Board of Funeral Service Education. Have completed a minimum of 32 semester hours or 48 quarter hours of instruction, including the subjects set out in sub-part e.1. of this subdivision, as prescribed by a mortuary science college approved by the Board or a school of mortuary science accredited by the American Board of Funeral Service Education.

d.   Have completed 12 months of resident traineeship as a funeral director, pursuant to the procedures and conditions set out in G.S. 90-210.25(a)(4), either before or after satisfying the educational requirement under sub-subdivision c. of this subdivision.

e.   Have passed an oral or written funeral director examination on the following subjects:

1. Psychology, sociology, pathology, funeral directing, business law, funeral law, funeral management, and accounting.

2. Repealed by Session Laws 1997-399, s. 5.

3. Laws of North Carolina and rules of the Board and other agencies dealing with the care, transportation and disposition of dead human bodies.

(2) To be licensed for the practice of embalming under this Article, a person must:

a. Be at least 18 years of age.

b. Be of good moral character.

c. Be a graduate of a mortuary science college approved by the Board.

d. Have completed 12 months of resident traineeship as an embalmer pursuant to the procedures and conditions set out in G.S. 90-210.25(a)(4), either before or after satisfying the educational requirement under sub-subdivision c. of this subdivision.

e. Have passed an oral or written embalmer examination on the following subjects:

1. Embalming, restorative arts, chemistry, pathology, microbiology, and anatomy.

2. Repealed by Session Laws 1997-399, s. 6.

3. Laws of North Carolina and rules of the Board and other agencies dealing with the care, transportation and disposition of dead human bodies.

(3) To be licensed for the practice of funeral service under this Article, a person must:

a. Be at least 18 years of age.

b. Be of good moral character.

c. Be a graduate of and receive an associate degree from a mortuary science college approved by the Board or a school of mortuary science accredited by the American Board of Funeral Service Education. Have completed a minimum of 60 semester hours or 90 quarter hours of instruction, including the subjects set out in sub-part e.1. of this subdivision, as prescribed by a mortuary science college approved by the Board or a school of mortuary science accredited by the American Board of Funeral Service Education.

d. Have completed 12 months of resident traineeship as a funeral service licensee, pursuant to the procedures and conditions set out in G.S. 90-210.25(a)(4), either before or after satisfying the educational requirement under sub-subdivision c. of this subdivision.

e. Have passed an oral or written funeral service examination on the following subjects:

1. Psychology, sociology, funeral directing, business law, funeral law, funeral management, and accounting.

2. Embalming, restorative arts, chemistry, pathology, microbiology, and anatomy.

3. Repealed by Session Laws 1997-399, s. 7.

4. Laws of North Carolina and rules of the Board and other agencies dealing with the care, transportation and disposition of dead human bodies.

(4) a. A person desiring to become a resident trainee shall apply to the Board on a form provided by the Board. The application shall state that the applicant is not less than 18 years of age, of good moral character, and is the graduate of a high school or the equivalent thereof, and shall indicate the licensee under whom the applicant expects to train. A person training to become an embalmer may serve under either a licensed embalmer or a funeral service licensee. A person training to become a funeral director may serve under either a licensed funeral director or a funeral service licensee. A person training to become a funeral service licensee shall serve under a funeral service licensee. The application must be sustained by oath of the applicant and be accompanied by the appropriate fee. When the Board is satisfied as to the qualifications of an applicant it shall instruct the secretary to issue a certificate of resident traineeship.

b.   Within 30 days of a resident trainee leaving the proctorship of the licensee under whom the trainee has worked, the licensee shall file with the Board an affidavit showing the length of time served with the licensee by the trainee, and the affidavit shall be made a matter of record in the Board's office. The licensee shall deliver a copy of the affidavit to the trainee.

c.   A person who has not completed the traineeship and wishes to do so under a licensee other than the one whose name appears on the original certificate may reapply to the Board for approval.

d.   A certificate of resident traineeship shall be signed by the resident trainee and upon payment of the renewal fee shall be renewable one year after the date of original registration; but the certificate may not be renewed more than two times. The Board shall mail to each registered trainee at his last known address a notice that the renewal fee is due and that, if not paid within 30 days of the notice, the certificate will be canceled. A late fee, in addition to the renewal fee, shall be charged for a late renewal, but the renewal of the registration of any resident trainee who is engaged in active service in the Armed Forces of the United States at the time renewal is due may, at the discretion of the Board, be held in abeyance for the duration of that service without penalties. No credit shall be allowed for the 12-month period of resident traineeship that shall have been completed more than five years preceding the examination for a license.

e.   All registered resident trainees shall report to the Board at least once every month during traineeship upon forms provided by the Board listing the work which has been completed during the preceding month of resident traineeship. The data contained in the reports shall be certified as correct by the licensee under whom the trainee has served during the period and by the licensed person who is managing the funeral service establishment. Each report shall list the following:

1.   For funeral director trainees, the conduct of any funerals during the relevant time period,

2.   For embalming trainees, the embalming of any bodies during the relevant time period,

3.   For funeral service trainees, both of the activities named in 1 and 2 of this subsection, engaged in during the relevant time period.

f. To meet the resident traineeship requirements of G.S. 90-210.25(a)(1), G.S. 90-210.25(a)(2) and G.S. 90-210.25(a)(3) the following must be shown by the affidavit(s) of the licensee(s) under whom the trainee worked:

1. That the funeral director trainee has, under supervision, assisted in directing at least 25 funerals during the resident traineeship,

2. That the embalmer trainee has, under supervision, assisted in embalming at least 25 bodies during the resident traineeship,

3. That the funeral service trainee has, under supervision, assisted in directing at least 25 funerals and, under supervision, assisted in embalming at least 25 bodies during the resident traineeship.

g. The Board may suspend or revoke a certificate of resident traineeship for violation of any provision of this Article.

h. Each sponsor for a registered resident trainee must during the period of sponsorship be actively employed with a funeral establishment. The traineeship shall be a primary vocation of the trainee.

i. Only one resident trainee may register and serve at any one time under any one person licensed under this Article.

j., k. Repealed by Session Laws 1991, c. 528, s. 4.

l. The Board shall register no more than one resident trainee at a funeral establishment that served 100 or fewer families during the 12 months immediately preceding the date of the application, and shall register no more than one resident trainee for each additional 100 families served at the funeral establishment during the 12 months immediately preceding the date of the application.

(5) The Board by regulation may recognize other examinations that the Board deems equivalent to its own.

a. All licenses shall be signed by the president and secretary of the Board and the seal of the Board affixed thereto. All licenses shall be issued, renewed or duplicated for a period not exceeding one year upon payment of the renewal fee, and all licenses, renewals or duplicates thereof shall expire and terminate the thirty-first day of December following the date of their issue unless sooner revoked and canceled; provided, that the date of expiration may be changed by unanimous consent of the Board and upon 90 days' written notice of such change to all persons licensed for the practice of funeral directing, embalming and funeral service in this State.

b. The holder of any license issued by the Board who shall fail to renew the same on or before February 1 of the calendar year for which the license is to be renewed shall have forfeited and surrendered the license as of that date. No license forfeited or surrendered pursuant to the preceding sentence shall be reinstated by the Board unless it is shown to the Board that the applicant has, throughout the period of forfeiture, engaged full time in another state of the United States or the District of Columbia in the practice to which the applicant's North Carolina license applies and has completed for each such year continuing education substantially equivalent in the opinion of the Board to that required of North Carolina licensees; or has completed in North Carolina a total number of hours of accredited continuing education computed by multiplying five times the number of years of forfeiture; or has passed the North Carolina examination for the forfeited license. No additional resident traineeship shall be required. The applicant shall be required to pay all delinquent annual renewal fees and a reinstatement fee. The Board may waive the provisions of this section for an applicant for a forfeiture which occurred during the applicant's service in the Armed Forces of the United States provided the applicant applies within six months following severance therefrom.

c. All licensees now or hereafter licensed in North Carolina shall take continuing education courses in subjects relating to the practice of the profession for which they are licensed, to the end that the benefits of learning and reviewing skills will be utilized and applied to assure proper service to the public.

d. As a prerequisite to the annual renewal of a license, the licensee must complete, during the year immediately preceding renewal, at least five hours of continuing education courses, of which the Board may require licensees to take up to two hours specified by the Board. All continuing education courses must be approved by the Board prior to enrollment. A licensee who completes more than five hours in a year may carry over a maximum of five hours as a credit to the following year's requirement. A licensee who is issued an initial license on or after July 1 does not have to satisfy the continuing education requirement for that year.

e. The Board shall not renew a license unless fulfillment of the continuing education requirement has been certified to it on a form provided by the Board, but the Board may waive this requirement for renewal in cases of certified illness or undue hardship or where the licensee lives outside of North Carolina and does not practice in North Carolina, and the Board shall waive the requirement for all licensees who were licensed on or before December 31, 2003, and have been licensed in North Carolina for a continuous period of 25 years or more, for all licensees who are licensed on or after January 1, 2004, who have been licensed for a continuous period of 25 years or more and have attained the age of 60 years, and for all licensees who are, at the time of renewal, members of the General Assembly.

f. The Board shall cause to be established and offered to the licensees, each calendar year, at least eight hours of continuing education courses. The Board may charge licensees attending these courses a reasonable registration fee in order to meet the expenses thereof and may also meet those expenses from other funds received under the provisions of this Article.

g. Any person who having been previously licensed by the Board as a funeral director or embalmer prior to July 1, 1975, shall not be required to satisfy the requirements herein for licensure as a funeral service licensee, but shall be entitled to have such license renewed upon making proper application therefor and upon payment of the renewal fee provided by the provisions of this Article. Persons previously licensed by the Board as a funeral director may engage in funeral directing, and persons previously licensed by the Board as an embalmer may engage in embalming. Any person having been previously licensed by the Board as both a funeral director and an embalmer may upon application therefor receive a license as a funeral service licensee.

h. The Department of Justice may provide a criminal record check to the Board for a person who has applied for a new or renewal license, or certification through the Board. The Board shall provide to the Department of Justice, along with the request, the fingerprints of the applicant, any additional information required by the Department of Justice, and a form signed by the applicant consenting to the check of the criminal record and to the use of the fingerprints and other identifying information required by the State or national repositories. The applicant's fingerprints shall be forwarded to the State Bureau of Investigation for a search of the State's criminal history record file, and the State Bureau of Investigation shall forward a set of the fingerprints to the Federal Bureau of Investigation for a national criminal history check. The Board shall keep all information pursuant to this subdivision privileged, in accordance with applicable State law and federal guidelines, and the information shall be confidential and shall not be a public record under Chapter 132 of the General Statutes.

The Department of Justice may charge each applicant a fee for conducting the checks of criminal history records authorized by this subdivision.

(a1) Inactive Licenses. - Any person holding a license issued by the Board for funeral directing, for embalming, or for the practice of funeral service may apply for an inactive license in the same category as the active license held. The inactive license is renewable annually. Continuing education is not required for the renewal of an inactive license. The holder of an inactive license may not engage in any activity requiring an active license. The holder of an inactive license may apply for an active license in the same category, and the Board shall issue an active license if the applicant has completed a total number of hours of accredited continuing education equal to five times the number of years the applicant held the inactive license. No application fee is required for the reinstatement of an active license pursuant to this subsection. The holder of an inactive license who returns to active status shall surrender the inactive license to the Board.

(a2) In order to engage in the practice of funeral directing or funeral service, such a licensee must own, be employed by, or otherwise be an agent of a licensed funeral establishment; except that such a licensee may practice funeral directing or funeral service if:

(1) Employed by a college of mortuary science; or

(2) The licensee:

a. Maintains all of his or her business records at a location made known to the Board and available for inspection by the Board under the same terms and conditions as the business records of a licensed funeral establishment;

b. Complies with rules and regulations imposed on funeral establishments and the funeral profession that are designed to protect consumers, to include, but not be limited to, the Federal Trade Commission's laws and rules requiring General Price Lists and Statements of Goods and Services; and

c. Pays to the Board the funeral establishment license fee required by law and set by the Board.

Nothing in this subdivision shall preclude a licensee from arranging cremations and cremating human remains while employed by a crematory.

(b) Persons Licensed under the Laws of Other Jurisdictions. -

(1) The Board shall grant licenses to funeral directors, embalmers and funeral service licensees, licensed in other states, territories, the District of Columbia, and foreign countries, when it is shown that the applicant holds a valid license as a funeral director, embalmer or funeral service licensee issued by the other jurisdiction, has demonstrated knowledge of the laws and rules governing the profession in North Carolina and has submitted proof of his good moral character; and either that the applicant has continuously practiced the profession in the other jurisdiction for at least three years immediately preceding his application, or the Board has determined that the licensing requirements for the other jurisdiction are substantially similar to those of North Carolina.

(2) The Board shall periodically review the mortuary science licensing requirements of other jurisdictions and shall determine which licensing requirements are substantially similar to the requirements of North Carolina.

(3) The Board may issue special permits, to be known as courtesy cards, permitting nonresident funeral directors, embalmers and funeral service licensees to remove bodies from and to arrange and direct funerals and embalm bodies in this State, but these privileges shall not include the right to establish a place of business in or engage generally in the business of funeral directing and embalming in this State. Except for special permits issued by the Board for teaching continuing education programs and for work in connection with disasters, no special permits may be issued to nonresident funeral directors, embalmers, and funeral service licensees from states that do not issue similar courtesy cards to persons licensed in North Carolina pursuant to this Article.

(c) Registration, Filing and Transportation. -

(1) The holder of any license granted by this State for those within the funeral service profession or renewal thereof provided for in this Article shall cause registration to be filed in the office of the board of health of the county or city in which he practices his profession, or if there be no board of health in such county or city, at the office of the clerk of the superior court of such county. All such licenses, certificates, duplicates and renewals thereof shall be displayed in

a conspicuous place in the funeral establishment where the holder renders service.

(2) It shall be unlawful for any railway agent, express agency, baggage master, conductor or other person acting as such, to receive the dead body of any person for shipment or transportation by railway or other public conveyance, to a point outside of this State, unless the body is accompanied by a burial-transit permit.

(3) The "transportation or removal of a dead human body" shall mean the removal of a dead human body for a fee from the location of the place of death or discovery of death or the transportation of the body to or from a medical facility, funeral establishment or facility, crematory or related holding facility, place of final disposition, or place designated by the Medical Examiner for examination or autopsy of the dead human body.

(4) Any individual, not otherwise exempt from this subsection, shall apply for and receive a permit from the Board before engaging in the transportation or removal of a dead human body in this State. Unless otherwise exempt from this subsection, no corporation or other business entity shall engage in the transportation or removal of a dead human body unless it has in its employ at least one individual who holds a permit issued under this section. No individual permit holder shall engage in the transportation or removal of a dead human body for more than one person, firm, or corporation without first providing the Board with written notification of the name and physical address of each such employer.

(5) The following persons shall be exempt from the permit requirements of this section but shall otherwise be subject to subdivision (9) of this subsection and any rules relating to the proper handling, care, removal, or transportation of a dead human body:

a. Licensees under this Article and their employees.

b. Employees of common carriers.

c. Except as provided in sub-subdivision (6)c. of this section, employees of the State and its agencies and employees of local governments and their agencies.

d. Funeral directors licensed in another state and their employees.

(6) The following persons shall be exempt from this section:

a. Emergency medical technicians, rescue squad workers, volunteer and paid firemen, and law enforcement officers while acting within the scope of their employment.

b. Employees of public or private hospitals, nursing homes, or long-term care facilities, while handling a dead human body within such facility or while acting within the scope of their employment.

c. State and county medical examiners and their investigators.

d. Any individual transporting cremated remains.

e. Any individual transporting or removing a dead human body of their immediate family or next of kin.

f. Any individual who has exhibited special care and concern for the decedent.

(7) Individuals eligible to receive a permit under this section for the transportation or removal of a dead human body for a fee, shall:

a. Be at least 18 years of age.

b. Possess and maintain a valid drivers license issued by this State and provide proof of all liability insurance required for the registration of any vehicle in which the person intends to engage in the business of the removal or transportation of a dead human body.

c. Affirmatively state under oath that the person has read and understands the statutes and rules relating to the removal and transportation of dead human bodies and any guidelines as may be adopted by the Board.

d. Provide three written character references on a form prescribed by the Board, one of which must be from a licensed funeral director.

e. Be of good moral character.

(8) The permit issued under this section shall expire on December 31 of each year. The application fee for the individual permit shall not exceed one hundred twenty-five dollars ($125.00). A fee, not to exceed one hundred dollars ($100.00), in addition to the renewal fee not to exceed seventy-five dollars ($75.00), shall be charged for any application for renewal received by the Board after February 1 of each year.

(9) No person shall transport a dead human body in the open cargo area or passenger area of a vehicle or in any vehicle in which the body may be viewed by the public. Any person removing or transporting a dead human body shall either cover the body, place it upon a stretcher designed for the purpose of transporting humans or dead human bodies in a vehicle, and secure such stretcher in the vehicle used for transportation, or shall enclose the body in a casket or container designed for common carrier transportation, and secure the casket or container in the vehicle used for transportation. No person shall fail to treat a dead human body with respect at all times. No person shall take a photograph or video recording of a dead human body without the consent of a member of the deceased's immediate family or next of kin or other authorizing agent.

(10) The Board may adopt rules under this section including permit application procedures and the proper procedures for the removal, handling, and transportation of dead human bodies. The Board shall consult with the Office of the Chief Medical Examiner before initiating rule making under this section and before adopting any rules pursuant to this section. Nothing in this section prohibits the Office of the Chief Medical Examiner from adopting policies and procedures regarding the removal, transportation, or handling of a dead human body under the jurisdiction of that office that are more stringent than the laws in this section or any rules adopted under this section. Any violation of this section or rules adopted under this section may be punished by the Board by a suspension or revocation of the permit to transport or remove dead human bodies or by a term of probation. The Board may, in lieu of any disciplinary measure, accept a penalty not to exceed five thousand dollars ($5,000) per violation.

(11) Each applicant for a permit shall provide the Board with the applicant's home address, name and address of any corporation or business entity employing such individual for the removal or transportation of dead human bodies, and the make, year, model, and license plate number of any vehicle in which a dead human body is transported. A permittee shall provide written notification to the Board of any change in the information required to be

provided to the Board by this section or by the application for a permit within 30 days after such change takes place.

(12)   If any person shall engage in or hold himself out as engaging in the business of transportation or removal of a dead human body without first having received a permit under this section, the person shall be guilty of a Class 2 misdemeanor.

(13)   The Board shall have the authority to inspect any place or premises that the business of removing or transporting a dead human body is carried out and shall also have the right of inspection of any vehicle and equipment used by a permittee for the removal or transportation of a dead human body.

(d)   Establishment Permit. -

(1)   No person, firm or corporation shall conduct, maintain, manage or operate a funeral establishment unless a permit for that establishment has been issued by the Board and is conspicuously displayed in the establishment. Each funeral establishment at a specific location shall be deemed to be a separate entity and shall require a separate permit and compliance with the requirements of this Article.

(2)   A permit shall be issued when:

a.   It is shown that the funeral establishment has in charge a person, known as a manager, licensed for the practice of funeral directing or funeral service, who shall not be permitted to manage more than one funeral establishment. The manager shall be charged with overseeing the daily operation of the funeral establishment. If the manager leaves the employment of the funeral establishment and is the only licensee employed who is eligible to serve as manager, the funeral establishment may operate without a manager for a period not to exceed 30 days so long as: (i) the funeral establishment retains one or more licensees to perform all services requiring a license under this Article; (ii) the licensees are not practicing under the exception authorized by G.S. 90-210.25(a2) and would otherwise be eligible to serve as manager; and (iii) the funeral establishment registers the name of the licensees with the Board.

b.   The Board receives a list of the names of all part-time and full-time licensees employed by the establishment.

c. It is shown that the funeral establishment satisfies the requirements of G.S. 90-210.27A.

d. The Board receives payment of the permit fee.

(3) Applications for funeral establishment permits shall be made on forms provided by the Board and filed with the Board by the owner, a partner, a member of the limited liability company, or an officer of the corporation by January 1 of each year, and shall be accompanied by the application fee or renewal fee, as the case may be. All permits shall expire on December 31 of each year. If the renewal application and renewal fee are not received in the Board's office on or before February 1, a late renewal fee, in addition to the regular renewal fee, shall be charged.

(4) The Board may place on probation, refuse to issue or renew, suspend, or revoke a permit when an owner, partner, manager, member, operator, or officer of the funeral establishment violates any provision of this Article or any regulations of the Board, or when any agent or employee of the funeral establishment, with the consent of any person, firm or corporation operating the funeral establishment, violates any of those provisions, rules or regulations. In any case in which the Board is entitled to place a funeral establishment permittee on a term of probation, the Board may also impose a penalty of not more than five thousand dollars ($5,000) in conjunction with the probation. In any case in which the Board is entitled to suspend, revoke, or refuse to renew a permit, the Board may accept from the funeral establishment permittee an offer to pay a penalty of not more than five thousand dollars ($5,000). The Board may either accept a penalty or revoke or refuse to renew a license, but not both. Any penalty under this subdivision may be in addition to any penalty assessed against one or more licensed individuals employed by the funeral establishment.

(5) Funeral establishment permits are not transferable. A new application for a permit shall be made to the Board within 30 days of a change of ownership of a funeral establishment.

(d1) Embalming Outside Establishment. - An embalmer who engages in embalming in a facility other than a funeral establishment or in the residence of the deceased person shall, no later than January 1 of each year, register the facility with the Board on forms provided by the Board.

(e) Revocation; Suspension; Compromise; Disclosure. -

(1) Whenever the Board finds that an applicant for a license or a person to whom a license has been issued by the Board is guilty of any of the following acts or omissions and the Board also finds that the person has thereby become unfit to practice, the Board may suspend or revoke the license or refuse to issue or renew the license, in accordance with the procedures set out in Chapter 150B of the General Statutes:

a. Conviction of a felony or a crime involving fraud or moral turpitude.

a1. Denial, suspension, or revocation of an occupational or business license by another jurisdiction.

b. Fraud or misrepresentation in obtaining or renewing a license or in the practice of funeral service.

c. False or misleading advertising as the holder of a license.

d. Solicitation of dead human bodies by the licensee, his agents, assistants, or employees; but this paragraph shall not be construed to prohibit general advertising by the licensee.

e. Employment directly or indirectly of any resident trainee agent, assistant or other person, on a part-time or full-time basis, or on commission, for the purpose of calling upon individuals or institutions by whose influence dead human bodies may be turned over to a particular licensee.

f. The payment or offer of payment of a commission by the licensee, his agents, assistants or employees for the purpose of securing business except as authorized by Article 13D of this Chapter.

g. Gross immorality, including being under the influence of alcohol or drugs while practicing funeral service.

h. Aiding or abetting an unlicensed person to perform services under this Article, including the use of a picture or name in connection with advertisements or other written material published or caused to be published by the licensee.

i. Failing to treat a dead human body with respect at all times.

j. Violating or cooperating with others to violate any of the provisions of this Article or Articles 13D, 13E, or 13F of Chapter 90 of the General Statutes, any rules and regulations of the Board, or the standards set forth in Funeral Industry Practices, 16 C.F.R. 453 (1984), as amended from time to time.

k.   Violation of any State law or municipal or county ordinance or regulation affecting the handling, custody, care or transportation of dead human bodies.

l.   Refusing to surrender promptly the custody of a dead human body or cremated remains upon the express order of the person lawfully entitled to the custody thereof.

m.   Knowingly making any false statement on a certificate of death or violating or cooperating with others to violate any provision of Article 4 or 16 of Chapter 130A of the General Statutes or any rules or regulations promulgated under those Articles as amended from time to time.

n.   Indecent exposure or exhibition of a dead human body while in the custody or control of a licensee.

In any case in which the Board is entitled to suspend, revoke or refuse to renew a license, the Board may accept from the licensee an offer to pay a penalty of not more than five thousand dollars ($5,000). The Board may either accept a penalty or revoke or refuse to renew a license, but not both.

(2)   Where the Board finds that a licensee is guilty of one or more of the acts or omissions listed in subdivision (e)(1) of this section but it is determined by the Board that the licensee has not thereby become unfit to practice, the Board may place the licensee on a term of probation in accordance with the procedures set out in Chapter 150B of the General Statutes. In any case in which the Board is entitled to place a licensee on a term of probation, the Board may also impose a penalty of not more than five thousand dollars ($5,000) in conjunction with the probation. The Board may also require satisfactory completion of remedial or educational training as a prerequisite to license reinstatement or for completing the term of probation.

No person licensed under this Article shall remove or cause to be embalmed a dead human body when he or she has information indicating crime or violence of any sort in connection with the cause of death, nor shall a dead human body be cremated, until permission of the State or county medical examiner has first been obtained. However, nothing in this Article shall be construed to alter the duties and authority now vested in the office of the coroner.

No funeral service establishment shall accept a dead human body from any public officer (excluding the State or county medical examiner or his agent), or employee or from the official of any institution, hospital or nursing home, or from a physician or any person having a professional relationship with a decedent, without having first made due inquiry as to the desires of the persons who have the legal authority to direct the disposition of the decedent's body. If any persons are found, their authority and directions shall govern the disposal of the remains of the decedent. Any funeral service establishment receiving the remains in violation of this subsection shall make no charge for any service in connection with the remains prior to delivery of the remains as stipulated by the persons having legal authority to direct the disposition of the body. This section shall not prevent any funeral service establishment from charging and being reimbursed for services rendered in connection with the removal of the remains of any deceased person in case of accidental or violent death, and rendering necessary professional services required until the persons having legal authority to direct the disposition of the body have been notified.

When and where a licensee presents a selection of funeral merchandise to the public to be used in connection with the service to be provided by the licensee or an establishment as licensed under this Article, a card or brochure shall be directly associated with each item of merchandise setting forth the price of the service using said merchandise and listing the services and other merchandise included in the price, if any. When there are separate prices for the merchandise and services, such cards or brochures shall indicate the price of the merchandise and of the items separately priced.

At the time funeral arrangements are made and prior to the time of rendering the service and providing the merchandise, a funeral director or funeral service licensee shall give or cause to be given to the person or persons making such arrangements a written statement duly signed by a licensee of said funeral establishment showing the price of the service as selected and what services are included therein, the price of each of the supplemental items of services or merchandise requested, and the amounts involved for each of the items for which the funeral establishment will advance moneys as an accommodation to the person making arrangements, insofar as any of the above items can be specified at that time. If fees charged by a finance company for expediting payment of life insurance proceeds to the establishment will be passed on to the person or persons responsible for payment of the funeral expenses, information regarding the fees, including the total dollar amount of the fee, shall be disclosed in writing. The statement shall have printed, typed or stamped on the face thereof: "This statement of disclosure is provided under the requirements of

North Carolina G.S. 90-210.25(e)." The Board may prescribe other disclosures that a licensee shall give to consumers upon finding that the disclosure is necessary to protect public health, safety, and welfare.

(e1) The taking or recovery of human tissue at a funeral establishment by any person is prohibited. The prohibition does not apply to any of the following:

(1) A licensee under this Article that performs embalming or otherwise prepares a dead human body in the ordinary course of business.

(2) The Chief Medical Examiner or anyone acting under the Chief Medical Examiner's authority.

(3) An autopsy technician who takes or recovers tissue from a dead human body if all of the following apply:

a. The taking or recovery is the subject of an academic research program.

b. The academic research program has appropriate Institutional Review Board supervision.

c. The academic research program has obtained informed consent of the donor or the person legally authorized to provide consent.

No funeral establishment or person licensed under this Article shall permit the taking or recovery of human tissue from a dead human body in its custody or control for human transplantation purposes or for research purposes, except that a funeral establishment or person licensed under this Article may permit an autopsy technician to take or recover tissue at a funeral establishment pursuant to subdivision (3) of this subsection. No funeral establishment or any of its licensees, agents, or employees shall accept, solicit, or offer to accept any payment, gratuity, commission, or compensation of any kind for referring potential tissue donors to a tissue bank or tissue broker or to an eye bank or eye broker. For purposes of this subsection, the term "tissue" does not include an eye.

(f) Unlawful Practices. - If any person shall practice or hold himself or herself out as practicing the profession or art of embalming, funeral directing or practice of funeral service or operating a funeral establishment without having complied with the provisions of this Article, the person shall be guilty of a Class 2 misdemeanor.

(g) Whenever it shall appear to the Board that any person, firm or corporation has violated, threatens to violate or is violating any provisions of this Article, the Board may apply to the courts of the State for a restraining order and injunction to restrain these practices. If upon application the court finds that any provision of this Article is being violated, or a violation is threatened, the court shall issue an order restraining and enjoining the violations, and this relief may be granted regardless of whether criminal prosecution is instituted under the provisions of this subsection. The venue for actions brought under this subsection shall be the superior court of any county in which the acts are alleged to have been committed or in the county where the defendant in the action resides. (1901, c. 338, ss. 9, 10, 14; Rev., ss. 3644, 4388; 1917, c. 36; 1919, c. 88; C.S., ss. 6781, 6782; 1949, c. 951, s. 4; 1951, c. 413; 1957, c. 1240, ss. 2, 21/2; 1965, cc. 719, 720; 1967, c. 691, s. 48; c. 1154, s. 2; 1969, c. 584, ss. 3, 3a, 4; 1975, c. 571; 1979, c. 461, ss. 11-21; 1981, c. 619, ss. 1-4; 1983, c. 69, s. 5; 1985, c. 242; 1987, c. 430, ss. 4-11; c. 827, s. 1; c. 879, s. 6.2; 1991, c. 528, ss. 4, 5; 1993, c. 539, s. 638; 1994, Ex. Sess., c. 24, s. 14(c); 1997-399, ss. 5-13; 2001-294, s. 3; 2002-147, s. 9; 2003-420, ss. 1, 7; 2007-297, s. 1; 2007-531, s. 4; 2011-183, s. 63.)

§ 90-210.25A: Recodified as G.S. 65-77 by Session Laws 2003-420, s. 8(b), effective October 1, 2003.

§ 90-210.25B. Persons who shall not be licensed under this Article.

(a) The board shall not issue or renew any licensure, permit, or registration to any person or entity who has been convicted of a sexual offense against a minor.

(b) For purposes of this Article, the term "sexual offense against a minor" means a conviction of any of the following offenses: G.S. 14-27.4A(a) (sex offense with a child; adult offender), G.S. 14-27.7A (statutory rape or sexual offense of person who is 13, 14, or 15 years old where the defendant is at least six years older), G.S. 14-190.16 (first-degree sexual exploitation of a minor), G.S. 14-190.17 (second degree sexual exploitation of a minor), G.S. 14-190.17A (third degree sexual exploitation of a minor), G.S. 14-190.18 (promoting prostitution of a minor), G.S. 14-190.19 (participating in prostitution of a minor), G.S. 14-202.1 (taking indecent liberties with children), G.S. 14-202.3 (solicitation of child by computer or certain other electronic devices to commit an unlawful sex act), G.S. 14-202.4(a) (taking indecent liberties with a student), G.S. 14-318.4(a1) (parent or caretaker commit or permit act of prostitution with or by a juvenile), or G.S. 14-318.4(a2) (commission or allowing of sexual act upon a juvenile by parent or guardian). The term shall also include a conviction of the following: any attempt, solicitation, or conspiracy to commit any of these offenses or any aiding and abetting any of these offenses. The term shall also include a conviction in another jurisdiction for an offense which if committed in this State has the same or substantially similar elements to an offense against a minor as defined by this section.

(c) If a person or entity holding a license, permit, or registration in another jurisdiction has the license revoked, suspended, or placed on probation because of a felony conviction other than those enumerated above, the board shall impose a sanction equal to or greater than to the sanction imposed by the other jurisdiction.

(d) If a person or entity holding a license, permit, or registration in another jurisdiction has the license revoked, suspended, or placed on probation because of conduct related to fitness to practice as described in G.S. 90-210.25(e), the board shall impose a sanction equal to or greater than the sanction imposed by the other jurisdiction. (2012-194, s. 71.)

§ 90-210.25C. Notification forms for deceased voters.

(a) At the time funeral arrangements are made, a funeral director or funeral service licensee is encouraged to make available to near relatives of the deceased a form upon which the near relative may report the status of the deceased voter to the board of elections of the county in which the deceased was a registered voter.

(b) A funeral director or funeral service licensee may obtain forms for reporting the status of deceased voters from the county board of elections. (2013-381, s. 39.2.)

§ 90-210.26. Good moral character.

Evidence of good moral character may be shown by the affidavits of three persons who have been acquainted with the applicant for three years immediately preceding the submission of the affidavit. (1979, c. 461, s. 22.)

§ 90-210.27. Repealed by Session Laws 1987, c. 430, s. 12.

§ 90-210.27A. Funeral establishments.

(a) Every funeral establishment shall contain a preparation room which is strictly private, of suitable size for the embalming of dead bodies. Each preparation room shall:

(1) Contain one standard type operating table.

(2) Contain facilities for adequate drainage.

(3) Contain a sanitary waste receptacle.

(4) Contain an instrument sterilizer.

(5) Have wall-to-wall floor covering of tile, concrete, or other material which can be easily cleaned.

(6) Be kept in sanitary condition and subject to inspection by the Board or its agents at all times.

(7) Have a placard or sign on the door indicating that the preparation room is private.

(8) Have a proper ventilation or purification system to maintain a nonhazardous level of airborne contamination.

(b) No one is allowed in the preparation room while a dead human body is being prepared except licensees, resident trainees, public officials in the discharge of their duties, members of the medical profession, officials of the funeral home, next of kin, or other legally authorized persons.

(c)   Every funeral establishment shall contain a reposing room for dead human bodies, of suitable size to accommodate a casket and visitors.

(d)   Repealed by Session Laws 1997-399, s. 14.

(e)   If a funeral establishment is solely owned by a natural person, that person must be licensed by the Board as a funeral director or a funeral service licensee. If it is owned by a partnership, at least one partner must be licensed by the Board as a funeral director or a funeral service licensee. If it is owned by a corporation, the president, vice-president, or the chairman of the board of directors must be licensed by the Board as a funeral director or a funeral service licensee. If it is owned by a limited liability company, at least one member must be licensed by the Board as a funeral director or a funeral service licensee. The licensee required by this subsection must be actively engaged in the operation of the funeral establishment.

(f)   If a funeral establishment uses the name of a living person in the name under which it does business, that person must be licensed by the Board as a funeral director or a funeral service licensee.

(g)   No funeral establishment shall own, operate, or maintain a chapel without first having registered the name, location, and ownership thereof with the Board; own or maintain more than two chapels, or own or maintain a chapel outside of a radius of 50 miles from the funeral establishment. A duly licensed person may use a chapel for making arrangements for funeral services, selling funeral merchandise to the public by photograph, video, or computer based presentation, or making financial arrangements for the rendering of the service or sale of supplies, provided that the uses are secondary and incidental to and do not interfere with the reposing of dead human bodies, visitation, or funeral ceremony.

(h)   All public health laws and rules apply to funeral establishments. In addition, all funeral establishments must comply with all of the standards established by the rules adopted by the Board.

(i)   No funeral establishment shall use an unregistered or misleading name. Misleading names include, but are not limited to, names in the plural form when there is only one funeral establishment, the use of names of deceased individuals, unless the establishment is licensed using the name at the time the new application is made, the use of names of individuals not associated with the establishment, and the use of the word "crematory" or "crematorium" in the name of a funeral establishment that does not own a crematory. If an owner of a funeral establishment owns more than one funeral establishment, the owner may not use the word "crematory" or "crematorium" in the name of more than one of its funeral establishments; except that each funeral home having a crematory on the premises may contain the term "crematory" or "crematorium" in its name.

(j)   A funeral establishment will not use any name other than the name by which it is properly registered with the Board. (1987, c. 430, s. 13; c. 879, s. 6.2; 1997-399, s. 14; 2001-294, s. 4; 2003-420, s. 9(a), (b); 2007-531, s. 5.)

§ 90-210.28. Fees.

The Board may set and collect fees, not to exceed the following amounts:

Establishment permit

Application $400.00

Annual renewal 250.00

Late renewal 150.00

Establishment and embalming facility reinspection fee
.... 100.00

Courtesy card

Application 100.00

Annual renewal 75.00

Out-of-state licensee

Application 250.00

Embalmer, funeral director, funeral service

Application-North

   Carolina-Resident 200.00

   -Non-Resident 250.00

Annual Renewal-embalmer or

   funeral director 75.00

Total fee, embalmer and funeral director

   when both are held by the same person 100.00

   -funeral service 100.00

   Inactive Status 50.00

   Reinstatement fee 50.00

Resident trainee permit

   Application 50.00

   Voluntary change in supervisor 50.00

   Annual renewal 35.00

   Late renewal 25.00

   Duplicate license certificate 25.00

Chapel registration

   Application 150.00

   Annual renewal 100.00

   Late renewal 75.00

The Board shall provide, without charge, one copy of the current statutes and regulations relating to Funeral Service to every person applying for and paying the appropriate fees for licensing pursuant to this Article. The Board may charge all others requesting copies of the current statutes and regulations, and the licensees or applicants requesting additional copies, a fee equal to the costs of production and distribution of the requested documents. (1979, c. 461, s. 22; 1981, c. 619, s. 5; 1985, c. 447, ss. 1, 2; 1987, c. 710; 1989 (Reg. Sess., 1990), c. 968; 1997-399, s. 15; 2001-294, s. 5; 2007-531, s. 6.)

§ 90-210.29. Students.

(a) Students who are enrolled in duly accredited mortuary science colleges in North Carolina may engage in the practices defined in this Article if the practices are part of their academic training and if the practices are under the supervision of a licensed instructor of mortuary science or a licensee designated by the mortuary science college upon registration with the Board.

(b) Repealed by Session Laws 2001-294, s. 6. (1979, c. 461, s. 22; 2001-294, s. 6.)

§ 90-210.29A. Identification of bodies before burial or cremation.

The funeral director or person otherwise responsible for the final disposition of a dead body shall, prior to the interment or entombment of the dead body, affix on the ankle or wrist of the dead body, or, if cremated, on the inside of the temporary container or urn containing the remains of the dead body, a tag of durable, noncorroding material permanently marked with the name of the deceased, the date of death, the social security number of the deceased, the county and state of death, and the site of interment or entombment. (1995, c. 312, s. 1; 2003-420, s. 10.)

§ 90-210.29B. Examination scores not public record.

The examination scores of applicants for licensure shall not be subject to the provisions of Chapter 132 of the General Statutes. The Board shall release to any person requesting examination scores whether or not the applicant has obtained a passing score at the time of the request. (2007-484, s. 43.9; 2007-531, s. 7.)

Article 13B.

Funeral and Burial Trust Funds.

§ 90-210.30 through 90-210.39: Repealed by 1991 (Regular Session, 1992), c. 901, s. 1.

Article 13C.

Cremations.

§§ 90-210.40 through 90-210.54: Recodified as Article 13F of Chapter 90, G.S. 90-210.120 through 90-210.134.

§§ 90-210.55 through 90-210.59. Reserved for future codification purposes.

Article 13D.

Preneed Funeral Funds.

§ 90-210.60. Definitions.

As used in this Article, unless the context requires otherwise:

(1) "Board" means the North Carolina Board of Funeral Service as created pursuant to Article 13A of Chapter 90 of the General Statutes;

(2) "Financial institution" means a bank, credit union, trust company, savings bank, or savings and loan association authorized by law to do business in this State;

(3) "Insurance company" means any corporation, limited liability company, association, partnership, society, order, individual or aggregation of individuals engaging in or proposing or attempting to engage as principals in any kind of insurance business, including the exchanging of reciprocal or interinsurance contracts between individuals, partnerships, and corporations;

(3a) "Legal representative" means the person authorized by G.S. 130A-420 who would be otherwise authorized to dispose of the remains of the preneed funeral contract beneficiary.

(4) "Prearrangement insurance policy" means a life insurance policy, annuity contract, or other insurance contract, or any series of contracts or agreements in any form or manner, issued by an insurance company authorized by law to do business in this State, which, whether by assignment or otherwise, has for a purpose the funding of a preneed funeral contract or an insurance-funded funeral or burial prearrangement, the insured or annuitant being the person for whose service the funds were paid;

(5) "Preneed funeral contract" means any contract, agreement, or mutual understanding, or any series or combination of contracts, agreements, or mutual understandings, whether funded by trust deposits or prearrangement insurance policies, or any combination thereof, which has for a purpose the furnishing or performance of funeral services, or the furnishing or delivery of personal property, merchandise, or services of any nature in connection with the final disposition of a dead human body, to be furnished or delivered at a time determinable by the death of the person whose body is to be disposed of, but does not mean the furnishing of a cemetery lot, crypt, niche, or mausoleum;

(6) "Preneed funeral contract beneficiary" means the person upon whose death the preneed funeral contract will be performed; this person may also be the purchaser of the preneed funeral contract;

(7) "Preneed funeral funds" means all payments of cash made to any person, partnership, association, corporation, or other entity upon any preneed

funeral contract or any other agreement, contract, or prearrangement insurance policy, or any series or combination of preneed funeral contracts or any other agreements, contracts, or prearrangement insurance policies, but excluding the furnishing of cemetery lots, crypts, niches, and mausoleums, which have for a purpose or which by operation provide for the furnishing or performance of funeral or burial services, or the furnishing or delivery of personal property, merchandise, or services of any nature in connection with the final disposition of a dead human body, to be furnished or delivered at a time determinable by the death of the person whose body is to be disposed of, or the providing of the proceeds of any insurance policy for such use;

(8) "Preneed funeral planning" means offering to sell or selling preneed funeral contracts, or making other arrangements prior to death for the providing of funeral services or merchandise;

(9) "Preneed licensee" means a funeral establishment which has applied for and has been granted a license to sell preneed funeral contracts under the Article. Such license is also referred to in this Article as a "preneed funeral establishment license." (1969, c. 187, s. 1; 1983, c. 657, s. 1; 1985, c. 12, s. 1; 1991 (Reg. Sess., 1992), c. 901, s. 2; 1993, c. 553, s. 27; 1997-399, s. 23; 2001-294, ss. 7, 8; 2003-420, s. 1; 2007-531, s. 7.1; 2010-96, s. 38; 2010-102, s. 6; 2010-191, s. 3.)

§ 90-210.61. Deposit or application of preneed funeral funds.

(a) Preneed funeral funds are subject to the provisions of this Article and shall be deposited or applied as follows:

(1) If the preneed funeral contract purchaser chooses to fund the preneed funeral contract by a trust deposit or deposits, the preneed licensee shall deposit all funds in an insured account in a financial institution, in trust, in the preneed licensee's name as trustee within five business days. The preneed licensee, at the time of making the deposit as trustee, shall furnish to the financial institution the name of each preneed funeral contract purchaser and the amount of payment on each for which the deposit is being made. The preneed licensee may establish an individual trust fund for each preneed funeral contract or a common trust fund for all preneed funeral contracts. The trust accounts shall be carried in the name of the preneed licensee as trustee, but accounting records shall be maintained for each individual preneed funeral

contract purchaser showing the amounts deposited and invested, and interest, dividends, increases, and accretions earned. Except as provided in this Article, all interest, dividends, increases, or accretions earned by the funds shall remain with the principal. The trust fund may be charged with applicable taxes and for reasonable charges paid by the trustee to itself or others for the preparation of fiduciary tax returns. Penalties charged by a financial institution for early withdrawals caused by a transfer pursuant to G.S. 90-210.63 shall be paid by the preneed licensee. Penalties charged as a result of other early withdrawals as permitted by this Article shall be paid from the trust fund, and the financial institution shall give the preneed funeral contract purchaser prompt notice of these penalties.

(2) Notwithstanding any other provision of law, if a preneed funeral contract is funded by a trust deposit or trust deposits, a preneed licensee may retain, free of the trust, up to ten percent (10%) of any payments made on a preneed funeral contract, provided that the preneed licensee fully discloses in writing in advance to the preneed funeral contract purchaser the percentage of the payments to be retained. If there is no substitution pursuant to G.S. 90-210.63(a), the preneed licensee shall give credit for the amount retained upon the death of the preneed funeral contract beneficiary and performance of the preneed funeral contract.

(3) If the preneed funeral contract purchaser chooses to fund the contract by a prearrangement insurance policy, the preneed licensee shall apply all funds received for this purpose to the purchase of the prearrangement insurance policy within five business days. The preneed licensee shall notify the insurance company of the name of each preneed funeral contract purchaser and the amount of each payment when the prearrangement insurance policy or policies are purchased.

(b) Except as provided by this Article or by the preneed funeral contract, all payments made by the purchaser of a preneed funeral contract or prearrangement insurance policy shall remain trust funds within a financial institution or as paid insurance premiums with an insurance company, as the case may be, until the death of the preneed funeral contract beneficiary and until full performance of the preneed funeral contract.

(c) Each preneed licensee may establish and maintain with a financial institution of its choice, a preneed funeral fund clearing account. Preneed funeral funds received by a preneed licensee may be deposited and held in such an account until disbursed by the preneed licensee to fund a preneed funeral contract pursuant to subdivisions (a)(1) or (a)(3) of this section. This account shall be used solely for the receipt and disbursement of preneed funeral funds.

(d)   Funds deposited in trust under a revocable standard preneed funeral contract may, with the written permission of the preneed funeral contract purchaser, be withdrawn by the trustee and used to purchase a prearrangement insurance policy. Except as provided in this subsection, no funds deposited in trust in a financial institution pursuant to this Article shall be withdrawn by the trustee to purchase a prearrangement insurance policy.

(e)   Except as provided by G.S. 90-210.61(c), at no time before making a deposit or purchasing a prearrangement insurance policy may a preneed licensee, or its agents or employees, deposit in its own account or the account of any other person any monies coming into its hands for the purpose of purchasing services, merchandise, or prearrangement insurance policies under the provisions of this Article. (1969, c. 187, ss. 2, 4; 1981 (Reg. Sess., 1982), c. 1336, s. 1; 1983, c. 657, ss. 2, 4; 1985, c. 12, ss. 1-3; 1987, c. 430, ss. 15, 16; c. 879, s. 6.2; 1989, c. 485, s. 16; c. 738, s. 2; 1991 (Reg. Sess., 1992), c. 901, s. 2.)

§ 90-210.62. Types of preneed funeral contracts; forms.

(a)   A preneed licensee may offer standard preneed funeral contracts and inflation-proof preneed funeral contracts. A standard preneed funeral contract applies the trust funds or insurance proceeds to the purchase price of funeral services and merchandise at the time of death of the contract beneficiary without protection against potential future price increases. An inflation-proof contract establishes an agreement between the preneed licensee and the purchaser for funeral services and merchandise without regard to potential future price increases. Upon written disclosure to the purchaser of a preneed funeral contract, inflation-proof contracts may permit the preneed licensee to retain all of the preneed funeral contract trust funds on deposit, and all insurance proceeds, even those in excess of the retail cost of goods and services provided, when the preneed licensee has fully performed the preneed funeral contract. Preneed funeral contracts may be revocable or irrevocable, at the option of the preneed funeral contract purchaser.

(b) The Board may prescribe forms for preneed funeral contracts consistent with this Article. All contracts must be in writing on forms prescribed by the Board. Any use or attempted use of any oral preneed funeral contract or any written contract in a form not prescribed by the Board shall be deemed a violation of this Article. (1991 (Reg. Sess., 1992), c. 901, s. 2; 2007-531, s. 8.)

§ 90-210.63. Substitution of licensee.

(a) If the preneed funeral contract is irrevocable, the preneed funeral contract purchaser, or after his death the preneed funeral contract beneficiary or his legal representative, upon written notice to the financial institution or insurance company and the preneed licensee who is a party to the preneed funeral contract, may direct the substitution of a different funeral establishment to furnish funeral services and merchandise.

(1) If the substitution is made after the death of the preneed funeral contract beneficiary, a funeral establishment providing any funeral services or merchandise need not be a preneed licensee under this Article to receive payment for such services or merchandise. The original contracting preneed licensee shall be entitled to payment for any services or merchandise provided pursuant to G.S. 90-210.65(d). If the substitution is made before the death of the preneed funeral contract beneficiary, the substitution must be to a preneed licensee. If the preneed funeral contract is funded by a trust deposit or deposits, the financial institution shall immediately pay the funds held to the original contracting preneed licensee.

(2) The original contracting preneed licensee shall immediately pay all funds received to the successor funeral establishment designated. Regardless of whether the substitution is made before or after the death of the preneed funeral contract beneficiary, the original contracting preneed licensee shall not be required to give credit for the amount retained pursuant to G.S. 90-210.61(a)(2), except when there was a substitution under G.S. 90-210.68(d1) and (e). Upon making payments pursuant to this subsection, the financial institution and the original contracting preneed licensee shall be relieved from all further contractual liability thereon.

(3) If the preneed funeral contract is funded by a prearrangement insurance policy, the insurance company shall not pay any of the funds until the death of

the preneed funeral contract beneficiary, and the insurance company shall pay the funds in accordance with the terms of the policy.

(b) The person giving notice of the substitution of a preneed licensee and the successor preneed licensee shall enter into a new preneed funeral contract for the funds transferred, and this Article shall apply, including the duty of the successor preneed licensee to deposit all of the funds in a financial institution if the death of the preneed funeral contract beneficiary has not occurred. Nothing in this subsection shall be construed to permit the use of the transferred funds to purchase a prearrangement insurance policy, nor to permit an irrevocable preneed funeral contract to be made revocable or to result in the payment of any of the transferred funds to the preneed funeral contract purchaser or to the preneed funeral contract beneficiary or his estate, except as provided by G.S. 90-210.64(b). (1991 (Reg. Sess., 1992), c. 901, s. 2; 1993, c. 242, s. 1; 1997-399, s. 24; 2003-420, s. 11.)

§ 90-210.63A. Amendment of preneed funeral contracts.

(a) Unless otherwise provided by this Article, preneed funeral contracts may be modified by mutual consent of the contracting preneed funeral establishment and the preneed contract purchaser, or after the death of the preneed contract purchaser, the preneed contract beneficiary or his or her legal representative.

(b) When the preneed contract purchaser and preneed contract beneficiary are the same, the preneed contract purchaser may designate one or more individuals to change the arrangements or performing funeral establishment, or may designate that the arrangements or performing funeral establishment may not be changed without an order from the clerk of superior court in the county where probate proceedings are instituted upon a finding that the change is in the best interest of the estate.

(c) If the preneed purchaser, or after his or her death, the preneed contract beneficiary or his or her legal representative, and the contracting preneed funeral establishment agree to modify any goods or services selected under an inflation-proof contract, the preneed licensee shall not be required to guarantee the price of the modified goods and services at the time of death and all other funeral goods and service selected shall remain guaranteed. If the modifications increase the purchase price, the provisions of G.S. 90-210.64(b) shall apply as if the modified contract had been executed on the original date. If the modifications decrease the purchase price, the preneed licensee shall refund all monies according to the provisions of G.S. 90-210.64(d). (2007-531, s. 9.)

§ 90-210.64. Death of preneed funeral contract beneficiary; disposition of funds.

(a) After the death of a preneed funeral contract beneficiary and full performance of the preneed funeral contract by the preneed licensee, the preneed licensee shall promptly complete a certificate of performance and present it to the financial institution that holds funds in trust under G.S. 90-210.61(a)(1) or to the insurance company that issued a preneed insurance policy pursuant to G.S. 90-210.61(a)(3). Upon receipt of the certificate of performance or similar claim form, the financial institution shall pay the trust funds to the contracting preneed licensee and the insurance company shall pay the insurance proceeds according to the terms of the policy. Within 10 days after receiving payment, the preneed licensee shall file a copy of the certificate of performance or other claim form to the Board.

(b) Unless otherwise specified in the preneed funeral contract, the preneed licensee shall have no obligation to deliver merchandise or perform any services for which payment in full has not yet been deposited with a financial institution or that will not be provided by the proceeds of a prearrangement insurance policy. Any such amounts received which do not constitute payment in full shall be refunded to the estate of the deceased preneed funeral contract beneficiary or credited against the cost of merchandise or services contracted for by a representative of the deceased. Any balance remaining after payment for the merchandise and services as set forth in the preneed funeral contract shall be paid to the estate of the preneed funeral contract beneficiary or the prearrangement insurance policy beneficiary named to receive any such balance. Provided, however, unless the parties agree to the contrary, there shall be no refund to the estate of the preneed funeral contract beneficiary of an inflation-proof preneed funeral contract except as required by G.S. 90-210.63A(c).

(c) In the event that any person other than the contracting preneed licensee performs any funeral service or provides any merchandise as a result of the death of the preneed funeral contract beneficiary, the financial institution shall pay the trust funds to the contracting preneed licensee and the insurance company shall pay the insurance proceeds according to the terms of the policy.

The preneed licensee shall, subject to the provisions of G.S. 90-210.65(d), immediately pay the monies so received to the other provider.

(d) When the balance of a preneed funeral fund is one hundred dollars ($100.00) or less and is payable to the estate of a deceased preneed funeral contract beneficiary and there has been no representative of the estate appointed, the balance due may be paid directly to a beneficiary or to the beneficiaries of the estate. If the balance of a preneed funeral fund exceeds one hundred dollars ($100.00) or is not payable to the estate, the balance must be paid into the office of the clerk of superior court in the county where probate proceedings could be filed for the deceased preneed funeral contract beneficiary.

(e) Upon the fulfillment of a preneed contract, all of the following items shall be completed within 30 days:

(1) The contracting preneed licensee must submit a certificate of performance or similar claim form to the financial institution holding the preneed trust funds and close the preneed account.

(2) The proceeds of this trust account shall be distributed according to the terms of the preneed contract.

(3) A completed copy of the certificate of performance or similar claim form evidencing the final disposition of any financial institution preneed trust account funds must be filed with the Board by the contracting licensee. (1991 (Reg. Sess., 1992), c. 901, s. 2; 1997-399, s. 25; 2001-294, s. 9; 2003-420, s. 12; 2007-531, s. 10.)

§ 90-210.65. Refund of preneed funeral funds.

(a) Within 30 days of receipt of a written request from the purchaser of a revocable preneed funeral contract who has trust funds deposited with a financial institution pursuant to G.S. 90-210.61(a), the financial institution shall refund to the preneed funeral contract purchaser the entire amount held by the financial institution.

(b) Within 30 days of receipt of a written notice of cancellation of any prearrangement insurance policy purchased pursuant to G.S. 90-210.61(a)(3), the issuing insurance company shall pay such amounts to such person or persons as is provided under the terms of the prearrangement insurance policy.

(c)   After making refund pursuant to this section and giving notice of the refund to the preneed licensee, the financial institution or insurance company shall be relieved from all further liability.

(d)   Notwithstanding any other provision of this Article, if a preneed funeral contract is revoked or transferred following the death of the preneed funeral contract beneficiary, the purchaser of the preneed funeral contract may be charged according to the contracting preneed licensee's price lists for any services performed or merchandise provided prior to revocation or transfer.

(e)   This section shall not apply to irrevocable preneed funeral contracts. Irrevocable preneed funeral contracts may only be revoked or any proceeds refunded by the order of a court of competent jurisdiction, except as follows:

(1)   The Board may order an irrevocable contract revoked when the preneed contract beneficiary is no longer domiciled in this State and has submitted a written copy to the Board of a new preneed funeral contract executed under the laws of the state where the preneed contract beneficiary is domiciled. Upon receipt of the Board's order, the original contracting preneed licensee shall immediately follow the provisions of G.S. 90-210.63 to transfer the funds to the successor firm.

(2)   Irrevocable preneed funeral contracts purchased pursuant to G.S. 90-210.61(a)(3) shall also be revocable when the underlying insurance policy lapses or is otherwise cancelled and the lapsed or cancelled policy no longer provides any funding for the preneed funeral contract. (1969, c. 187, s. 3; 1981 (Reg. Sess., 1982), c. 1336, s. 2; 1983, c. 657, s. 3; 1985, c. 12, ss. 1, 2; 1991 (Reg. Sess., 1992), c. 901, s. 2; 2003-420, s. 13; 2007-531, s. 11.)

§ 90-210.66. Recovery fund.

(a)   There is established the Preneed Recovery Fund. The Fund shall be administered by the Board. The purpose of the Fund is to reimburse purchasers of preneed funeral contracts who have suffered financial loss as a result of the malfeasance, misfeasance, default, failure or insolvency of any licensee under this Article, and includes refunds due a preneed funeral contract beneficiary from a preneed licensee who has retained any portion of the preneed funeral contract payments pursuant to G.S. 90-210.61(a)(2).

(b) From the fee for each preneed funeral contract as required by G.S. 90-210.67(d), the Board shall deposit two dollars ($2.00) into the Fund. The Board may suspend the deposits into the Fund at any time and for any period for which the Board determines that a sufficient amount is available to meet likely disbursements and to maintain an adequate reserve.

(c) All sums received by the Board pursuant to this section shall be held in a separate account known as the Preneed Recovery Fund. Deposits to and disbursements from the Fund account shall be subject to rules established by the Board.

(d) The Board shall adopt rules governing management of the Fund, the presentation and processing of applications for reimbursement, and subrogation or assignment of the rights of any reimbursed applicant.

(e) The Board may expend monies in the Fund for the following purposes:

(1) To make reimbursements on approved applications;

(2) To purchase insurance to cover losses as deemed appropriate by the Board and not inconsistent with the purposes of the Fund;

(3) To invest such portions of the Fund as are not currently needed to reimburse losses and maintain adequate reserves, as are permitted to be made by fiduciaries under State law; and

(4) To pay the expenses of the Board for administering the Fund, including employment of legal counsel to prosecute subrogation claims.

(f) Reimbursements from the Fund shall be made only to the extent to which such losses are not bonded or otherwise covered, protected or reimbursed and only after the applicant has complied with all applicable rules of the Board.

(g) The Board shall investigate all applications made and may reject or allow such claims in whole or in part to the extent that monies are available in the Fund. The Board shall have complete discretion to determine the order and manner of payment of approved applications. All payments shall be a matter of privilege and not of right, and no person shall have any right in the Fund as a third-party beneficiary or otherwise. No attorney may be compensated by the Board for prosecuting an application for reimbursement.

(h)   In the event reimbursement is made to an applicant under this section, the Board shall be subrogated in the reimbursed amount and may bring any action it deems advisable against any person, including a preneed licensee. The Board may enforce any claims it may have for restitution or otherwise and may employ and compensate consultants, agents, legal counsel, accountants and any other persons it deems appropriate.

(i)   The Fund shall apply to losses arising after July 9, 1992, regardless of the date of the underlying preneed funeral contract. (1991 (Reg. Sess., 1992), c. 901, s. 2; 1997-399, s. 26.)

§ 90-210.67. Application for license.

(a)   No person may offer or sell preneed funeral contracts or offer to make or make any funded funeral prearrangements without first securing a license from the Board. Notwithstanding any other provision of law, any person who offers to sell or sells a casket, to be furnished or delivered at a time determinable by the death of the person whose body is to be disposed of in the casket, shall first comply with the provisions of this Article. There shall be two types of licenses: a preneed funeral establishment license and a preneed sales license. Only funeral establishments holding a valid establishment permit pursuant to G.S. 90-210.25(d) shall be eligible for a preneed funeral establishment license. Employees and agents of such entities, upon meeting the qualifications to engage in preneed funeral planning as established by the Board, shall be eligible for a preneed sales license. The Board shall establish the preneed funeral planning activities that are permitted under a preneed sales license. The Board shall adopt rules establishing such qualifications and activities no later than 12 months following the ratification of this act [Session Laws 1991 (Reg. Sess., 1992), c. 901, s. 2]. Preneed sales licensees may sell preneed funeral contracts, prearrangement insurance policies, and make funded funeral prearrangements only on behalf of one preneed funeral establishment licensee; provided, however, they may sell preneed funeral contracts, prearrangement insurance policies, and make funeral prearrangements for any number of licensed preneed funeral establishments that are wholly owned by or affiliated with, through common ownership or contract, the same entity; provided further, in the event they engage in selling prearrangement insurance policies, they shall meet the licensing requirements of the Commissioner of Insurance. Every preneed funeral contract shall be signed by a person licensed as a funeral director or funeral service licensee pursuant to Article 13A of Chapter 90 of the General Statutes.

Application for a license shall be in writing, signed by the applicant and duly verified on forms furnished by the Board. Each application shall contain at least the following: the full names and addresses (both residence and place of business) of the applicant, and every partner, member, officer and director thereof if the applicant is a partnership, limited liability company, association, or corporation and any other information as the Board shall deem necessary. A preneed funeral establishment license shall be valid only at the address stated in the application or at a new address approved by the Board.

(b) An application for a preneed funeral establishment license shall be accompanied by a nonrefundable application fee of not more than four hundred dollars ($400.00). The Board shall set the amounts of the application fees and renewal fees, by rule. A funeral establishment receiving a new preneed establishment license after January 1, 2008, or whose preneed establishment license has lapsed or was terminated for any reason after January 1, 2008, shall obtain a surety bond in an amount not less than fifty thousand dollars ($50,000) for five years, or upon demonstrating that it is solvent, no less than one year from the date the original license is issued. The Board may extend the bonding requirement in the event there is a claim paid from the bond.

If the license is granted, the application fee shall be applied to the annual license fee for the first year or part thereof. Upon receipt of the application and payment of the application fee, the Board shall issue a renewable preneed funeral establishment license unless it determines that the applicant has violated any provision of G.S. 90-210.69(c) or has made false statements or representations in the application, or is insolvent, or has conducted or is about to conduct, its business in a fraudulent manner, or is not duly authorized to transact business in this State. The license shall expire on December 31 and each preneed funeral establishment licensee shall pay annually to the Board on or before that date a license renewal fee of not more than two hundred fifty dollars ($250.00). On or before the first day of February immediately following expiration, a license may be renewed without paying a late fee. After that date, a license may be renewed by paying a late fee of not more than one hundred dollars ($100.00) in addition to the annual renewal fee.

(c) An application for a preneed sales license shall be accompanied by a nonrefundable application fee of not more than fifty dollars ($50.00). The Board shall set the amounts of the application fees and renewal fees by rule, but the fees shall not exceed fifty dollars ($50.00). If the license is granted, the application fee shall be applied to the annual license fee for the first year or part thereof. Upon receipt of the application and payment of the application fee, the Board shall issue a renewable preneed sales license provided the applicant has met the qualifications to engage in preneed funeral planning as established by the Board unless it determines that the applicant has violated any provision of G.S. 90-210.69(c). The license shall expire on December 31 and each preneed sales licensee shall pay annually to the Board on or before that date a license renewal fee of not more than fifty dollars ($50.00). On or before the first day of February, a license may be renewed without paying a late fee. After that date, a license may be renewed by paying a late fee of not more than twenty-five dollars ($25.00) in addition to the annual renewal fee.

(d) Any person selling a preneed funeral contract, whether funded by a trust deposit or a prearrangement insurance policy, shall remit to the Board, within 10 days of the sale, a fee not to exceed twenty dollars ($20.00) for each sale and a copy of each contract. The person shall pay a late fee of not more than twenty-five dollars ($25.00) for each late filing and payment. The fees shall not be remitted in cash.

(d1) The Board may also set and collect a fee of not more than twenty-five dollars ($25.00) for the late filing of a certificate of performance and a fee of not more than one hundred and fifty dollars ($150.00) for the late filing of an annual report.

(e), (f). Repealed by Session Laws 2003-420, s. 14, effective October 1, 2003. (1969, c. 187, s. 5; 1981, c. 671, ss. 16, 17; 1983, c. 657, s. 4; 1985, c. 12, ss. 1, 2; 1991 (Reg. Sess., 1992), c. 901, s. 2; 1995 (Reg. Sess., 1996), c. 665, s. 1; 1997-399, s. 27; 2001-294, s. 10; 2003-420, s. 14; 2007-531, s. 12.)

§ 90-210.68. Licensee's books and records; notice of transfers, assignments and terminations.

(a) Every preneed licensee shall keep for examination by the Board accurate accounts, books, and records in this State of all preneed funeral contract and prearrangement insurance policy transactions, copies of all agreements, insurance policies, instruments of assignment, the dates and amounts of payments made and accepted thereon, the names and addresses of the contracting parties, the persons for whose benefit funds are accepted, and the names of the financial institutions holding preneed funeral trust funds and insurance companies issuing prearrangement insurance policies. The Board, its inspectors appointed pursuant to G.S. 90-210.24 and its examiners, which the Board may appoint to assist in the enforcement of this Article, may during normal hours of operation and periods shortly before or after normal hours of operation, investigate the books, records, and accounts of any licensee under this Article with respect to trust funds, preneed funeral contracts, and prearrangement insurance policies. Any preneed licensee who, upon inspection, fails to meet the requirements of this subsection or who fails to keep an appointment for an inspection shall pay a reinspection fee to the Board in an amount not to exceed one hundred dollars ($100.00). The Board may require the attendance of and examine under oath all persons whose testimony it may require. Every preneed licensee shall submit a written report to the Board, at least annually, in a manner and with such content as established by the Board, of its preneed funeral contract sales and performance of such contracts. The Board may also require other reports.

(b)   A preneed licensee may transfer preneed funds held by it as trustee from the financial institution which is a party to a preneed funeral contract to a substitute financial institution that is not a party to the contract. Within 10 days after the transfer, the preneed licensee shall notify the Board, in writing, of the name and address of the transferee financial institution. Before the transfer may be made, the transferee financial institution shall agree to make disclosures required under the preneed funeral contract to the Board or its inspectors or examiners. If the contract is revocable, the licensee shall notify the contracting party of the intended transfer.

(c)   If any preneed licensee transfers or assigns its assets or stock to a successor funeral establishment or terminates its business as a funeral establishment, the preneed licensee and assignee shall notify the Board at least 15 days prior to the effective date of the transfer, assignment or termination: provided, however, the successor funeral establishment must be a preneed licensee or shall be required to apply for and be granted such license by the Board before accepting any preneed funeral contracts, whether funded by trust deposits or preneed insurance policies. Provided further, a successor funeral establishment shall be liable to the preneed funeral contract purchasers for the amount of contract payments retained by the assigning or transferring funeral home pursuant to G.S. 90-210.61(a)(2).

(d) Financial institutions that accept preneed funeral trust funds and insurance companies that issue prearrangement insurance policies shall, upon request by the Board or its inspectors or examiners, disclose any information regarding preneed funeral trust accounts held or prearrangement insurance policies issued by it for a preneed licensee.

Financial institutions that accept preneed funeral trust funds and insurance companies that assign policy proceeds or designate a preneed funeral establishment as beneficiary shall also forward an account balance to the contracting preneed funeral establishment at the end of each calendar year.

(d1) When a preneed funeral establishment license lapses or is terminated for any reason, the preneed licensee shall immediately divest of all the unperformed preneed funeral contracts and shall transfer them and any amounts retained under G.S. 90-210.61(a)(2) to another preneed funeral establishment licensee pursuant to the procedures of subsection (e) of this section.

(e) In the event that any preneed licensee is unable or unwilling or is for any reason relieved of its responsibility to perform as trustee or to perform any preneed funeral contract, the Board shall order the contract and any amounts retained pursuant to G.S. 90-210.61(a)(2) to be assigned to a substitute preneed licensee provided that neither the substitute preneed licensee or preneed contract purchaser, or after the death of the preneed contract purchaser, the preneed contract beneficiary or his or her legal representative, shall be obligated to perform the agreement without executing a new preneed funeral contract. Any lapse or transfer of a preneed contract pursuant to this section shall not be grounds to revoke an irrevocable preneed funeral contract.

(f) The substitute preneed licensee under subsections (d1) and (e) of this section shall be liable to the preneed funeral contract purchasers for the amount of contract payments that had been retained by, and that the substitute preneed licensee has received from, the assigning preneed licensee. (1969, c. 187, s. 6; 1983, c. 657, ss. 4, 5; 1985, c. 12, s. 1; 1991 (Reg. Sess., 1992), c. 901, s. 2; 1993, c. 164, s. 3; 1997-399, s. 28; 2007-531, ss. 13, 14.)

§ 90-210.69. Rulemaking; enforcement of Article; judicial review; determination of penalty amount.

(a) The Board is authorized to adopt rules for the carrying out and enforcement of the provisions of this Article. The Board may perform such other acts and exercise such other powers and duties as are authorized by this Article and by Article 13A of this Chapter to carry out its powers and duties.

(b) The Board may administer oaths and issue subpoenas requiring the attendance of persons and the production of papers and records in any investigation conducted by it. Members of the Board's staff or the sheriff or other appropriate official of any county of this State shall serve all notices, subpoenas and other papers given to them by the Board for service in the same manner as process issued by any court of record. Any person who does not obey a subpoena issued by the Board shall be guilty of a misdemeanor and, upon conviction thereof, shall be fined or imprisoned in the discretion of the court.

(c) In accordance with the provisions of Chapter 150B of the General Statutes, if the Board finds that a licensee, an applicant for a license or an applicant for license renewal is guilty of one or more of the following, the Board may refuse to issue or renew a license or may suspend or revoke a license or place the holder thereof on probation upon conditions set by the Board, with revocation upon failure to comply with the conditions:

(1) Offering to engage or engaging in activities for which a license is required under this Article but without having obtained such a license.

(2) Aiding or abetting an unlicensed person, firm, partnership, association, corporation or other entity to offer to engage or engage in such activities.

(3) A crime involving fraud or moral turpitude by conviction thereof.

(4) Fraud or misrepresentation in obtaining or receiving a license or in preneed funeral planning.

(5) False or misleading advertising.

(6) Violating or cooperating with others to violate any provision of this Article, the rules and regulations of the Board, or the standards set forth in Funeral Industry Practices, 16 C.F.R. 453 (1984), as amended from time to time.

(7) Denial, suspension, or revocation of an occupational or business license by another jurisdiction.

In any case in which the Board is authorized to take any of the actions permitted under this subsection, the Board may instead accept an offer in compromise of the charges whereby the accused shall pay to the Board a penalty of not more than five thousand dollars ($5,000). In any case in which the Board is entitled to place a licensee on a term of probation, the Board may also impose a penalty of not more than five thousand dollars ($5,000) in conjunction with such probation.

(d) Any proceedings pertaining to or actions against a funeral establishment under this Article may be in addition to any proceedings or actions permitted by G.S. 90-210.25(d)(4). Any proceedings pertaining to or actions against a person licensed for funeral directing or funeral service may be in addition to any proceedings or actions permitted by G.S. 90-210.25 (e)(1) and (2).

(e) Judicial review shall be pursuant to Article 4 of Chapter 150B of the General Statutes.

(f) In determining the amount of any penalty imposed or assessed under Article 13 of Chapter 90 of the General Statutes, the Board shall consider:

(1) The degree and extent of harm to the public health, safety, and welfare, or to property, or the potential for harm.

(2) The duration and gravity of the violation.

(3) Whether the violation was committed willfully or intentionally or reflects a continuing pattern.

(4) Whether the violation involved elements of fraud or deception either to the public or to the Board, or both.

(5) The violator's prior disciplinary record with the Board.

(6) Whether and the extent to which the violator profited by the violation.
(1969, c. 187, s. 7; 1983, c. 657, s. 4; 1985, c. 12, s. 1; 1991 (Reg. Sess., 1992), c. 901, s. 2; 1997-399, ss. 29, 30; 2001-294, s. 11; 2004-203, s. 7; 2007-531, s. 15.)

§ 90-210.70. Penalties.

(a)   Anyone who embezzles or who fraudulently, or knowingly and willfully misapplies, or in any manner converts preneed funeral funds to his own use, or for the use of any partnership, corporation, association, or entity for any purpose other than as authorized by this Article; or anyone who takes, makes away with or secretes, with intent to embezzle or fraudulently or knowingly and willfully misapply or in any manner convert preneed funeral funds for his own use or the use of any other person for any purpose other than as authorized by this Article shall be guilty of a felony. If the value of the preneed funeral funds is one hundred thousand dollars ($100,000) or more, violation of this section is a Class C felony. If the value of the preneed funeral funds is less than one hundred thousand dollars ($100,000), violation of this section is a Class H felony. Each such embezzlement, conversion, or misapplication shall constitute a separate offense and may be prosecuted individually. Upon conviction, all licenses issued under this Article shall be revoked.

(b)   Any person who willfully violates any other provision of this Article shall be guilty of a Class 1 misdemeanor. Each such violation shall constitute a separate offense and may be prosecuted individually.

(c)   If a corporation or limited liability company embezzles or fraudulently or knowingly and willfully misapplies or converts preneed funeral funds as provided in subsection (a) hereof or otherwise violates any provision of this Article, the officers, directors, members, agents, or employees responsible for committing the offense shall be fined or imprisoned as herein provided.

(d)   The Board shall have the power to investigate violations of this section and shall deliver all evidence of violations of subsection (a) of this section to the district attorney in the county where the offense occurred. The Board shall, with the fees collected under this Article, employ legal counsel and other staff to monitor preneed trusts, investigate complaints, audit preneed trusts, and be responsible for delivering evidences to the district attorney when there is evidence that a felony has been committed by a licensee. The record of complaints, auditing, and enforcement shall be presented in an annual report from the Board to the General Assembly.

(e)   Whenever it shall appear to the Board that any person, firm, or corporation has violated, threatens to violate, or is violating any provisions of this Article, the Board may apply to the courts of the State for a restraining order and injunction to restrain these practices. If upon application the court finds that any provision of this Article is being violated, or a violation is threatened, the court shall issue an order restraining and enjoining the violations, and this relief may be granted regardless of whether criminal prosecution is instituted under the provisions of this subsection. The venue for actions brought under this subsection shall be the superior court of any county in which the acts are alleged to have been committed or in the county where the defendant in the action resides. (1969, c. 187, s. 8; 1985, c. 12, s. 1; 1991 (Reg. Sess., 1992), c. 901, s. 2; 1993 (Reg. Sess., 1994), c. 767, s. 28; 1997-399, ss. 31, 32; 1997-443, s. 19.25(o); 2003-420, s. 15.)

§ 90-210.71. Nonregulation of insurance sales.

The provisions of this Article do not regulate the issuance and sale of insurance policies, but apply only to the underlying preneed funeral contracts. (1991 (Reg. Sess., 1992), c. 901, s. 2.)

§ 90-210.72. Nonapplication to certain funeral contracts.

This Article does not apply to contracts for funeral services or merchandise sold as preneed burial insurance policies pursuant to Part 13 of Article 10 of Chapter 143B of the North Carolina General Statutes or to replacements or conversions of such policies pursuant to G.S. 143B-472.28. (1991 (Reg. Sess., 1992), c. 901, s. 2.)

§ 90-210.73. Not public record.

The names and addresses of the purchasers and beneficiaries of preneed funeral contracts filed with the Board shall not be subject to Chapter 132 of the General Statutes. (1997-399, s. 33.)

§§ 90-210.74 through 90-210.79. Reserved for future codification purposes.

Article 13E.

Mutual Burial Associations.

§ 90-210.80. Duties of Board; meetings.

It shall be the duty of the North Carolina Board of Funeral Service to supervise, pursuant to this Article, all burial associations authorized by this Article to operate in North Carolina, to determine that such associations are operated in conformity with this Article and the rules adopted pursuant to this Article; to prosecute violations of this Article or rules adopted pursuant thereto; and to protect the interest of members of mutual burial associations.

The North Carolina Board of Funeral Service, after a public hearing, may promulgate reasonable rules and regulations for the enforcement of this Article and in order to carry out the intent thereof. The Board is authorized and directed to adopt specific rules to provide for the orderly transfer of a member's benefits in cash or merchandise and services from the funeral director sponsoring the member's association to the funeral establishment which furnishes a funeral service, or merchandise, or both, for the burial of the member, provided that any funeral establishment to which the member's benefits are transferred in accordance with such rules shall, if located in North Carolina, be a funeral establishment registered and permitted under the provisions of G.S. 90-210.25 or shall, if located in any other state, territory or foreign country, be a funeral establishment recognized by and operating in conformity with the laws of such other state, territory or foreign country. One or more burial associations operating in North Carolina may merge into another burial association operating in North Carolina and two or more burial associations operating in North Carolina may consolidate into a new burial association provided that any such plan of merger or plan of consolidation shall be adopted and carried out in accordance with rules adopted by the Board pursuant to this Article.

All rules heretofore adopted by the North Carolina Mutual Burial Association Commission or the North Carolina Board of Funeral Service in accordance with prior law and which have not been amended, rescinded, revoked or otherwise changed, or which have not been nullified or made inoperative or unenforceable because of any statute enacted after the adoption of any such rule, shall remain in full force and effect until amended, rescinded, revoked or otherwise changed by action of the North Carolina Board of Funeral Service as set out above, or until nullified or made inoperative or unenforceable because of statutory enactment or court decision.

Members of the Board shall receive, when attending such regular or special meetings such per diem, expense allowance and travel allowance as are allowed other commissions and boards of the State. The legal adviser to the Board shall be entitled to actual expenses when attending regular or special meetings of the Board held other than in Raleigh. All expenses of the Board shall be paid from funds coming to the Board pursuant to this Article or appropriated for this purpose. (1967, c. 1197, s. 2; 1971, c. 1151; 1973, c. 1147, s. 1; 1975, c. 837; 1987, c. 864, s. 12; 1997-313, ss. 3, 5; 1999-425, s. 1; 2003-420, ss. 1, 17(b).)

§ 90-210.81. Requirements as to rules and bylaws.

All burial associations now operating within the State of North Carolina shall have and maintain rules and bylaws embodying the following:

Article 1. The name of this association shall be _____, which shall indicate that said association is a mutual burial association.

Article 2. The objects and purposes for which this association is formed and the purposes for which it has been organized, and the methods and plan of operation of this association shall be to provide a plan for each member of this association for the payment of one funeral benefit for each member, which shall consist of a funeral benefit in cash or merchandise and service, with no free embalming or free ambulance service included in this benefit. No other free service or any other thing free shall be held out, promised or furnished, in any case. Such funeral benefit shall be in the amount of one hundred dollars ($100.00) of cash or merchandise and service, without free embalming or free ambulance service, for persons of the age of 10 years and over, or in the amount of fifty dollars ($50.00) for persons under the age of 10 years; provided, however, that any member of this association of the age of 10 years or more may purchase a double benefit (for a total benefit of two hundred dollars ($200.00)), and provided further, however, that any member of this association under the age of 10 years may purchase a double benefit (for a total benefit of one hundred dollars ($100.00)) or a quadruple benefit (for a total benefit of two hundred dollars ($200.00)); however, any additional benefit (as set out herein) shall be based on the assessment rate, as provided in Article 6 of this section, at the attained age of applicant at the time the additional benefit takes effect.

The purchase of an additional benefit shall not be available to any member who cannot fulfill the requirements as set forth in Article 3 of this section.

Provided, further, that mutual burial associations organized and operating pursuant to this Article may offer for sale to its members in good standing, funeral benefits payable only in cash in excess of two hundred dollars ($200.00), but those sales shall be subject to all applicable insurance laws of this State and shall in no manner be subject to the provisions of this Article or impair whatsoever funds heretofore or hereafter collected and held by that Association pursuant to this Article. All mutual burial association policies heretofore or hereafter sold in this State in an amount of two hundred dollars ($200.00) or less shall continue to be administered by the Board of Funeral Service and shall be subject to all provisions of this Article.

Article 3. Any person who has passed his or her first birthday, and who has not passed his or her sixty-fifth birthday, and who is in good health and not under treatment of any physician, nor confined in any institution for the treatment of mental or other disease, may become a member of this burial association by the payment by such person, or for such person, of a membership fee in accordance with the provisions of this Article and the first assessment due on the membership issued for such member in accordance with the provisions of Article 6 herein. The membership fee for any person joining prior to July 1, 1975, is twenty-five cents (25¢). The membership fee of any person joining after July 1, 1975, is twenty-five cents (25¢) for each one hundred dollars ($100.00) of benefits provided in such membership, with a minimum membership fee of twenty-five cents (25¢). The payment of the membership fee, without the payment of the first quarterly assessment due on the membership, shall not authorize the issuance of a certificate of membership in this burial association, and a certificate of membership for such person shall not be issued until the first such assessment is paid. Any member of this association joining after July 1, 1975, and who shall thereafter purchase an increased benefit shall pay an additional membership fee in accordance with this Article so that the total membership fee paid by such person shall equal twenty-five [cents] (25¢) for each one hundred dollars ($100.00) of benefits in such member's membership; provided, that any member with a fifty-dollar ($50.00) benefit who increases his benefit from fifty dollars ($50.00) to one hundred dollars ($100.00) shall not be required to pay any additional membership fee. The payment of any additional membership fee, without the payment of the first additional assessment due for the increased benefit, shall not make such member eligible for any additional benefit, and such member shall not be eligible for any additional benefit until the first such additional assessment due for such additional benefit is paid.

Notwithstanding the foregoing, the provisions of the last paragraph of Article 6, hereinafter set out, shall control the increase of benefits from fifty dollars ($50.00) to one hundred dollars ($100.00) for any member of this association joining under the age of 10 whose benefits in force upon such member attaining his or her tenth birthday are in the amount of fifty dollars ($50.00).

Applicant's birthday must be written in the application and subject to verification by any record the Board of Funeral Service may deem necessary to prove or establish a true date of the birth of any applicant.

Article 4. The annual meeting of the association shall be held at ____ (here insert the place, date and hour); each member shall have one vote at said annual meeting and 15 members of the association shall constitute a quorum. There shall be elected at the annual meeting of said association a board of directors of seven members, each of whom shall serve for a period of from one to five years as the membership may determine and until his or her successor shall have been elected and qualified. Any member of the board of directors who shall fail to maintain his or her membership, as provided in the rules and bylaws of said association, shall cease to be a member of the board of directors and a director shall be appointed by the president of said association for the unexpired term of such disqualified member. There shall be at least an annual meeting of the board of directors, and such meeting shall be held immediately following the annual meeting of the membership of the association. The directors of the association may, by a majority vote, hold other meetings of which notice shall be given to each member by mailing such notice five days before the meeting to be held. At the annual meetings of the directors of the association, the board of directors shall elect a president, a vice-president, and a secretary-treasurer. The president and vice-president shall be elected from among the directors, but the secretary-treasurer may be selected from the director membership or from the membership of the association, it being provided that it is not necessary that the secretary-treasurer shall be a member of the board of directors. Among other duties that the secretary-treasurer may perform, he shall be chargeable with keeping an accurate and faithful roll of the membership of this association at all times and he shall be chargeable with the duty of faithfully preserving and faithfully applying all moneys coming into his hands by virtue of his said office. The president, vice-president and secretary-treasurer shall constitute a board of control who shall direct the affairs of the association in accordance with these Articles and bylaws of the association, and subject to such modification as may be made or authorized by an act of the General Assembly. The secretary-treasurer shall keep a record of all assessments made, dues collected and benefits paid. The books of the association, together with all records and bank accounts shall be at all times open to the inspection of the Board of Funeral Service or its duly constituted auditors or representatives. It shall be the duty of the secretary or secretary-treasurer of each association to keep the books of the association posted up-to-date so that the financial standing of the association may be readily ascertained by the Board of Funeral Service or any auditor or representative employed by it. Upon the failure of any secretary or secretary-treasurer to comply with this provision, it shall be the duty of the Board of Funeral Service to take charge of the books of the association and do whatever work is necessary to bring the books up-to-date. The actual costs of said work may be charged the burial association and shall be paid from the thirty percent (30%) allowed by law for the operation of the burial association.

Whenever in the opinion of the Board of Funeral Service, it is necessary to audit the books of any burial association more than once in any calendar year, the Board of Funeral Service shall have authority to assess such burial association the actual cost of any audit in excess of one per calendar year, provided that no more than one audit may be deemed necessary unless a discrepancy exists at the last regular audit. Such cost shall be paid from the thirty percent (30%) allowed by law for the operation of the burial association.

Every burial association shall file with the Board of Funeral Service an annual report of its financial condition on a form furnished to it by the Board of Funeral Service. Such report shall be filed on or before February 15 of each calendar year and shall cover the complete financial condition of the burial association for the immediate preceding calendar year. The Board of Funeral Service shall levy and collect a penalty of twenty-five dollars ($25.00) for each day after February 15 that the report called for herein is not filed. The Board may, in its discretion, grant any reasonable extension of the above filing date without the penalty provided in this section. Such penalty shall be paid from the thirty percent (30%) allowed by law for the operation of the burial association. Any secretary or secretary-treasurer who fails to file such financial report on or before February 15 of each calendar year or on or before the last day of any period of extension for the filing of such report granted by the Board to the burial association of such secretary or secretary-treasurer shall be guilty of a Class 3 misdemeanor. Each day after February 15, or the last day of any period of extension for the filing of the report granted by the Board to the burial association of such secretary or secretary-treasurer, that said report is not filed by the secretary or secretary-treasurer of a burial association, shall constitute a separate offense.

Article 5. Upon the death of any officer, his successor shall be elected by the board of directors for the unexpired term. The president, vice-president and secretary-treasurer shall be elected for a term of from one to five years, and shall hold office until his successor is elected and qualified, subject to the power of the board of directors to remove any officer for good cause shown; provided, that any officer removed by the board of directors shall have the right of appeal to the membership of the association, such appeal to be heard at the next ensuing annual meeting of said membership.

Article 6. Each member shall be assessed according to the following schedule for the benefit indicated (or in multiples thereof for additional benefit) at the age of entry of the member.

Assessment Rate for Age Groups:

First to tenth birthday

($50.00) benefit   five
cents (5¢)

Tenth to thirtieth birthday

($100.00) benefit   ten cents
(10¢)

Thirtieth to fiftieth birthday

($100.00) benefit   twenty
cents (20¢)

Fiftieth to sixty-fifth birthday

($100.00) benefit   thirty
cents (30¢)

(Ages shall be defined as having passed a certain birthday instead of nearest birthday.) Assessment shall always be made on the entire membership in good standing.

Any member joining under the age of 10 shall, upon attaining his or her tenth birthday, pay thereafter the assessment for a member age 10 as set out above.

Any member joining under the age of 10 whose benefits in force upon such member attaining his or her tenth birthday are in the amount of fifty dollars ($50.00) shall, if such member is in good standing upon attaining his or her tenth birthday, thereafter have benefits in force in the amount of one hundred dollars ($100.00) without the necessity of making application for such increased benefit. Assessments made thereafter for such member shall be the same as an assessment for a member age 10 as set out above. Such one-hundred-dollar ($100.00) benefit shall be in full force and effect for any such member in good standing immediately upon such member attaining his or her tenth birthday even though the increased assessment provided for herein shall not yet be due and payable, it being the intent of this Article that, notwithstanding any other provisions in these Articles, any member in good standing with a fifty-dollar ($50.00) benefit shall immediately upon attainment of his or her tenth birthday have a one-hundred-dollar ($100.00) benefit in force whether or not the increased assessment is then due and payable by such member in accordance with the assessment period of this association.

Article 7. No benefit will be paid for natural death occurring within 30 days from the date of the certificate of membership, which certificate shall express the true date such person becomes a member of this association, and the certificate issued shall be in acknowledgment of membership in this association. Benefits will be paid for death caused by accidental means occurring any time after date of membership certificate. No benefits will be paid in case of suicidal death of any member within one year from the date of the membership certificate. No agent or other person shall have authority to issue membership certificates in the field, but such membership certificates shall be issued at the home office of the association by duly authorized officers: the president, vice-president or secretary, and a record thereof duly made.

Article 8. Any member failing to pay any assessment within 30 days after notice shall be in bad standing, and unless and until restored, shall not be entitled to benefits. Notice shall be presumed duly given when mailed, postage paid, to the last known address of such members: Provided, moreover, that notice to the head of a family shall be construed as notice to the entire membership of such family in said association. Any member or head of a family changing his or her address shall give notice to the secretary-treasurer in writing of such change, giving the old address as well as the new, and the head of a family notifying the secretary-treasurer of change in address shall list with the secretary in such notice all the members of his or her family having membership in said association. Any member in bad standing may, within 90 days after the date of an assessment notice, be reinstated to good standing by the payment of all delinquent dues and assessments: Provided such person shall at the same time submit to the secretary-treasurer satisfactory evidence of good health, in writing, and no benefit will be paid for natural death occurring within 30 days after reinstatement. In case of death caused by accidental means, benefit will be in force immediately after reinstatement. Any person desiring to discontinue his membership for any reason shall communicate such desire to the secretary-treasurer immediately and surrender his or her certificate of membership. Any adult member who is the head of a family and who, with his family, has become in bad standing, shall furnish to the secretary-treasurer satisfactory evidence of the good health of each member desired to be reinstated in writing.

Article 9. The benefits herein provided are for the purpose of furnishing a funeral and burial benefit, in cash or merchandise and service, for a deceased member. The funeral and burial benefit, if furnished in merchandise and service, shall be in keeping with and similar to the merchandise and service sold and furnished at the same price by reputable funeral directors of this or other like communities.

Article 10. It is understood and stipulated that the benefits provided for shall be payable only to a funeral establishment which provides a funeral service for a deceased member and which, if located in North Carolina, is a funeral establishment registered under the provisions of G.S. 90-210.25 or which, if located in any other state, territory or foreign country, is a funeral establishment recognized by and operating in conformity with the laws of such other state, territory or foreign country. Upon the death of any member, it shall be the duty of the person or persons making the funeral arrangements for such deceased member to notify the secretary of the member's burial association of the death of such member. The person or persons making the funeral arrangements for such deceased member shall have 30 days from the date of the death of such member in which to make demand upon the burial association for the funeral benefits to which such member is entitled.

The benefits provided for are to be paid by the burial association to the funeral director providing such funeral and burial service either in cash or in merchandise and service as elected by the person or persons making the funeral arrangements for such deceased member. If the burial association shall fail, on demand, to provide the benefits to which the deceased member was entitled to the funeral establishment which provided the funeral service for the deceased member, then the benefits shall be paid in cash to the representative of the deceased member qualified under law to receive such benefits.

Article 11. Assessments shall be made as provided in G.S. 90-210.96. Whenever possible, assessments will be made at definitely stated intervals so as to reduce the cost of collection and to prevent lapse.

Article 12. In the event the proceeds of the annual assessments imposed on the entire membership for one year, as provided in G.S. 90-210.96, do not prove sufficient at any time to yield the benefit provided for in these bylaws, then the secretary-treasurer shall notify the Board of Funeral Service who shall be authorized, unless the membership is increased to that point where such assessments are sufficient, to cause liquidation of said association, and may transfer all members in good standing to a like organization or association.

Article 13. (a) All legitimate operating expenses of the association shall be paid out of the assessments, but in no case shall the entire expenses exceed thirty percent (30%) of the total of the assessments collected and the investment income of the burial association in one calendar year.

(b) Each burial association shall establish and maintain a reserve account for the payment of member's benefits. On the thirty-first day of December following July 1, 1975, each burial association shall transfer to such burial association's reserve account established in accordance with this Article all funds which such burial association is maintaining on that date in an account designated by such burial association as either a surplus account or a reserve account. Thereafter, beginning on January 1, 1976, each burial association shall place in such reserve account five percent (5%) of the assessments collected from and after that date and five percent (5%) of the investment income of the association earned from and after that date. These sums shall continue to be placed in the association's reserve account until the association's reserve account shall equal twenty-one dollars ($21.00) per member. Thereafter if the reserve account shall fall below twenty-one dollars ($21.00) per member, such sums shall again be deposited in the account until such time as the reserve account shall again be equal to twenty-one dollars ($21.00) per member. If the reserve account shall at any time exceed twenty-one dollars ($21.00) per member, amounts in excess of twenty-one dollars ($21.00) per member may be withdrawn from the reserve account.

Article 14. Special meetings of the association membership may be called by the secretary-treasurer when by him deemed necessary or advisable, and he shall call a meeting when petitioned to do so by sixty-six and two-thirds percent (66 2/3%) of the members of said association who are in good standing.

Article 15. The secretary-treasurer shall, upon satisfactory evidence that membership was granted to any person not qualified at the time of entry as provided under Article 3 of these bylaws, refund any amounts paid as assessment, and shall remove the name from the membership roll.

Article 16. Any member may pay any number of assessments in advance, in which case such member will not be further assessed until a like number of assessments shall have been levied against the remaining membership.

Article 17. No person may maintain active membership in two or more separate burial associations. Any person who is found to have membership in two or more separate burial associations shall forfeit all benefits and fees paid in all associations of which he is a member except in the association which he first joined and of which he is still then a member. A person is not a member of an association for purposes of this Article if he has discontinued his membership in such association or if such association has been placed in liquidation.

Article 18. Each year, before the annual meeting of the membership of this association, the association shall cause to be published in a newspaper of general circulation in the county in which such association has its principal place of business, or shall cause to be mailed to each member in good standing a statement showing total income collected, expenses paid and burial benefits provided for by such association during the next preceding year.

Article 19. These rules and bylaws shall not be modified, canceled or abridged by any association or other authority except by act of the General Assembly of North Carolina. (1941, c. 130, s. 4; 1943, c. 272, ss. 1, 2; 1945, c. 125, s. 1; 1947, c. 100, s. 1; 1949, c. 201, ss. 1, 2; 1953, c. 1201; 1955, c. 259, ss. 3, 4; 1967, c. 1197, s. 4; 1969, c. 1041, ss. 2, 3; 1973, c. 688; 1975, c. 837; 1977, c. 748, ss. 1, 2, 6; 1981, c. 989, s. 4; 1987, c. 864, ss. 12, 50; 1991, c. 62, s. 1; 1991 (Reg. Sess., 1992), c. 1007, s. 39; 1993, c. 539, s. 1042; c. 553, ss. 48, 49; 1994, Ex. Sess., c. 24, s. 14(c); 1997-313, ss. 4-6; 1999-425, s. 2; 2003-420, ss. 1, 17(b).)

§ 90-210.82. Limitation of soliciting agents; licensing and qualifications; officers exempt from license; issuance of membership certificates.

Each burial association shall have for each funeral home sponsoring the said burial association not more than five agents or representatives soliciting members other than the secretary-treasurer and president, and before any agent or representative shall or may represent any burial association in North Carolina, he or she shall first apply to the Board of Funeral Service for a license, and the Board of Funeral Service shall have full power and authority to issue such license upon proof satisfactory to such Board that such person is capable of soliciting burial association memberships, is of good moral character and recommended by the association in behalf of which such membership solicitations are to be made. The Board of Funeral Service may reject the application of any person who does not meet the requirements as to capacity and moral fitness. The Board of Funeral Service may, upon proof satisfactory to it that said licensed agent has violated any section of this law, revoke said license. Upon the issuing of a license to solicit membership in any burial association, such person shall be required to pay in cash, at the time of issuing license to such applicant, to the Board of Funeral Service, the sum of five dollars ($5.00); moneys derived from this fee or charge, are to be and remain in the department or office of such Board of Funeral Service, for supervision of burial associations in this State, subject to withdrawal for expenses of supervision by authority of the Board of Funeral Service. It shall not be necessary that the president or secretary-treasurer of any burial association obtain a license for soliciting membership in the association of which such person is president or secretary-treasurer. Membership certificates shall not be issued by a solicitor in the field, but shall be reported to the office of the association and there issued and a record made of such issuance at the time such certificate is so issued. (1941, c. 130, s. 5; 1945, c. 125, s. 2; 1947, c. 100, s. 2; 1949, c. 201, s. 3; 1975, c. 837; 1987, c. 864, s. 12; 1997-313, ss. 5, 6, 7; 2003-420, ss. 1, 17(b).)

§ 90-210.83. Assessments against associations.

In order to meet the expenses of the supervision of the burial associations, the Board of Funeral Service shall prepare an annual budget for the office of the Board of Funeral Service. Thereafter, the Board of Funeral Service shall assess each burial association one hundred dollars ($100.00) and shall prorate the remaining amount of this budget, over and above any other funds made available to it for this purpose, and assess each association on a pro rata basis in accordance with the number of members of each association. Each burial association shall remit to the Board of Funeral Service its pro rata part of the total assessment, which expense shall be included in the thirty per centum (30%) expense allowance as provided in G.S. 90-210.81. This assessment shall be made on the first day of July of each and every year and said assessment shall be paid within 30 days thereafter. If any association shall fail or refuse to pay such assessment within 30 days, the Board of Funeral Service is authorized to transfer all memberships and assets of every kind and description to the nearest association that is found by the Board of Funeral Service to be in good sound financial condition. (1941, c. 130, s. 6; 1943, c. 272, s. 3; 1945, c. 125, s. 3; 1947, c. 100, s. 3; 1949, c. 201, s. 4; 1951, c. 901, s. 1; 1955, c. 259, ss. 1, 2; 1967, c. 985, s. 1; 1969, c. 1006, s. 2; 1973, c. 1476, s. 1; 1975, c. 837; 1977, c. 748, s. 3; 1981, c. 989, s. 6; 1983, c. 717, s. 12; 1987, c. 864, ss. 12, 14; 1997-313, ss. 5, 6, 7; 2003-420, ss. 16, 17(b).)

§ 90-210.84. Unlawful to operate without written authority of Board.

It shall be unlawful for any person, firm or corporation, association or organization to organize, operate, or in any way solicit members for a burial association, or for participation in any plan, scheme, or device similar to burial associations, without the written authority of the Board of Funeral Service, and any person, firm or corporation violating the provisions of this section shall be guilty of a Class 1 misdemeanor; provided, however, the Board of Funeral Service shall not withhold authority for the organization or operation of a bona fide burial association, meeting the requirements of this Article, unless it shall be found and established to the satisfaction of the Board of Funeral Service that the person or persons applying for authority to organize and operate such bona fide burial association is disqualified or does not meet the requirements of this Article. (1941, c. 130, s. 7; 1975, c. 837; 1987, c. 864, s. 12; 1993, c. 539, s. 1043; 1994, Ex. Sess., c. 24, s. 14(c); 1997-313, s. 5; 2003-420, ss. 1, 17(b).)

§ 90-210.85. Revocation of license.

In the event it is proven to the satisfaction of the Board of Funeral Service that any burial association is being operated not in conformity with any provision of this Article, then it shall become the duty of the Board of Funeral Service upon hearing to revoke the license of said burial association and transfer said burial association, its membership and all its assets of every kind and description to another burial association that is found by the Board of Funeral Service to be in good sound financial condition; provided, that if said burial association gives notice of appeal as provided for in G.S. 90-210.94, then said burial association may continue to operate as before the revocation and until final adjudication. (1945, c. 125, s. 4; 1975, c. 837; 1987, c. 864, ss. 12, 15; 1997-313, s. 5; 2003-420, ss. 1, 17(b).)

§ 90-210.86. Deposit or investment of funds of mutual burial associations.

Funds belonging to each mutual burial association over and above the amount determined by the Board of Funeral Service to be necessary for operating capital shall be invested in:

(1)   Deposits in any bank or trust company in this State.

(2)   Obligations of the United States of America.

(3)   Obligations of any agency or instrumentality of the United States of America if the payment of interest and principal of such obligations is fully guaranteed by the United States of America.

(4)   Obligations of the State of North Carolina.

(5)   Bonds and notes of any North Carolina local government or public authority, subject to such restrictions as the Board of Funeral Service may impose.

(6)   Shares of or deposits in any savings and loan association organized under the laws of this State and shares of or deposits in any federal savings and loan association having its principal office in this State, provided that any such savings and loan association is insured by the United States of America or any agency thereof or by any mutual deposit guaranty association authorized by the Commissioner of Insurance of North Carolina to do business in North Carolina pursuant to Article 7A of Chapter 54 of the General Statutes.

(7) Obligations of the Federal Intermediate Credit Banks, the Federal Home Loan Banks, Fannie Mae, the Banks for Cooperatives, and the Federal Land Banks, maturing no later than 18 months after the date of purchase.

Violation of the provisions of this section shall, after hearing, be cause for revocation or suspension of license to operate a mutual burial association. (1957, c. 820, s. 1; 1975, c. 837; 1987, c. 864, s. 12; 1997-313, s. 5; 2001-487, s. 14(l); 2003-420, ss. 1, 17(b).)

§ 90-210.87. Unclaimed funds of defunct burial association.

All unclaimed funds of any burial association that is no longer in operation shall be disposed of in accordance with Chapter 116B. (1969, c. 1083; 1975, c. 837; 1979, 2nd Sess., c. 1311, s. 7; 1987, c. 864, s. 12; 2003-420, s. 17(b).)

§ 90-210.88. Penalty for failure to operate in substantial compliance with bylaws.

If any burial association or other organization or official thereof, or any person operates or allows to be operated a burial association on any plan, scheme or bylaws not in substantial compliance with the bylaws set forth in G.S. 90-210.81, the Board of Funeral Service may revoke any authority or license granted for the operation of such burial association, and any person, firm or corporation or association convicted of the violation of this section shall be guilty of a Class 1 misdemeanor. (1941, c. 130, s. 8; 1975, c. 837; 1987, c. 864, ss. 12, 16; 1993, c. 539, s. 1044; 1994, Ex. Sess., c. 24, s. 14(c); 1997-313, s. 5; 2003-420, ss. 1, 17(b).)

§ 90-210.89. Penalty for wrongfully inducing person to change membership.

Any burial association official, agent or representative thereof or any person who shall use fraud or make any promise not part of the printed bylaws, or who shall offer any rebate, gratuity or refund to cause a member of one association to change membership to another association, shall be guilty of a Class 1 misdemeanor. (1941, c. 130, s. 9; 1975, c. 837; 1987, c. 864, s. 12; 1993, c. 539, s. 1045; 1994, Ex. Sess., c. 24, s. 14(c); 2003-420, s. 17(b).)

§ 90-210.90. Penalty for making false and fraudulent entries.

Any person or burial association official who makes or allows to be made any false entry on the books of the association with intent to deceive or defraud any member thereof, or with intent to conceal from the Board of Funeral Service or its deputy or agent, or any auditor authorized to examine the books of such association, under the supervision of the Board of Funeral Service, shall be guilty of a Class 1 misdemeanor. (1941, c. 130, s. 10; 1945, c. 125, s. 5; 1975, c. 837; 1987, c. 864, s. 12; 1993, c. 539, s. 1046; 1994, Ex. Sess., c. 24, s. 14(c); 1997-313, ss. 5, 6; 2003-420, ss. 1, 17(b).)

§ 90-210.91. Accepting applications without collecting fee and first assessment.

Any burial association official, agent or representative, or any other person who shall accept any application for membership in any association without collecting the membership fee and first assessment due thereon from any such person making such an application for membership, shall be guilty of a Class 1 misdemeanor.

Any burial association official, agent or representative, or any other person who shall accept an application for an additional benefit from a member of a burial association without collecting the additional membership fee and the additional assessment due thereon from any such person making such an application for an additional benefit shall be guilty of a Class 1 misdemeanor. (1941, c. 130, s. 11; 1975, c. 837; 1987, c. 864, s. 12; 1993, c. 539, s. 1047; 1994, Ex. Sess., c. 24, s. 14(c); 2003-420, s. 17(b).)

§ 90-210.92. Removal of secretary-treasurer for failure to maintain proper records.

Any burial association secretary-treasurer who fails to maintain records to the minimum standards required by the Board of Funeral Service shall be by such

Board removed from office and another elected in his stead, such election to be immediate and by the board of directors of said burial association upon notice of such removal. (1941, c. 130, s. 12; 1975, c. 837; 1987, c. 864, s. 12; 1997-313, s. 5; 2003-420, ss. 1, 17(b).)

§ 90-210.93. Free services; failure to make proper assessments, etc., made a misdemeanor.

Any person or persons who offer free funeral services or free embalming, free ambulance service or any other thing free of charge, acting for any burial association, directly or indirectly, or who so acting shall in any way fail to assess for the amount needed to pay death losses and allowable expenses, shall be guilty of a Class 1 misdemeanor. (1941, c. 130, s. 13; 1967, c. 1197, s. 5; 1975, c. 837; 1987, c. 864, s. 12; 1993, c. 539, s. 1048; 1994, Ex. Sess., c. 24, s. 14(c); 2003-420, ss. 1, 17(b).)

§ 90-210.94. Right of appeal upon revocation or suspension of license.

Upon the revocation or suspension of any license or authority by the Board of Funeral Service, under any of the provisions of this Article, the said association or individual whose license or authority has been revoked or suspended shall have the right of appeal from the action of the Board of Funeral Service in revoking or suspending such license or authority to the Superior Court of Wake County or to the superior court of the county in which the said association or the said individual is domiciled or, upon agreement of the parties to the appeal, to any other superior court of the State. The association or individual appealing from the order of the Board of Funeral Service shall give notice of appeal in writing to the Board of Funeral Service, with a copy of such notice to the clerk of the superior court to which the appeal is taken, within 10 days of the date of notice of the order revoking or suspending the said license or authority and shall pay such appeal fees to the clerk of superior court as are required by law. Within 30 days after receipt of the notice of appeal, the Board of Funeral Service shall file with the clerk of the superior court of the county in which the appeal is to be heard the decision of the Board of Funeral Service. Upon receipt of such decision, the clerk of superior court shall place the matter upon the civil issue docket of the superior court and the same shall be heard de novo. Pending such appeal, the burial association or individual whose license or authority has been suspended or revoked shall continue to operate or function as before the revocation or suspension and until final adjudication by the superior court. (1941, c. 130, s. 14; 1943, c. 272, s. 4; 1957, c. 820, s. 3; 1973, c. 108, s. 20; 1975, c. 837; 1987, c. 864, s. 12; 1997-313, s. 5; 2003-420, ss. 1, 17(b).)

§ 90-210.95. Bond of secretary or secretary-treasurer of burial associations.

The secretary or secretary-treasurer of each burial association shall, before entering upon the duties of his office, and for the faithful performance thereof, execute a bond payable to the Board of Funeral Service as trustee for the burial association in some bonding company licensed to do business in this State, to be approved by the Board of Funeral Service. Said bond shall be in an amount not less than one thousand dollars ($1,000), nor more than ten thousand dollars ($10,000), in the discretion of the Board, for those associations whose assets, as determined by the Board's audit, are ten thousand dollars ($10,000) or less. For those associations whose assets, as determined by the Board's audit, are in excess of ten thousand dollars ($10,000), said bond shall be in an amount of ten thousand dollars ($10,000) plus twenty-five per centum (25%) of all assets over ten thousand dollars ($10,000); provided, however, that the bond required by this section shall not in any event exceed fifty thousand dollars ($50,000). If any association operates a branch or subsidiary and the officers of both associations are the same, for purposes of this section, it shall be treated as one association. Any burial association, with the consent of the Board of Funeral Service, may give a bond secured by a deed of trust on real estate situated in North Carolina, in lieu of procuring said bond from a bonding company. The bond thus given shall not be acceptable in excess of the ad valorem tax value for the current year of the real estate securing said bond. The deed of trust shall be recorded in the county or counties wherein the land lies and shall be deposited with the Board of Funeral Service, name the Board as trustee for the burial association and must constitute a first lien on the property secured by the deed of trust. Said deed of trust shall contain a description of the encumbered property by metes and bounds together with evidence by title insurance policy or by certificate of an attorney-at-law, certifying that said trustor is the owner of a marketable fee simple title to such lands. (1941, c. 130, s. 15; 1943, c. 272, s. 5; 1967, c. 985, s. 2; 1975, c. 837; 1987, c. 864, s. 12; 1997-313, s. 5; 2003-420, ss. 1, 17(b).)

§ 90-210.96. Assessments.

Every burial association now or hereinafter organized shall make 12 assessments, or their equivalent, per year per member. The Board of Funeral Service shall order any association to make more than 12 assessments per year when, after notice and hearing, it shall appear to the Board of Funeral Service that the death loss of any association so requires in order to protect the interest of the members. (1943, c. 272, s. 6; 1969, c. 1041, s. 1; 1971, c. 650; 1975, c. 837; 1987, c. 864, s. 12; 1997-313, s. 5; 2003-420, ss. 1, 17(b).)

§ 90-210.97. Making false or fraudulent statement a misdemeanor.

Any officer or employee of any burial association authorized to do business under this Article, who shall knowingly or willfully make any false or fraudulent statement or representation in or with reference to any application for membership or for the purpose of obtaining money or any benefit from any burial association transacting business under this Article, or who shall make any false financial statement to the Board of Funeral Service or to the membership of the burial association of which such person is an officer or employee shall be guilty of a Class 1 misdemeanor. (1943, c. 272, s. 6; 1975, c. 837; 1987, c. 864, s. 12; 1993, c. 539, s. 1049; 1994, Ex. Sess., c. 24, s. 14(c); 1997-313, s. 5; 2003-420, ss. 1, 17(b).)

§ 90-210.98. Statewide organization of associations.

It shall be lawful for the several mutual burial associations of the State of North Carolina, in good standing, to organize and provide for a statewide organization of mutual burial associations, which organization shall be for the mutual and general suggestive control of mutual burial associations in the State of North Carolina. Such organization shall be known as the North Carolina Burial Association, Incorporated, and shall be composed of members who are lawfully operating burial associations in this State and who pay their dues to such association. (1941, c. 130, s. 16; 1975, c. 837; 1987, c. 864, s. 12; 2003-420, s. 17(b).)

§ 90-210.99. Article deemed exclusive authority for organization, etc., of mutual burial associations.

This Article shall be deemed and held exclusive authority for the organization and operation of mutual burial associations within the State of North Carolina, and such associations shall not be subject to any other laws respecting insurance companies of any class. (1941, c. 130, s. 17; 1975, c. 837; 1987, c. 864, s. 12; 2003-420, s. 17(b).)

§ 90-210.100. Operation of association in violation of law prohibited.

No person, firm or corporation shall operate as a burial association in this State unless incorporated under the laws of the State of North Carolina and unless such association shall be operated in compliance with all the provisions of this Article, and unless such association shall be licensed and approved by the Board of Funeral Service. (1941, c. 130, s. 18; 1975, c. 837; 1987, c. 864, s. 12; 1997-313, s. 5; 2003-420, ss. 1, 17(b).)

§ 90-210.101. Member of Armed Forces failing to pay assessments; reinstatement.

If a member of a burial association who is in the Armed Forces of the United States fails to pay any assessment, the member shall be in bad standing, and unless and until restored, shall not be entitled to benefits. However, the member shall be reinstated in the burial association upon application made by the member at any time until 12 months after the member's discharge from the Armed Forces of the United States, notwithstanding the member's physical condition and without the payment of assessments which have become due during the member's service in the Armed Forces of the United States. Benefits will be in force immediately after such reinstatement. (1943, c. 732, s. 2; 1975, c. 837; 1987, c. 864, s. 12; 2003-420, s. 17(b); 2011-183, s. 64.)

§ 90-210.102. Hearing by Board of dispute over liability for funeral benefits; appeal.

In case of a disagreement between the representative of a deceased member of any burial association and such deceased member's burial association a hearing may be held by the Board of Funeral Service, on request of either party, to determine whether the association is liable for the benefits set forth in the policy issued to the said deceased member of said burial association. The Board of Funeral Service shall render a decision which shall have the same force and effect as judgments rendered by courts of competent jurisdiction in North Carolina. Either party may appeal from the decision of the Board of Funeral Service. Appeal shall be to the district court division of the General Court of Justice in the county in which the burial association is located. The procedure for appeal shall be the same as the appeal procedure set forth in Article 19 of Chapter 7A of the General Statutes of North Carolina regulating appeals from the magistrate to the district court. (1947, c. 100, s. 5; 1975, c. 837; 1987, c. 864, s. 12; 1997-313, s. 5; 2003-420, ss. 1, 17(b); 2007-531, s. 16.)

§ 90-210.103. Board authorized to subpoena witnesses, administer oaths and compel attendance at hearings.

For the purpose of holding hearings the Board of Funeral Service shall have power to subpoena witnesses, administer oaths, and compel attendance of witnesses and parties. (1957, c. 820, s. 2; 1975, c. 837; 1987, c. 864, s. 12; 1997-313, s. 5; 2003-420, ss. 1, 17(b).)

§ 90-210.104. Authority of Board to examine financial records.

The Board of Funeral Service shall have authority to examine all records relating to a burial association's financial condition wherever such records are located, including records maintained by any corporation, building and loan association, savings and loan association, credit union, or other legal entity organized and operating pursuant to the authority contained in Chapters 53 and 54 of the General Statutes. (1977, c. 748, s. 4; 1987, c. 864, s. 12; 1997-313, s. 5; 2003-420, ss. 1, 17(b).)

§ 90-210.105. Board authorized to freeze certain funds of Association.

Whenever in the opinion of the Board of Funeral Service it deems it necessary for the protection of the interest of members of a burial association, it shall have authority by written order to direct that the funds of any burial association on deposit in any institution organized and operating under Chapters 53 and 54 of the General Statutes be frozen and not paid out by such legal entity. Any legal entity freezing the funds of a burial association pursuant to the directive of the Board of Funeral Service shall not be liable to any burial association for freezing said account pursuant to the order of the Board. (1977, c. 748, s. 5; 1987, c. 864, s. 12; 1997-313, ss. 5, 6; 2003-420, ss. 1, 17(b).)

§ 90-210.106. Authority of foreign or domestic mutual burial association or domestic or foreign insurance company to purchase, merge or consolidate with North Carolina mutual burial associations.

(a) Any mutual burial association or insurance company operating pursuant to the laws of this State or any other state may purchase the assets of, merge, or consolidate with a North Carolina chartered mutual burial association in accordance with the laws of this State and any rules promulgated by the Board of Funeral Service to protect the interest of members of mutual burial associations prior to the purchase, merger, or consolidation of the association.

(b) Notwithstanding any provision of Chapter 55 or Chapter 55A, any domestic or foreign insurance company which if organized in North Carolina would have to be organized under Chapter 55 may merge or consolidate with any domestic mutual burial association. When a domestic or foreign insurance company consolidates or merges with a domestic mutual burial association and sells insurance or burial benefits in excess of two hundred dollars ($200.00), it shall be subject to all of the provisions of the insurance laws of North Carolina.

(c) If the assets and liabilities of a North Carolina mutual burial association are purchased, and no merger, consolidation or dissolution is effectuated in connection with the purchase, the management and administrative operations of the North Carolina mutual burial association shall be transferred to the purchasing entity.

(d) In any purchase, merger, or consolidation pursuant to this section, the membership of the mutual burial association shall be guaranteed coverage in the amounts held by each member at the time of such purchase, merger, or consolidation. During the life of the member, this coverage shall not exceed the annual rate charged by the mutual burial association that is being purchased, merged, or consolidated. An insurance company which purchases, merges with, or consolidates with a North Carolina mutual burial association shall establish and maintain life insurance reserves in accordance with the insurance laws of North Carolina for those burial insurance policies existing at the time of the purchase, merger, or consolidation. A North Carolina mutual burial association or foreign mutual burial association which purchases, merges with, or consolidates with a North Carolina mutual burial association shall establish and maintain burial insurance reserves in accordance with the burial insurance laws of North Carolina for those burial insurance policies existing at the time of the purchase, merger, or consolidation. (1981, c. 989, s. 5; 1983, c. 766; 1987, c. 864, s. 12; 1997-313, s. 5; 2003-420, ss. 1, 17(b).)

§ 90-210.107. Acquisition, merger, dissolution, and liquidation of mutual burial associations.

(a) Any insurance company which desires to purchase the assets of or to merge with a burial association as provided in G.S. 90-210.106 shall submit to the Board of Funeral Service and to the secretary of the association a written proposal containing the terms and conditions of the proposed purchase or merger. A proposal may be conditioned upon an increase in the assessments of an association in the manner set out in subsection (g) of this section. In such a case, the issues of purchase or merger and an increase in assessments may be considered at the same meeting of the association.

(b) Upon receipt of a written proposal:

(1) The Board shall issue an order directing the association to hold a meeting of the membership within 30 days following receipt of the order for the purpose of voting on the proposal.

(2) Within 10 days of receiving the order from the Board, the association shall give at least 10 days' written notice of the meeting to each of its members. The notice shall:

a. State the date, time, and place of the meeting.

b. State the purpose of the meeting.

c.	Contain or have attached the proposal submitted by the insurance company.

d.	Contain a statement limiting the time that each member will be permitted to speak to the proposal, if the association deems it advisable.

e.	Contain a written proxy form and instructions concerning the proxy prescribed by the Board.

(c)	A representative of the insurance company shall be permitted to attend the meeting held by the association for the purposes of explaining the proposal and answering any questions from the members. The officers of the association may present their views concerning the proposal. Any member of the association who wishes to speak to the proposal shall be permitted to do so subject to any time limitation stated in the notice of the meeting.

(d)	The secretary of the association shall record the name of every member who is present at the meeting or has issued a written proxy pursuant to G.S. 55A-7-24 and shall determine whether there is a quorum. The presence of 15 members or ten percent (10%) of the membership, whichever is greater, shall constitute a quorum. Acceptance or rejection of the proposal shall be by majority vote of the members voting. Any member who is at least 18 years of age shall be permitted to vote. A parent or guardian of any member who is under 18 years of age may vote on behalf of his or her child or ward, but only one vote may be cast on behalf of that member.

(e)	The secretary of the association shall certify the result of the vote and the presence of a quorum to the Board within five days following the meeting and shall include with the certification a copy of the notice of the meeting that was sent to the members of the association.

(f)	The Board shall immediately review the certification, the notice, and any other records that may be necessary to determine the adequacy of notice, the presence of a quorum, and the validity of the vote. Upon determining that the meeting and vote were regular and held following proper notice and that a majority of a quorum of the members voted in favor of the proposal, the Board shall issue an order approving the purchase or merger and directing that the purchase or merger proceed in accordance with the proposal.

(g) Any burial association whose current assessments are not, or are unlikely to be within the next three years, adequate to reach or maintain a reserve of at least twenty-one dollars ($21.00) per member or are inadequate to meet the requirements of a proposal from an insurance company to acquire the assets of or to merge with the association may increase its assessments by an amount necessary to reach and maintain the reserve or to meet the proposal. The increase shall be approved by a vote of the members of the association at a regular meeting of the association or at a special meeting called for the purpose of increasing assessments.

(1) Any officer or director of the association may call a special meeting for the purpose of increasing assessments, and the secretary shall call a special meeting for such purpose upon the request of at least ten percent (10%) of the members or upon receipt of a proposal from an insurance company that is conditioned upon an increase in assessments.

(2) Written notice setting out the date, time, place, and the purpose of the meeting shall be hand delivered or sent by first-class mail, postage prepaid, to the last known address of each member of the association at least 10 days in advance of the meeting.

(3) No vote may be had on the question of an increase in assessments unless a quorum of the members of the association is present at the meeting. A quorum shall be conclusively presumed if 15 members or ten percent (10%) of the membership of the association, whichever is greater, is present at the meeting.

(4) The proposal to increase the assessments shall be approved by an affirmative vote of a majority of the members present and voting.

(5) The secretary of the association within five days following the meeting shall certify the result of the vote and the presence of a quorum to the Board in the manner and for the purposes set out in subsections (e) and (f) of this section.

(h) Upon a written request from an association that has held a valid meeting and voted for voluntary dissolution in accordance with G.S. 90-210.81, the Board shall issue an order of liquidation for that association.

(i) Upon receipt of a request for voluntary dissolution under subsection (h) of this section or if the sponsoring funeral establishment has its permit revoked or ceases operation for any reason, the Board shall issue an order of liquidation. The Board's order may direct that the agreements for members' benefits be transferred to a financially sound mutual burial association, as well as all records, property, and unexpended balances of funds of the association to be liquidated, if the financially sound mutual burial association agrees in writing to accept the transfer. The Board's order shall direct the burial association to complete the liquidation and to file a final report with the Board no later than December 31 of the year of the liquidation. Upon receipt of the order of liquidation, the burial association shall:

(1)   Cease accepting new members.

(2)   Collect all debts owed to the association and pay all debts owed by the association from monies on hand, including the reserve.

(3)   Distribute pro rata any remaining monies on hand and in the reserve among those who were members of the association and whose transfer could not be accomplished on the date that the liquidation order was issued by the Board. Each member's distributive share shall be determined by dividing the amount of the member's benefit by the aggregate benefits of all members of the association and then multiplying the total amount of money available for distribution by the percentage so derived. Assessments owed by the members to the association at the time of distribution shall be taken into account and shall be offset against the members' distributive shares.

(4)   Issue a certificate to members in an amount that equals the difference between the distributive share issued in subdivision (3) of this subsection and the full amount of the member's association benefit. Any certificate issued shall supersede and supplant any other certificate already issued by the association. The certificate shall be on a form prescribed by the Board and shall be prepared and distributed by the association at its expense.

(5)   File a final report with the Board on or before December 31 in the year in which the order of liquidation was issued. This report shall show all receipts and disbursements, including the amount distributed to each member, since the last annual report of the association was filed with the Board.

(j)   A certificate issued under subsection (i) of this section may be used as a credit toward the cost of funeral services, facilities, and merchandise at any funeral establishment that agrees on forms prescribed by the Board to accept such certificates. A funeral establishment that agrees to accept certificates shall do so until the agreement with the Board expires. The Board shall maintain and distribute to the public a list of funeral establishments that will accept certificates.

(k)   Upon receipt of the final report of dissolution by the association, which is required by subsection (i) of this section, the Board shall immediately review the final report and shall notify the association whether the report is complete and has been accepted. Upon acceptance of the final report by the Board, all licenses issued to soliciting agents of the association pursuant to G.S. 90-210.84 are automatically cancelled. (1999-425, s. 3; 2003-420, ss. 1, 17(b); 2007-531, s. 17.)

§§ 90-210.108 through 90-210.119: Reserved for future codification purposes.

Article 13F.

Cremations.

§ 90-210.120. Short title.

This Article shall be known and may be cited as the North Carolina Crematory Act. (1989 (Reg. Sess., 1990), c. 988, s. 1; 2003-420, s. 2.)

§ 90-210.121. Definitions.

As used in this Article, unless the context requires otherwise:

(1)   "Authorizing agent" means a person legally entitled to authorize the cremation of human remains in accordance with G.S. 90-210.124.

(2)   "Board" means the North Carolina Board of Funeral Service.

(3)   "Body parts" means limbs or other portions of the anatomy that are removed from a person or human remains for medical purposes during

treatment, surgery, biopsy, autopsy, or medical research; or human bodies or any portion thereof that have been donated to science for medical purposes.

(4)   "Casket" means a rigid container that is designed for the encasement of human remains and that is usually constructed of wood, metal, or other material and ornamented and lined with fabric, and which may or may not be combustible.

(5)   "Certificate of cremation" means a certificate provided by the crematory manager who performed the cremation containing, at a minimum, the following information:

a.   Name of decedent;

b.   Date of cremation;

c.   Name and address of crematory; and

d.   Signature of crematory manager or person acting as crematory manager.

(6)   "Cremated remains" means all human remains recovered after the completion of the cremation process, including pulverization which leaves only bone fragments reduced to unidentifiable dimensions.

(7)   "Cremation" means the technical process, using intense heat and flame, that reduces human remains to bone fragments. Cremation includes the processing and may include the pulverization of the bone fragments.

(8)   "Cremation chamber" means the enclosed space within which the cremation process takes place. Cremation chambers covered by this Article shall be used exclusively for the cremation of human remains.

(9)   "Cremation container" means the container in which the human remains are transported to the crematory or placed therein upon arrival for storage and placement in a cremation chamber for cremation. A cremation container shall comply with all of the following standards:

a.   Be composed of readily combustible materials suitable for cremation;

b. Be able to be closed in order to provide a complete covering for the human remains;

c. Be resistant to leakage or spillage;

d. Be rigid enough for handling with ease;

e. Be able to provide protection for the health, safety, and personal integrity of crematory personnel; and

f. Be easily identifiable. The covering of the cremation container shall contain the following information:

1. The name of the decedent;

2. The date of death;

3. The sex of the decedent; and

4. The age at death of the decedent.

(10) "Cremation interment container" means a rigid outer container composed of concrete, steel, fiberglass, or some similar material in which an urn is placed prior to being interred in the ground and which is designed to withstand prolonged exposure to the elements and to support the earth above the urn.

(11) "Crematory" or "crematorium" means the building or buildings or portion of a building on a single site that houses the cremation equipment, the holding and processing facilities, the business office, and other parts of the crematory business. A crematory must comply with all applicable public health and environmental laws and rules and must contain the equipment and meet all of the standards established by the rules adopted by the Board.

(12) "Crematory licensee" means the individual or legal entity that is licensed by the Board to operate a crematory and perform cremations.

(13) "Crematory manager" means the person who is responsible for the management and operation of the crematory. A crematory manager must either be licensed to practice funeral directing or funeral service and be qualified as a

crematory technician or must obtain a crematory manager permit issued by the Board. In order to receive a crematory manager permit, a person must:

a. Be at least 18 years of age.

b. Be of good moral character.

c. Be qualified as a crematory technician.

Notwithstanding any other provision of law, a crematory that is licensed by the Board prior to January 1, 2004, and as of that date is not managed by a crematory manager who is licensed to practice funeral directing or funeral service, or who has a crematory manager permit, may continue to be managed by a crematory manager who is not licensed to practice funeral directing or funeral service or who does not have a crematory manager permit so long as there is no sale, transfer, devise, gift, or any other disposal of a controlling interest in the crematory.

(13a) "Cremation society" means any person, firm, corporation, or organization that is affiliated with a crematory licensed under this Article and provides cremation information to consumers.

(14) "Crematory technician" means any employee of a crematory licensee who has a certificate confirming that the crematory technician has attended a training course approved by the Board. The Board shall recognize the cremation certificate program that is conducted by the Cremation Association of North America (CANA).

(15) "Final disposition" means the cremation and the ultimate interment, entombment, inurnment, or scattering of the cremated remains or the return of the cremated remains by the crematory licensee to the authorizing agent or such agent's designee as provided in this Article. Upon the written direction of the authorizing agent, cremated remains may take various forms.

(16) "Holding and processing facility" means an area or areas that are designated for the retention of human remains prior to, and the retention and processing of cremated remains after, cremation; that comply with all applicable public health and environmental laws; preserve the health and safety of the crematory technician and other personnel of the crematory; and that are secure from access by anyone other than authorized persons. A holding facility and processing facility must be located in a crematory.

(17) "Human remains" means the body of a deceased person, including a separate human fetus, regardless of the length of gestation, or body parts.

(17a) "Initial container" means a receptacle for cremated remains, for which the intended use and design is to hold cremated remains, usually composed of cardboard, plastic, or similar material that can be closed in a manner so as to prevent the leakage or spillage of the cremated remains or the entrance of foreign material and is a single container of sufficient size to hold the cremated remains.

(18) "Niche" means a compartment or cubicle for the memorialization or final disposition of an urn or container containing cremated remains.

(19) "Processing" means the removal of bone fragments from the cremation chamber for the reduction in size, labeling and packaging, and placing in an urn or initial container.

(20) "Pulverization" means the reduction of identifiable or unidentifiable bone fragments after the completion of the cremation to granulated particles by mechanical means.

(21) "Scattering area" means an area permitted by North Carolina law including, but not limited to, an area designated by a cemetery and located on dedicated cemetery property where cremated remains that have been removed from their container can be mixed with or placed on top of the soil or ground cover.

(22) Repealed by Session Laws 2007-531, s. 18, effective August 31, 2007.

(23) "Urn" means a receptacle designed to permanently encase the cremated remains. (1989 (Reg. Sess., 1990), c. 988, s. 1; 1997-399, s. 16; 2003-420, s. 2; 2007-531, s. 18; 2011-284, s. 64.)

§ 90-210.122. Crematory Authority established.

(a) The North Carolina Crematory Authority is established as a Committee within the Board. The Crematory Authority shall suggest rules to the Board for the carrying out and enforcement of the provisions of this Article.

(b) The Crematory Authority shall initially consist of five members appointed by the Governor and two members of the Board appointed by the Board. The Governor may consider a list of recommendations from the Cremation Association of North Carolina.

(c) The initial terms of the members of the Crematory Authority shall be staggered by the appointing authorities so that the terms of three members (two of which shall be appointees of the Governor) expire December 31, 1991, the terms of two members (both of which shall be appointees of the Governor) expire December 31, 1992, and the terms of the remaining two members (one of which shall be an appointee of the Governor) expire December 31, 1993.

As the terms of the members appointed by the Governor expire, their successors shall be elected from among a list of nominees in an election conducted by the Board in which all licensed crematory operators are eligible to vote. The Board shall conduct the election for members of the Crematory Authority and shall prescribe the procedures and establish the time and date for nominations and elections to the Crematory Authority. A nominee who receives a majority of the votes cast shall be declared elected. The Board shall appoint the successors to the two positions for which it makes initial appointments pursuant to this section.

The terms of the elected members of the Crematory Authority shall be three years. The terms of the members appointed by the Board, including the members initially appointed pursuant to this subsection, shall be coterminous with their terms on the Board. Any vacancy occurring in an elective seat shall be filled for the unexpired term by majority vote of the remaining members of the Crematory Authority. Any vacancy occurring in a seat appointed by the Governor shall be filled by the Governor. Any vacancy occurring in a seat appointed by the Board shall be filled by the Board.

(d) The members of the Crematory Authority shall receive per diem and necessary travel and subsistence expenses in accordance with the provisions of G.S. 93B-5 for all time actually spent upon the business of the Crematory Authority. All expenses, salaries and per diem provided for in this Article shall be paid from funds received and shall in no manner be an expense to the State.

(e) The Crematory Authority shall select from its members a chairman, a vice chairman and a secretary who shall serve for one year or until their successors are elected and qualified. No two offices may be held by the same person. The Crematory Authority, with the concurrence of the Board, shall have the authority to engage adequate staff as deemed necessary to perform its duties.

(f) The Crematory Authority shall hold at least one meeting in each year. In addition, the Crematory Authority may meet as often as the proper and efficient discharge of its duties shall require. Four members shall constitute a quorum. (1989 (Reg. Sess., 1990), c. 988, s. 1; 2003-420, s. 2; 2007-531, s. 19.)

§ 90-210.123. Licensing and inspection.

(a) Any person doing business in this State, or any cemetery, funeral establishment, corporation, partnership, joint venture, voluntary organization, or any other entity may erect, maintain, and operate a crematory in this State and may provide the necessary employees, facilities, structure, and equipment for the cremation of human remains, provided that the person or entity has secured a license as a crematory licensee in accordance with this Article.

(b) A crematory may be constructed on or adjacent to any cemetery, on or adjacent to any funeral establishment that is zoned commercial or industrial, or at any other location consistent with local zoning and environmental regulations.

(c) Application for a license as a crematory licensee shall be made on forms furnished and prescribed by the Board. The Board shall inspect the premises, facilities, structure, and equipment to be used as a crematory, confirm that the crematory manager's and crematory technician's educational certificate is valid, and issue a renewable license to the crematory licensee if the applicant meets all the requirements and standards of the Board and the requirements of this Article.

(d) Every application for licensure shall identify the crematory manager and all crematory technicians employed by the crematory licensee providing that nothing in this Article shall prohibit the designation and identification by the crematory licensee of one individual to serve as a crematory manager and crematory technician. Each crematory licensed in North Carolina shall employ on a full-time basis at least one crematory technician. Every application for licensure and renewal thereof shall include all crematory technicians' educational certificates. The crematory licensee shall keep the Board informed at all times of the names and addresses of the crematory manager and all crematory technicians. In the event a licensee is in the process of replacing its only crematory technician at the time of license renewal, the licensee may continue to operate the crematory for a reasonable time period not to exceed 180 days.

(e) All licenses and permits shall expire on the last day of December of each year. A license or permit may be renewed without paying a late fee on or before the first day of February immediately following expiration. After that date, a license or permit may be renewed by paying a late fee as provided in G.S. 90-210.132 in addition to the annual renewal fee. Licenses and permits that remain expired six months or more require a new application for renewal. Licenses and permits are not transferable. A new application for a license or permit shall be made to the Board within 30 days following a change of ownership of more than fifty percent (50%) of the business.

(f) No person, cemetery, funeral establishment, corporation, partnership, joint venture, voluntary organization, or any other entity shall cremate any human remains, except in a crematory licensed for this express purpose and operated by a crematory licensee subject to the restrictions and limitations of this Article or unless otherwise permitted by statute.

(g) Whenever the Board finds that an owner, partner, crematory manager, member, officer, or any crematory technician of a crematory licensee or any applicant to become a crematory licensee, or that any authorized employee, agent, or representative has violated any provision of this Article, or is guilty of any of the following acts, and when the Board also finds that the crematory operator or applicant has thereby become unfit to practice, the Board may suspend, revoke, or refuse to issue or renew the license, in accordance with Chapter 150B of the General Statutes:

(1) Conviction of a felony or a crime involving fraud or moral turpitude.

(1a) Denial, suspension, or revocation of an occupational or business license by another jurisdiction.

(2) Fraud or misrepresentation in obtaining or renewing a license or in the practice of cremation.

(3) False or misleading advertising.

(4)   Solicitation of dead human bodies by the licensee, his agents, assistants, or employees; but this subdivision shall not be construed to prohibit general advertising by the licensee.

(5)   Employment directly or indirectly of any agent, assistant, or other person on a part-time or full-time basis or on commission for the purpose of calling upon individuals or institutions by whose influence dead human bodies may be turned over to a particular licensee.

(6)   The direct or indirect payment or offer of payment of a commission by the licensee or the licensee's agent, assistant, or employees for the purpose of securing business.

(7)   Gross immorality, including being under the influence of alcohol or drugs while performing cremation services.

(8)   Aiding or abetting an unlicensed person to perform services under this Article, including the use of a picture or name in connection with advertisements or other written material published or caused to be published by the licensee.

(9)   Failing to treat a dead human body with respect at all times.

(10)   Violating or cooperating with others to violate any of the provisions of this Article or of the rules of the Board.

(11)   Violation of any State law or municipal or county ordinance or regulation affecting the handling, custody, care, or transportation of dead human bodies.

(12)   Refusing to surrender promptly the custody of a dead human body or cremated remains upon the express order of the person lawfully entitled to the custody thereof, except as provided in G.S. 90-210.131(e).

(13)   Indecent exposure or exhibition of a dead human body while in the custody or control of a licensee.

(14)   Practicing funeral directing, embalming, or funeral service without a license.

In any case in which the Board is authorized to take any of the actions permitted under this subsection, the Board may instead accept an offer in compromise of the charges whereby the accused shall pay to the Board a penalty of not more than five thousand dollars ($5,000).

(h)   Where the Board finds a licensee is guilty of one or more of the acts or omissions listed in subsection (g) of this section but it is determined by the Board that the licensee has not thereby become unfit to practice, the Board may place the licensee on a term of probation in accordance with the procedures set out in Chapter 150B of the General Statutes. In any case in which the Board is entitled to place a licensee on a term of probation, the Board may also impose a penalty of not more than five thousand dollars ($5,000) in conjunction with the probation.

(i)   The Board may hold hearings in accordance with the provisions of this Article and Chapter 150B of the General Statutes. The Board shall conduct any such hearing. The Board shall constitute an "agency" under Article 3A of Chapter 150B of the General Statutes with respect to proceedings initiated pursuant to this Article. The Board is empowered to regulate and inspect crematories and crematory licensees and to enforce as provided by law the provisions of this Article and the rules adopted hereunder. Any crematory that, upon inspection, is found not to meet any of the requirements of this Article shall pay a reinspection fee to the Board for each additional inspection that is made to ascertain whether the deficiency or other violation has been corrected. The Board may obtain preliminary and final injunctions whenever a violation of this Article has occurred or threatens to occur.

In addition to the powers enumerated in Chapter 150B of the General Statutes, the Board shall have the power to administer oaths and issue subpoenas requiring the attendance of persons and the production of papers and records before the Board in any hearing, investigation, or proceeding conducted by it. Members of the Board's staff or the sheriff or other appropriate official of any county of this State shall serve all notices, subpoenas, and other papers given to them by the President of the Board for service in the same manner as process issued by any court of record. Any person who neglects or refuses to obey a subpoena issued by the Board shall be guilty of a Class 1 misdemeanor. (1989 (Reg. Sess., 1990), c. 988, s. 1; 1993, c. 539, s. 639; 1997-399, s. 17; 2003-420, s. 2; 2007-531, ss. 20, 21.)

§ 90-210.124. Authorizing agent.

(a) The following person, in the priority list below, shall have the right to serve as an "authorizing agent":

(1) An individual at least 18 years of age may authorize the type, place, and method of disposition of the individual's own dead body by methods provided under G.S. 130A-420(a). An individual may delegate his or her right to dispose of his or her own body to any person by one of the methods provided under G.S. 130A-420(a1).

When an individual has authorized his or her own cremation and disposition in accordance with this subsection, the individual or institution designated by that individual shall act as the authorizing agent for that individual.

(2) If a decedent has left no written authorization for the cremation and disposition of the decedent's body as permitted under subdivision (1) of this subsection, the following competent persons in the order listed may authorize the type, method, place, cremation, and disposition of the decedent's body:

a. The surviving spouse.

b. A majority of the surviving children who are at least 18 years of age and can be located after reasonable efforts.

c. The surviving parents.

d. A majority of the surviving siblings who are at least 18 years of age and can be located after reasonable efforts.

e. A majority of the persons in the classes of the next degrees of kinship, in descending order, who, under State law, would inherit the decedent's estate if the decedent died intestate who are at least 18 years of age and can be located after reasonable efforts.

f. A person who has exhibited special care and concern for the decedent and is willing and able to make decisions about the cremation and disposition.

g. In the case of indigents or any other individuals whose final disposition is the responsibility of the State or any of its instrumentalities, a public administrator, medical examiner, coroner, State-appointed guardian, or any other public official charged with arranging the final disposition of the decedent may serve as the authorizing agent.

h. In the case of individuals who have donated their bodies to science or whose death occurred in a nursing home or private institution and in which the institution is charged with making arrangements for the final disposition of the decedent, a representative of such institution may serve as the authorizing agent in the absence of any of the above.

i. In the absence of any of the above, any person willing to assume responsibility as authorizing agent, as specified in this act.

This subsection does not grant to any person the right to cancel a preneed funeral contract executed pursuant to Article 13D of Chapter 90 of the General Statutes or to cause or prohibit the substitution of a preneed licensee as authorized under G.S. 90-210.63 or permit modification of preneed contracts under G.S. 90-210.63A. If a person under this subsection is incompetent at the time of the decedent's death, the person shall be treated as if he or she predeceased the decedent. An attending physician may certify the incompetence of a person and the certification shall apply to the rights under this subsection only. Any person under this subsection may waive his or her rights under this subsection by any written statement notarized by a notary public or signed by two witnesses.

(b) A person who does not exercise his or her right to dispose of the decedent's body under subdivision (a)(2) of this section within five days of notification or 10 days from date of death, whichever is earlier, shall be deemed to have waived his or her right to authorize disposition of the decedent's body or to contest disposition in accordance with this section.

(c) An individual at least 18 years of age may, in a writing signed by the individual, authorize the cremation and disposition of one or more of the individual's body parts that has been or will be removed. If the individual does not authorize the cremation and disposition, a person listed in subdivision (a)(2) of this section may authorize the cremation and disposition as if the individual were deceased.

(d) This section does not apply to the disposition of dead human bodies as anatomical gifts under Part 3A of Article 16 of Chapter 130A of the General Statutes or the right to perform autopsies under Part 2 of Article 16 of Chapter 130A of the General Statutes. (2003-420, s. 2; 2007-531, s. 22; 2008-153, s. 5; 2010-191, s. 2.)

§ 90-210.125. Authorization to cremate.

(a) A crematory licensee shall not cremate human remains until it has received a cremation authorization form signed by an authorizing agent. The cremation authorization form shall be prescribed by the Board and shall contain at a minimum the following information:

(1) The identity of the human remains and confirmation that the human remains are in fact the individual so named.

(2) The time and date of death of the decedent.

(3) The name and address of the funeral establishment and/or the funeral director that obtained the cremation authorization.

(4) The name and address of the crematory to be in receipt of the human remains for the purpose of cremation.

(5) The name and address of the authorizing agent, the relationship between the authorizing agent and the decedent, and the date and time of signature of the authorizing agent.

(6) A representation that the authorizing agent does in fact have the right to authorize the cremation of the decedent and that the authorizing agent is not aware of any living person who has a superior priority right to that of the authorizing agent, as set forth in G.S. 90-210.124. Or, in the event that there is another living person who does have a superior priority right to that of the authorizing agent, a representation that the authorizing agent has made all reasonable efforts to contact such person, has been unable to do so, and has no reason to believe that such person would object to the cremation of the decedent.

(7) A representation that the authorizing agent has either disclosed the location of all living persons with an equal right to that of the authorizing agent, as set forth in G.S. 90-210.124, or does not know the location of any other living person with an equal right to that of the authorizing agent.

(8) Authorization for the crematory to cremate the human remains, including authorization to process or pulverize the cremated remains.

(9) A representation that the human remains do not contain a pacemaker or any other material or implant that may be potentially hazardous to the person performing the cremation.

(10) The name of the person authorized to receive the cremated remains from the crematory licensee.

(11) The manner in which final disposition of the cremated remains is to take place, if known. If the cremation authorization form does not specify final disposition in a grave, crypt, niche, or scattering area, then the form shall indicate that the cremated remains will be held by the crematory licensee for 30 days before they are disposed of, unless they are received from the crematory licensee prior to that time, in person, by the authorizing agent or his designee.

(12) The signature of the authorizing agent attesting to the accuracy of all representations contained on the cremation authorization form, except as set forth in subsection (b) of this section.

(13) If a cremation authorization form is being executed on a preneed basis, the cremation authorization form shall contain the disclosure required by G.S. 90-210.126. The authorizing agent may specify in writing religious practices that conflict with Article 13 of this Chapter. The crematory licensee and funeral director shall observe those religious practices except where they interfere with cremation in a licensed crematory as specified under G.S. 90-210.123 or the required documentation and record keeping.

(14) A licensed funeral director of the funeral establishment or crematory licensee that received the cremation authorization form shall also sign the cremation authorization form. Such individual shall not be responsible for any of the representations made by the authorizing agent, unless such individual has actual knowledge to the contrary, except for the information requested by subdivisions (a)(1), (2), (3), (4), and (9) of this section, which shall be considered to be representations of the individual. In addition, the funeral director shall warrant to the crematory that the human remains delivered to the crematory licensee are the human remains identified on the cremation authorization form with any other documentation required by this State, any county, or any municipality.

(b) An authorizing agent who signs a cremation authorization form shall be deemed to warrant the truthfulness of any facts set forth on the cremation authorization form, including that person's authority to order the cremation, except for the information required by subdivisions (a)(4) and (9) of this section, unless the authorizing agent has actual knowledge to the contrary. An authorizing agent signing a cremation authorization form shall be personally and individually liable for all damages occasioned thereby and resulting therefrom.

(c)   A crematory licensee shall have the legal right to cremate human remains upon the receipt of a cremation authorization form signed by an authorizing agent. There shall be no liability for a crematory licensee that cremates human remains pursuant to such authorization, or that releases or disposes of the cremated remains pursuant to such authorization, except for such crematory licensee's gross negligence, provided that the crematory licensee performs such functions in compliance with the provisions of this Article. There shall be no liability for a funeral establishment or licensee thereof that causes a crematory licensee to cremate human remains pursuant to such authorization, except for gross negligence, provided that the funeral establishment and licensee thereof and crematory licensee perform their respective functions in compliance with the provisions of this section.

(d)   After the authorizing agent has executed a cremation authorization form and prior to the commencement of the cremation, the authorizing agent may revoke the authorization and instruct the crematory licensee to cancel the cremation and to release or deliver the human remains to another crematory licensee or funeral establishment. Such instructions shall be provided to the crematory licensee in writing. A crematory licensee shall honor any instructions given to it by an authorizing agent under this section, provided that it receives such instructions prior to commencement of the cremation of the human remains. (2003-420, s. 2.)

§ 90-210.126. Preneed cremation arrangements.

(a)   Any person, on a preneed basis, may authorize the person's own cremation and the final disposition of the person's cremated remains by executing, as the authorizing agent, a cremation authorization form on a preneed basis and having the form signed by two witnesses. The person shall retain a copy of this form, and a copy shall be sent to the funeral establishment and/or the crematory licensee. Any person shall have the right to transfer or cancel this authorization at any time prior to the person's death by destroying the executed cremation authorization form and providing written notice to the party or parties that received the cremation authorization form.

(b)   Any cremation authorization form executed by an individual as the individual's own authorizing agent on a preneed basis shall contain the following disclosure, which shall be completed by the authorizing agent:

/ /   I do not wish to allow any of my survivors the option of canceling my cremation and selecting alternative arrangements, regardless of whether my survivors deem such a change to be appropriate.

/ /   I wish to allow only the survivors whom I have designated below the option of canceling my cremation and selecting alternative arrangements or continuing to honor my wishes for cremation and purchasing services and merchandise if they deem such a change to be appropriate.

(c)   Except as provided in subsection (b) of this section, at the time of the death of a person who has executed, as the authorizing agent, a cremation authorization form on a preneed basis, any person in possession of the executed form, and any person charged with making arrangements for the disposition of the decedent's human remains who has knowledge of the existence of the executed form, shall use the person's best efforts to ensure that the decedent's human remains are cremated and that the final disposition of the cremated remains is in accordance with the instructions contained on the cremation authorization form.

(d)   If a crematory licensee is in possession of a completed cremation authorization form, executed on a preneed basis, and the crematory licensee is in possession of the designated human remains, then the crematory licensee shall be required to cremate the human remains and dispose of the human remains according to the instructions contained on the cremation authorization form. A crematory licensee that complies with the preneed cremation authorization form under these circumstances may do so without any liability. A funeral establishment or licensee thereof that causes a crematory licensee to act in accordance with the preneed cremation authorization form under these circumstances may do so without any liability.

(e)   Any preneed contract sold by, or preneed arrangements made with, a funeral establishment that includes a cremation shall specify the final disposition of the cremated remains, pursuant to G.S. 90-210.130. In the event that no different or inconsistent instructions are provided to the crematory licensee by the authorizing agent at the time of death, the crematory licensee shall be authorized to release or dispose of the cremated remains as indicated in the preneed agreement. Upon compliance with the terms of the preneed agreement, the crematory licensee, and any funeral establishment or licensee thereof who caused the crematory licensee to act in compliance with the terms of the preneed agreement, shall be discharged from any legal obligation concerning such cremated remains.

(f)   The provisions of this section shall not apply to any cremation authorization form or preneed contract executed prior to the effective date of this act. Any funeral establishment, however, with the written approval of the authorizing agent or person who executed the preneed contract, may designate that such cremation authorization form or preneed contract shall be subject to this act. (2003-420, s. 2.)

§ 90-210.127. Record keeping.

(a)   The crematory licensee shall furnish to the person who delivers such human remains to the crematory licensee a receipt, signed by both the crematory licensee and the person who delivers the human remains, showing the date and time of the delivery; the type of casket or cremation container that was delivered; the name of the person from whom the human remains were received and the name of the funeral establishment or other entity with whom such person is affiliated; the name of the person who received the human remains on behalf of the crematory licensee; and the name of the decedent. The crematory licensee shall retain a copy of this receipt in its permanent records for three years.

(b)   Upon its release of cremated remains, the crematory licensee shall furnish to the person who receives such cremated remains from the crematory licensee a receipt, signed by both the crematory licensee and the person who receives the cremated remains, showing the date and time of the release; the name of the person to whom the cremated remains were released and the name of the funeral establishment, cemetery, or other entity with whom such person is affiliated; the name of the person who released the cremated remains on behalf of the crematory licensee; and the name of the decedent. The crematory shall retain a copy of this receipt in its permanent records for three years.

(c) A crematory licensee shall maintain at its place of business a record of all forms required by the Board of each cremation that took place at its facility for three years.

(d) The crematory licensee shall maintain a record for three years of all cremated remains disposed of by the crematory licensee in accordance with G.S. 90-210.126(d).

(e) Upon completion of the cremation, the crematory licensee shall issue a certificate of cremation.

(f) All records that are required to be maintained under this Article shall be subject to inspection by the Board or its agents upon request. (1989 (Reg. Sess., 1990), c. 988, s. 1; 1997-399, s. 18; 2003-420, s. 2.)

§ 90-210.128. Cremation containers.

(a) No crematory licensee shall make or enforce any rules requiring that any human remains be placed in a casket before cremation or that human remains be cremated in a casket, nor shall any crematory licensee refuse to accept human remains for cremation for the reason that they are not in a casket.

(b) No crematory licensee shall make or enforce any rules requiring that any cremated remains be placed in an urn or receptacle designed to permanently encase the cremated remains after the cremation process has been performed. (2003-420, s. 2.)

§ 90-210.129. Cremation procedures.

(a) In deaths certified by the attending physician, the body shall not be cremated before the crematory licensee receives a death certificate signed by the attending physician, which shall contain at a minimum the following information:

(1) Decedent's name;

(2) Date of death;

(3) Date of birth;

(4) Sex;

(5) Place of death;

(6) Facility name (if not institution, give street and number);

(7) County of death;

(8) City of death; and

(9) Time of death (if known).

(b) When required by G.S. 130A-388 and the rules adopted pursuant to that section or by successor statute and the rules pursuant to it, a cremation authorization form signed by a medical examiner shall be received by the crematory prior to cremation.

(c) In deaths coming under full investigation by the Office of the Chief Medical Examiner, a burial-transit permit/cremation authorization form must be received by the crematory before cremation.

(d) No body shall knowingly be cremated with a pacemaker or defibrillator or other potentially hazardous implant or condition in place. The authorizing agent for the cremation of the human remains shall be responsible for taking all necessary steps to ensure that any pacemaker or defibrillator or other potentially hazardous implant or condition is removed or corrected prior to cremation. If an authorizing agent informs the funeral director and the crematory licensee on the cremation authorization form of the presence of a pacemaker or defibrillator or other potentially hazardous implant or condition in the human remains, then the funeral director shall be responsible for ensuring that all necessary steps have been taken to remove the pacemaker or defibrillator or other potentially hazardous implant or to correct the hazardous condition before delivering the human remains to the crematory.

(e) Human remains shall not be cremated within 24 hours after the time of death, unless such death was a result of an infectious, contagious, or communicable and dangerous disease as listed by the Commission for Public Health, pursuant to G.S. 130A-134, and unless such time requirement is waived in writing by the medical examiner, county health director, or attending physician where the death occurred.

(f)   No unauthorized person shall be permitted in view of the cremation chamber or in the holding and processing facility while any human remains are being removed from the cremation container, processed, or pulverized. Relatives of the deceased and their invitees, the authorizing agent and the agent's invitees, medical examiners, Inspectors of the North Carolina Board of Funeral Service, and law enforcement officers in the execution of their duties shall be authorized to have access to the crematory area, subject to the rules adopted by the crematory licensee governing the safety of such individuals.

(g)   Human remains shall be cremated only while enclosed in a cremation container. Upon completion of the cremation, and insofar as is possible, all of the recoverable residue of the cremation process shall be removed from the cremation chamber. Insofar as is possible, all residue of the cremation process shall then be separated from any foreign residue or anything else other than bone fragments and then be processed by pulverization so as to reduce the cremated remains to unidentifiable particles. Any foreign residue and anything other than the particles of the cremated remains shall be removed from the cremated remains as far as possible and shall be disposed of by the crematory licensee. This section does not apply where law otherwise provides for commingling of human remains. The fact that there is incidental and unavoidable residue in the cremation chamber used in a prior cremation is not a violation of this subsection.

(h)   The simultaneous cremation of the human remains of more than one person within the same cremation chamber is forbidden.

(i)   Every crematory shall have a holding and processing facility, within the crematory, designated for the retention of human remains prior to cremation. The holding and processing facility must comply with any applicable public health laws and rules and must meet all of the standards established pursuant to rules adopted by the Board.

(j)   Crematory licensees shall comply with standards established by the Board for the processing and pulverization of human remains by cremation.

(k)   Nothing in this Article shall require a crematory licensee to perform a cremation that is impossible or impractical to perform.

(l) The cremated remains with proper identification shall be placed in an initial container or the urn selected or provided by the authorizing agent. The initial container or urn contents shall not be contaminated with any other object, unless specific authorization has been received from the authorizing agent or as provided in subsection (g) of this section.

(m) If the cremated remains are greater than the dimensions of an initial container or urn, the excess cremated remains shall be returned to the authorizing agent or its representative in a separate container or urn.

(n) If the cremated remains are to be shipped, the initial container or urn shall be packed securely in a suitable shipping container that complies with the requirements of the shipper. Cremated remains shall be shipped only by a method which has an internal tracing system available and which provides a receipt signed by the person accepting delivery, unless otherwise authorized in writing by the authorizing agent. Cremated remains shall be shipped to the proper address as stated on the cremation authorization form signed by the authorizing agent.

(o) Unless the provisions of G.S. 130A-114 apply, before cremation the crematory licensee shall receive a written statement, on a form prescribed by the Board and signed by the attending physician, acknowledging the circumstances, date, and time of the delivery of the fetal remains from the mother. If after reasonable efforts no physician can be identified with knowledge and information sufficient to complete the written statement required by this subsection, the crematory licensee shall obtain documentation of the circumstances, date, and time of delivery of the fetal remains prepared by a hospital, medical facility, law enforcement agency, or other entity. Notwithstanding any other provision of law, health care providers may release to a licensee, in accordance with the federal Standards for Privacy of Individually Identifiable Health Information under the Health Insurance Portability and Accountability Act of 1996 (HIPAA), medical records that document the circumstances, date, and time of delivery of fetal remains. If the crematory licensee cannot identify documents sufficient to meet the requirements of this subsection, the licensee shall report to the local medical examiner pursuant to G.S. 130A-383(a).

(p) If the provisions of Article 4 of Chapter 130A of the General Statutes apply, the crematory licensee shall receive a fetal report of death as prescribed in G.S. 130A-114.

(q) Before the cremation of amputated body parts, the crematory licensee shall receive a written statement, on a form prescribed by the Board and signed by the attending physician, acknowledging the circumstances of the amputation. If after reasonable efforts no physician can be identified with knowledge and information sufficient to complete the written statement required by this subsection, the crematory licensee shall notify the local medical examiner pursuant to G.S. 130A-383(b). This section does not apply to the disposition of body parts cremated pursuant to Part 3A of Article 16 of Chapter 130A of the General Statutes. (1989 (Reg. Sess., 1990), c. 988, s. 1; 1997-399, s. 19; 2003-420, s. 2; 2007-182, s. 1.2; 2007-531, s. 23; 2008-153, s. 6.)

§ 90-210.130. Final disposition of cremated remains.

(a) The authorizing agent shall provide the person with whom cremation arrangements are made with a signed statement specifying the ultimate disposition of the cremated remains, if known. The crematory licensee may store or retain cremated remains as directed by the authorizing agent. Records of retention and disposition of cremated remains shall be kept by the crematory licensee pursuant to G.S. 90-210.127.

(b) The authorizing agent is responsible for the disposition of the cremated remains. If, after a period of 30 days from the date of cremation, the authorizing agent or the agent's representative has not specified the final disposition or claimed the cremated remains, the crematory licensee or the person in possession of the cremated remains may release the cremated remains to another family member upon written notification to the authorizing agent delivered by certified mail or dispose of the cremated remains only in a manner permitted in this section. The authorizing agent shall be responsible for reimbursing the crematory licensee for all reasonable expenses incurred in disposing of the cremated remains pursuant to this section. A record of such disposition shall be made and kept by the person making the disposition. Upon disposing of cremated remains in accordance with this section, the crematory licensee or person in possession of the cremated remains shall be discharged from any legal obligation or liability concerning such cremated remains.

(c) In addition to the disposal of cremated remains in a crypt, niche, grave, or scattering garden located in a dedicated cemetery, or by scattering over uninhabited public land, the sea, or other public waterways pursuant to subsection (f) of this section, cremated remains may be disposed of in any manner on the private property of a consenting owner, upon direction of the authorizing agent. If cremated remains are to be disposed of by the crematory licensee on private property, other than dedicated cemetery property, the authorizing agent shall provide the crematory licensee with the written consent of the property owner.

(d)   Except with the express written permission of the authorizing agent, no person may:

(1)   Dispose of or scatter cremated remains in such a manner or in such a location that the cremated remains are commingled with those of another person. This subdivision shall not apply to the scattering of cremated remains at sea or by air from individual closed containers or to the scattering of cremated remains in an area located in a dedicated cemetery and used exclusively for such purposes.

(2)   Place cremated remains of more than one person in the same closed container. This subdivision shall not apply to placing the cremated remains of members of the same family in a common closed container designed for the cremated remains of more than one person with the written consent of the family.

(e)   Cremated remains shall be released by the crematory licensee to the individual specified by the authorizing agent on the cremation authorization form. The representative of the crematory licensee and the individual receiving the cremated remains shall sign a receipt indicating the name of the deceased, and the date, time, and place of the receipt, and contain a representation that the handling of the final disposition will be in a proper manner. After this delivery, the cremated remains may be transported in any manner in this State, without a permit, and disposed of in accordance with the provisions of this Article.

(f)   Cremated remains may be scattered over uninhabited public land, over a public waterway or sea, subject to health and environmental standards, or on the private property of a consenting owner pursuant to subsection (c) of this section. A person may utilize a boat or airplane to perform such scattering. Cremated remains shall be removed from their closed container before they are scattered. (1989 (Reg. Sess., 1990), c. 988, s. 1; 1997-399, s. 20; 2003-420, s. 2; 2007-531, s. 24.)

§ 90-210.131. Limitation of liability.

(a) Any person signing a cremation authorization form as authorizing agent shall be deemed to warrant the truthfulness of any facts set forth in the cremation authorization form, including the identity of the deceased whose remains are sought to be cremated and that person's authority to order such cremation.

(b) A crematory licensee shall have authority to cremate human remains only upon the receipt of a cremation authorization form signed by an authorizing agent. There shall be no liability of a crematory licensee that cremates human remains pursuant to such authorization or that releases or disposes of the cremated remains pursuant to such authorization. A crematory licensee and funeral establishment or licensee thereof who causes the crematory licensee to act shall have no liability for the final disposition or manner in which the cremated remains are handled after the cremated remains are released in accordance with the directions of the authorizing agent.

(c) A crematory licensee shall not be responsible or liable for any valuables delivered to the crematory licensee with human remains.

(d) A crematory licensee shall not be liable for refusing to accept a body or to perform a cremation until it receives a court order or other suitable confirmation that a dispute has been settled if:

(1) It is aware of any dispute concerning the cremation of human remains;

(2) It has a reasonable basis for questioning any of the representations made by the authorizing agent; or

(3) For any other lawful reason.

(e) If a crematory licensee is aware of any dispute concerning the release or disposition of the cremated remains, the crematory licensee may refuse to release the cremated remains until the dispute has been resolved or the crematory licensee has been provided with a court order authorizing the release or disposition of the cremated remains. A crematory licensee shall not be liable for refusing to release or dispose of cremated remains in accordance with this subsection. A crematory licensee may charge a reasonable storage fee if the dispute is not resolved within 30 days after it is received by the crematory licensee. (1989 (Reg. Sess., 1990), c. 988, s. 1; 1997-399, s. 21; 2003-420, s. 2.)

§ 90-210.132. Fees.

(a) The Board may set and collect fees not to exceed the following amounts from crematory licensees, crematory manager permit holders, and applicants:

(1)..... Licensee application fee. $400.00

(2)..... Annual renewal fee. 150.00

(3)..... Late renewal fee. 75.00

(4)..... Reinspection fee. 100.00

(5)..... Per cremation fee. 10.00

(6)..... Late fee, per cremation. 10.00

(7)..... Late fee, cremation report. .... 75.00 per month

(8)..... Crematory manager permit application fee. 150.00

(9)..... Annual crematory manager permit renewal fee. .... 40.00.

(b) The funds collected pursuant to this Article shall become part of the general fund of the Board. (1989 (Reg. Sess., 1990), c. 988, s. 1; 1997-399, s. 22; 2003-420, s. 2.)

§ 90-210.133. Crematory licensee rights.

(a) A crematory licensee may adopt reasonable rules consistent with this Article for the management and operation of a crematory. Nothing in this subsection may be construed to prevent a crematory licensee from adopting rules which are more stringent than the provisions of this Article.

(b) Nothing in this Article may be construed to relieve the crematory licensee from obtaining any other licenses or permits required by law.

(c) Nothing in this Article shall prohibit or require the performance of cremations by crematory licensees or crematory managers for or directly with the public or exclusively for or through licensed funeral directors. (1989 (Reg. Sess., 1990), c. 988, s. 1; 2003-420, s. 2.)

§ 90-210.134. Rulemaking, applicability, violations, and prohibitions of Article.

(a) The Board is authorized to adopt and promulgate such rules for the carrying out and enforcement of the provisions of this Article as may be necessary and as are consistent with the laws of this State and of the United States. The Board may develop a Standard Cremation Authorization Form and procedures for its execution that shall be used by the crematory licensee subject to this Article, unless a crematory has its own form approved by the Board. A crematory licensee that uses its own approved cremation authorization form must have the cremation authorization form reapproved if changed or after amendments are made to this Article or the rules adopted by the Board related to cremation authorization forms. The Board may perform such other acts and exercise such other powers and duties as may be provided in this Article, in Article 13A of this Chapter, and otherwise by law and as may be necessary to carry out the powers herein conferred.

(b) The provisions of this Article shall not apply to the cremation of medical waste performed by the North Carolina Anatomical Commission, licensed hospitals and medical schools, and the office of the Chief Medical Examiner when the disposition of such medical waste is the legal responsibility of the institutions.

(c) A violation of any of the provisions of this Article is a Class 2 misdemeanor.

(d) No person, firm, or corporation may request or authorize cremation or cremate human remains when the person, firm, or corporation has information indicating a crime or violence of any sort in connection with the cause of death unless such information has been conveyed to the State or county medical examiner and permission from the State or county medical examiner to cremate the human remains has thereafter been obtained. (1989 (Reg. Sess., 1990), c. 988, s. 1; 1993, c. 539, s. 640; 1994 Ex. Sess., c. 24, s. 14(c); 2003-420, s. 2.)

§ 90-210.135. Cremation societies.

No person, firm, or corporation licensed as a crematory under the provisions of this Article may operate a cremation society without first registering the name of the cremation society with the Board. (2007-531, s. 25.)

Article 14.

Cadavers for Medical Schools.

§ 90-211: Repealed by Session Laws 1973, c. 476, s. 128.

§§ 90-212 through 90-216. Repealed by Session Laws 1975, c. 694, s. 1.

Article 14A.

Bequest of Body or Part Thereof.

§§ 90-216.1 through 90-216.5. Repealed by Session Laws 1969, c. 84, s. 2.

Article 14B.

Disposition of Unclaimed Bodies.

§§ 90-216.6 through 90-216.11. Repealed by Session Laws 1983, c. 891, s. 3, effective January 1, 1984.

Article 14C.

Final Disposition or Transportation of Deceased Migrant Farm Workers and Their Dependents.

§ 90-216.12. Repealed by Session Laws 1983, c. 891, s. 4, effective January 1, 1984.

Article 15.

Autopsies.

§§ 90-217 through 90-220. Repealed by Session Laws 1983, c. 891, s. 5, effective January 1, 1984.

Article 15A.

Uniform Anatomical Gift Act.

§§ 90-220.1 through 90-220.11. Repealed by Session Laws 1983, c. 891, s. 6, effective January 1, 1984.

Article 15B.

Blood Banks.

§ 90-220.12. Supervision of licensed physician required; penalty for violation.

It shall be unlawful for any person, firm or corporation to engage in the selection of blood donors or in the collection, storage, processing, or transfusion of human blood, except at the direction or under the supervision of a physician licensed to practice medicine in North Carolina. Any person, firm or corporation convicted of the violation of this section shall be guilty of a Class 1 misdemeanor. (1971, c. 938; 1993, c. 539, s. 641; 1994, Ex. Sess., c. 24, s. 14(c).)

§ 90-220.13. Selection of donors; due care required.

In the selection of donors due care shall be exercised to minimize the risks of transmission of agents that may cause hepatitis or other diseases. (1971, c. 938.)

§ 90-220.14. Inapplicability.

Nothing in this Article shall be construed to affect the provisions of G.S. 20-16.2 and G.S. 20-139.1. (1971, c. 938.)

Article 16.

Dental Hygiene Act.

§ 90-221. Definitions.

(a) "Dental hygiene" as used in this Article shall mean the performance of the following functions: Complete oral prophylaxis, application of preventive agents to oral structures, exposure and processing of radiographs, administration of medicaments prescribed by a licensed dentist, preparation of diagnostic aids, and written records of oral conditions for interpretation by the dentist, together with such other and further functions as may be permitted by rules and regulations of the Board not inconsistent herewith.

(b) "Dental hygienist" as used in this Article, shall mean any person who is a graduate of a Board-accredited school of dental hygiene, who has been licensed by the Board, and who practices dental hygiene as prescribed by the Board.

(c) "License" shall mean a certificate issued to any applicant upon completion of requirements for admission to practice dental hygiene.

(d)   "Renewal certificate" shall mean the annual certificate of renewal of license to continue practice of dental hygiene in the State of North Carolina.

(e)   "Board" shall mean "The North Carolina State Board of Dental Examiners" created by Chapter 139, Public Laws of 1879, and Chapter 178, Public Laws of 1915 as continued in existence by G.S. 90-22.

(f)   "Supervision" as used in this Article shall mean that acts are deemed to be under the supervision of a licensed dentist when performed in a locale where a licensed dentist is physically present during the performance of such acts, except those acts performed under direction and in compliance with G.S. 90-233(a) or G.S. 90-233(a1), and such acts are being performed pursuant to the dentist's order, control and approval. (1945, c. 639, s. 1; 1971, c. 756, s. 1; 1981, c. 824, s. 1; 2007-124, s. 1.)

§ 90-222. Administration of Article.

The Board is hereby vested with the authority and is charged with the duty of administering the provisions of this Article. (1945, c. 639, s. 2.)

§ 90-223. Powers and duties of Board.

(a)   The Board is authorized and empowered to:

(1)   Conduct examinations for licensure,

(2)   Issue licenses and provisional licenses,

(3)   Issue annual renewal certificates,

(4)   Renew expired licenses, and

(5)   Contract with a regional or national testing agency to conduct clinical examinations. Prior to entering a contract with a regional or national testing agency, the Board shall evaluate the agency based on the following criteria:

a. The number of states that recognize the results of the testing agency's examination.

b. The cost to the applicant of the examination.

c. How long the testing agency has been conducting examinations.

d. Whether the examination includes procedures performed on human subjects as part of the assessment of clinical competencies.

(b) The Board shall have the authority to make or amend rules and regulations not inconsistent with this Article governing the practice of dental hygiene and the granting, revocation and suspension of licenses and provisional licenses of dental hygienists.

(1) Any rule adopted under this Article shall be distributed to all licensed dentists and all licensed dental hygienists within 30 days of final approval by the Board.

(2) The Board shall issue every two years a compilation or supplement of the Dental Hygiene Act and the Board rules and regulations, and, upon written request therefor, a directory of dental hygienists to each licensed dentist and dental hygienist.

(c) The Board shall keep on file in its office at all times a complete record of the names, addresses, license numbers and renewal certificate numbers of all persons entitled to practice dental hygiene in this State.

(d) The Board shall, in addition to any other requirements for Board approval of a school or program of dental hygiene for purposes of this Article, require that any school or program in North Carolina develop and implement a procedure for advanced placement of potentially qualified persons. This procedure shall be designed to encourage and allow credit for any person who has attained special capabilities in dental work through military service, on-the-job training or working experience, or other means not otherwise qualifying the person to be immediately eligible for licensure. The procedure shall include these elements: public announcement of the procedure, a method for persons who have special capabilities through training or experience to make application to the school or program for advanced placement, personal counseling on obtaining advanced placement, administration of specially prepared written and clinical examinations for all parts of the curriculum otherwise required for graduation, exemption from course requirements when results of the examinations so indicate, and appropriate modification of curriculum requirements, when necessary, to facilitate individual advancement in education programs. The procedure for advanced placement shall not be approved by the Board unless it is fairly designed to facilitate the substitution of military or civilian training and experience for regular curricula, taking into account that the special nature of military and certain civilian training and experience may be equivalent without necessarily being identical to the courses of the school or program.

(e) The Board shall have the authority to provide for programs for impaired dental hygienists as authorized in G.S. 90-48.3. (1945, c. 639, s. 3; 1971, c. 756, s. 2; 1973, c. 871, s. 2; 1979, 2nd Sess., c. 1195, s. 14; 1987, c. 827, s. 1; 1999-382, s. 2; 2000-189, s. 7; 2006-235, s. 1.)

§ 90-224. Examination.

(a) The applicant for licensure must be of good moral character, have graduated from an accredited high school or hold a high school equivalency certificate duly issued by a governmental agency or unit authorized to issue the same, and be a graduate of a program of dental hygiene in a school or college approved by the Board.

(b) The Board shall have the authority to establish in its rules and regulations:

(1) The form of application;

(2) The time and place of examination;

(3) The type of examination;

(4) The qualifications for passing the examination.

(b1) The Board also may grant a license to an applicant who is found to have passed an examination given by a Board-approved regional or national dental hygiene testing agency, provided that the Board deems the regional or national examination to be substantially equivalent to or an improvement upon the examination given by the Board, and the applicant meets the other qualifications set forth in this Article.

(c) The Department of Justice may provide a criminal record check to the Board for a person who has applied for a new or renewal license through the Board. The Board shall provide to the Department of Justice, along with the request, the fingerprints of the applicant, any additional information required by the Department of Justice, and a form signed by the applicant consenting to the check of the criminal record and to the use of the fingerprints and other identifying information required by the State or national repositories. The applicant's fingerprints shall be forwarded to the State Bureau of Investigation for a search of the State's criminal history record file, and the State Bureau of Investigation shall forward a set of the fingerprints to the Federal Bureau of Investigation for a national criminal history check. The Board shall keep all information pursuant to this subsection privileged, in accordance with applicable State law and federal guidelines, and the information shall be confidential and shall not be a public record under Chapter 132 of the General Statutes.

The Department of Justice may charge each applicant a fee for conducting the checks of criminal history records authorized by this subsection. (1945, c. 639, s. 4; 1971, c. 756, s. 3; 2002-147, s. 10; 2006-235, s. 2.)

§ 90-224.1. Licensure by credentials.

(a) The Board may issue a license by credentials to an applicant who has been licensed to practice dental hygiene in any state or territory of the United States if the applicant produces satisfactory evidence to the Board that the applicant has the required education, training, and qualifications; is in good standing with the licensing jurisdiction; has passed the National Board Dental Hygiene Examination administered by the Joint Commission on National Dental Examinations; has passed satisfactory examinations of proficiency in the knowledge and practice of dental hygiene as determined by the Board; and meets all other requirements of this section and rules adopted by the Board. The Board may, in its discretion, refuse to issue a license by credentials to an applicant who the Board determines is unfit to practice dental hygiene.

(b) The applicant for licensure shall be of good moral character, have graduated from an accredited high school or hold a high school equivalency certificate duly issued by a governmental agency or authorized unit, and have graduated from a dental hygiene program or school accredited by the

Commission on Dental Accreditation of the American Dental Association and approved by the Board.

(c)   The applicant must meet all of the following conditions:

(1)   Has been actively practicing dental hygiene, as defined in G.S. 90-221, under the supervision of a licensed dentist for a minimum of two years immediately preceding the date of application.

(2)   Has no history of disciplinary action or pending disciplinary action in the Armed Forces of the United States or in any state or territory in which the applicant is or has ever been licensed.

(3)   Has no felony convictions and has no other criminal convictions that would affect the applicant's ability to render competent dental hygiene care.

(4)   Has not failed a licensure examination administered by the North Carolina State Board of Dental Examiners.

(d)   The applicant for licensure by credentials shall submit an application, the form of which shall be determined by the Board, pay the fee required by G.S. 90-232, successfully complete examinations in Jurisprudence and Sterilization and Infection Control, and meet other criteria or requirements established by the Board, which may include an examination or interview before the Board or its authorized agents.

(e)   This section shall not be construed to include licensure by reciprocity, which is prohibited. (2002-37, s. 3; 2011-183, s. 65.)

§ 90-225. License issue and display.

(a)   The Board shall issue licenses to examinees who pass the Board's examination.

(b)   The Board shall determine:

(1)   The method and time of notifying successful candidates,

(2)   The time and form for issuing licenses, and

(3) The place license must be displayed. (1945, c. 639, s. 5; 1971, c. 756, s. 4.)

§ 90-225.1. Continuing education courses required.

All dental hygienists licensed under G.S. 90-225 shall be required to attend Board-approved courses of study in subjects relating to dental hygiene. The Board shall have authority to consider and approve courses, or providers of courses, to the end that those attending will gain (i) information on existing and new methods and procedures used by dental hygienists, (ii) information leading to increased safety and competence in their dealings with patients and supervising dentists, and (iii) information on other matters, as they develop, that are of continuing importance to the practice of dental hygiene as a part of the practice of dentistry. The Board shall determine the number of hours of study within a particular period and the nature of course work required. Failure to comply with continuing education requirements adopted under the authority of this section shall be grounds for the Board to decline to issue a renewal certificate under G.S. 90-227. (1993, c. 307, s. 3.)

§ 90-226. Provisional license.

(a) The North Carolina State Board of Dental Examiners shall, subject to its rules and regulations, issue a provisional license to practice dental hygiene to any person who is licensed to practice dental hygiene anywhere in the United States, or in any country, territory or other recognized jurisdiction, if the Board shall determine that said licensing jurisdiction imposed upon said person requirements for licensure no less exacting than those imposed by this State. A provisional licensee may engage in the practice of dental hygiene only in strict accordance with the terms, conditions and limitations of her license and with the rules and regulations of the Board pertaining to provisional license.

(b) A provisional license shall be valid until the date of the announcement of the results of the next succeeding Board examination of candidates for licensure to practice dental hygiene in this State, unless the same shall be earlier revoked or suspended by the Board.

(c) No person who has failed an examination conducted by the North Carolina State Board of Dental Examiners shall be eligible to receive a provisional license.

(d) Any person desiring to secure a provisional license shall make application therefor in the manner and form prescribed by the rules and regulations of the Board and shall pay the fee prescribed in G.S. 90-232.

(e) A provisional licensee shall be subject to those various disciplinary measures and penalties set forth in G.S. 90-229 upon a determination of the Board that said provisional licensee has violated any of the terms or provisions of this Article. (1971, c. 756, s. 5; 1975, c. 19, s. 5.)

§ 90-227. Renewal certificates.

(a) The Board shall issue annual renewal certificates to licensed dental hygienists.

(b) The Board shall have the authority to establish in its rules and regulations:

(1) The form of application for renewal certificates;

(2) The time the application must be submitted;

(3) The type of certificate to be issued;

(4) How the certificate must be displayed;

(5) The penalty for late application;

(6) The automatic loss of license if applications are not submitted. (1945, c. 639, s. 6; 1971, c. 756, s. 6.)

§ 90-228. Renewal of license.

The Board shall have the authority to renew the license of a dental hygienist who fails to obtain a renewal certificate for any year provided she

(1) Makes application for a renewal of license and

(2) Meets the qualifications established by the Board. (1945, c. 639, s. 7; 1971, c. 756, s. 7.)

§ 90-229. Disciplinary measures.

(a) The North Carolina State Board of Dental Examiners shall have the power and authority to (i) Refuse to issue a license to practice dental hygiene; (ii) Refuse to issue a certificate of renewal to practice dental hygiene; (iii) Revoke or suspend a license to practice dental hygiene; [and] (iv) Invoke such other disciplinary measures, censure or probative terms against a licensee as it deems proper; in any instance or instances in which the Board is satisfied that such applicant or licensee:

(1) Has engaged in any act or acts of fraud, deceit or misrepresentation in obtaining or attempting to obtain a license or the renewal thereof;

(2) Has been convicted of any of the criminal provisions of this Article or has entered a plea of guilty or nolo contendere to any charge or charges arising therefrom;

(3) Has been convicted of or entered a plea of guilty or nolo contendere to any felony charge or to any misdemeanor charge involving moral turpitude;

(4) Is a chronic or persistent user of intoxicants, drugs or narcotics to the extent that the same impairs her ability to practice dental hygiene;

(5) Is incompetent in the practice of dental hygiene;

(6) Has engaged in any act or practice violative of any of the provisions of this Article or violative of any of the rules and regulations promulgated and adopted by the Board, or has aided, abetted or assisted any other person or entity in the violation of the same;

(7) Has practiced any fraud, deceit or misrepresentation upon the public or upon any individual in an effort to acquire or retain any patient or patients;

(8) Has made fraudulent or misleading statements pertaining to her skill, knowledge, or method of treatment or practice;

(9) Has committed any fraudulent or misleading acts in the practice of dental hygiene;

(10) Has, in the practice of dental hygiene, committed an act or acts constituting malpractice;

(11) Has employed a person not licensed in this State to do or perform any act or service, or has aided, abetted or assisted any such unlicensed person to do or perform any act or service which cannot lawfully be done or performed by such person;

(12) Has engaged in any unprofessional conduct as the same may be from time to time, defined by the rules and regulations of the Board;

(13) Is mentally, emotionally, or physically unfit to practice dental hygiene or is afflicted with such a physical or mental disability as to be deemed dangerous to the health and welfare of patients. An adjudication of mental incompetency in a court of competent jurisdiction or a determination thereof by other lawful means shall be conclusive proof of unfitness to practice dental hygiene unless or until such person shall have been subsequently lawfully declared to be mentally competent.

(b) As used in this section the term "licensee" includes licensees and provisional licensees and the term "license" includes licenses and provisional licenses. (1945, c. 639, s. 8; 1971, c. 756, s. 8; 1997-456, s. 27.)

§ 90-230. Certificate upon transfer to another state.

Any dental hygienist duly licensed by the North Carolina State Board of Dental Examiners, desiring to move from North Carolina to another state, territory or foreign country, if a holder of a certificate of renewal of license from said Board, upon application to said Board and the payment to it of the fee in this Article provided, shall be issued a certificate showing her full name and address, the date of license originally issued to her, the date and number of her renewal of license, and whether any charges have been filed with the Board against her. The Board may provide forms for such certificate, requiring such additional information as it may determine proper. (1971, c. 756, s. 10.)

§ 90-231. Opportunity for licensee or applicant to have hearing.

(a) With the exception of applicants for reinstatement after revocation, every applicant for a license or provisional license to practice dental hygiene or licensee or provisional licensee to practice dental hygiene shall after notice have an opportunity to be heard before the North Carolina State Board of Dental Examiners shall take any action the effect of which would be:

(1) To deny permission to take an examination for licensing for which application has been duly made; or

(2) To deny a license after examination for any cause other than failure to pass an examination; or

(3) To withhold the renewal of a license for any cause other than failure to pay a statutory renewal fee; or

(4) To suspend a license; or

(5) To revoke a license; or

(6) To revoke or suspend a provisional license; or

(7) To invoke any other disciplinary measures, censure or probative terms against a licensee or provisional licensee,

such proceedings to be conducted in accordance with the provisions of Chapter 150B of the General Statutes of North Carolina.

(b) In lieu of or as a part of such hearing and subsequent proceedings the Board is authorized and empowered to enter any consent order relative to the discipline, censure, or probation of a licensee, provisional licensee or an applicant for a license or provisional license, or relative to the revocation or suspension of a license or provisional license.

(c) Following the service of the notice of hearing as required by Chapter 150B of the General Statutes, the Board and the person upon whom such notice is served shall have the right to conduct adverse examinations, take depositions, and engage in such further discovery proceedings as are permitted by the laws of this State in civil matters. The Board is hereby authorized and empowered to issue such orders, commissions, notices, subpoenas, or other process as might be necessary or proper to effect the purposes of this subsection; provided, however, that no member of the Board shall be subject to examination hereunder. (1945, c. 639, s. 10; 1967, c. 489, s. 1; 1971, c. 756, s. 11; 1973, c. 1331, s. 3; 1987, c. 827, s. 1.)

§ 90-232. Fees.

(a) In order to provide the means of carrying out and enforcing the provisions of this Article and the duties devolving upon the North Carolina State Board of Dental Examiners, it is authorized to charge and collect fees established by its rules not exceeding the following:

(1) Each applicant for examination.. $350.00

(2) Each renewal certificate, which fee shall be annually fixed by the Board and not later than November 30 of each year it shall give written notice of the amount of the renewal fee to each dental hygienist licensed to practice in this State by mailing such notice to the last address of record with the Board of each such dental hygienist.. 250.00

(3) Each restoration of license.. 150.00

(4) Each provisional license... 150.00

(5) Each certificate of license to a resident dental hygienist desiring to change to another state or territory.. 50.00

(6) Annual fee to be paid upon license renewal to assist in funding programs for impaired dental hygienists... 80.00

(7) Each license by credentials .... 1,500.

(b) In all instances where the Board uses the services of a regional or national testing agency for preparation, administration, or grading of examinations, the Board may require applicants to pay the actual cost of the testing agency in lieu of the fee authorized in subdivision (a)(1) of this section.

(c) In no event may the annual fee imposed on dental hygienists to fund the impaired dental hygienists program exceed the annual fee imposed on dentists to fund the impaired dentist program. All fees shall be payable in advance to the Board and shall be disposed of by the Board in the discharge of its duties under this Article. (1945, c. 639, s. 11; 1965, c. 163, s. 7; 1967, c. 489, s. 2; 1971, c. 756, s. 12; 1987, c. 555, s. 2; 1999-382, s. 3; 2002-37, s. 6; 2003-348, s. 2; 2006-235, s. 3.)

§ 90-233. Practice of dental hygiene.

(a) A dental hygienist may practice only under the supervision of one or more licensed dentists. This subsection shall be deemed to be complied with in the case of dental hygienists employed by or under contract with a local health department or State government dental public health program and especially trained by the Dental Health Section of the Department of Health and Human Services as public health hygienists, while performing their duties for the persons officially served by the local health department or State government program under the direction of a duly licensed dentist employed by that program or by the Dental Health Section of the Department of Health and Human Services.

(a1) A dental hygienist who has three years of experience in clinical dental hygiene or a minimum of 2,000 hours performing primarily prophylaxis or periodontal debridement under the supervision of a licensed dentist, who completes annual CPR certification, who completes six hours each year of Board-approved continuing education in medical emergencies in addition to the requirements of G.S. 90-225.1, and who is designated by the employing dentist as being capable of performing clinical hygiene procedures without the direct supervision of the dentist, may perform one or more dental hygiene functions as described in G.S. 90-221(a) without a licensed dentist being physically present if all of the following conditions are met:

(1)   A licensed dentist directs in writing the hygienist to perform the dental hygiene functions.

(2)   The licensed dentist has personally conducted an evaluation of the patient which shall include a complete oral examination of the patient, a thorough analysis of the patient's health history, a diagnosis of the patient's condition, and a specific written plan for treatment.

(3)   The dental hygiene functions directed to be performed in accordance with this subsection shall be conducted within 120 days of the dentist's evaluation.

(4)   The services are performed in nursing homes; rest homes; long-term care facilities; rural and community clinics operated by Board-approved nonprofits; rural and community clinics operated by federal, State, county, or local governments; and any other facilities identified by the Office of Rural Health and approved by the Board as serving dental access shortage areas.

(a2)   A dental hygienist shall not establish or operate a separate care facility that exclusively renders dental hygiene services.

(a3)   A dental hygienist who has been disciplined by the Board may not practice outside the direct supervision of a dentist under G.S. 90-233(a1). A dentist who has been disciplined by the Board may not allow a hygienist to work outside of that dentist's direct supervision under G.S. 90-233(a1).

(a4)   Each dentist who chooses to order dental hygiene services under G.S. 90-233(a1) shall report annually to the Board the number of patients who were treated outside the direct supervision of the dentist, the location in which the services were performed by the hygienist, and a description of any adverse circumstances which occurred during or after the treatment, if any. The dentist's report shall not identify hygienists or patients by name or any other identifier.

(a5)   Clinical dental hygiene services shall be provided in compliance with both CDC and OSHA standards for infection control and patient treatment.

(b)   A dentist in private practice may not employ more than two dental hygienists at one and the same time who are employed in clinical dental hygiene positions.

(c)   Dental hygiene may be practiced only by the holder of a license or provisional license currently in effect and duly issued by the Board. The following acts, practices, functions or operations, however, shall not constitute the practice of dental hygiene within the meaning of this Article:

(1)   The teaching of dental hygiene in a school or college approved by the Board in a board-approved program by an individual licensed as a dental hygienist in any state in the United States.

(2)   Activity which would otherwise be considered the practice of dental hygiene performed by students enrolled in a school or college approved by the Board in a board-approved dental hygiene program under the direct supervision of a dental hygienist or a dentist duly licensed in North Carolina or qualified for the teaching of dentistry pursuant to the provisions of G.S. 90-29(c)(3), acting as an instructor.

(3)   Any act or acts performed by an assistant to a dentist licensed to practice in this State when said act or acts are authorized and permitted by and performed in accordance with rules and regulations promulgated by the Board.

(4)   Dental assisting and related functions as a part of their instructions by students enrolled in a course in dental assisting conducted in this State and approved by the Board, when such functions are performed under the supervision of a dentist acting as a teacher or instructor who is either duly licensed in North Carolina or qualified for the teaching of dentistry pursuant to the provisions of G.S. 90-29(c)(3). (1945, c. 639, s. 12; 1971, c. 756, s. 13; 1973, c. 476, s. 128; 1981, c. 824, ss. 2, 3; 1989, c. 727, s. 219(6a); 1997-443, s. 11A.23; 1999-237, s. 11.65; 2007-124, s. 2.)

§ 90-233.1. Violation a misdemeanor.

Any person who shall violate, or aid or abet another in violating, any of the provisions of this Article shall be guilty of a Class 1 misdemeanor. (1945, c. 639, s. 13; 1971, c. 756, s. 14; 1993, c. 539, s. 642; 1994, Ex. Sess., c. 24, s. 14(c).)

Article 17.

Dispensing Opticians.

§ 90-234. Necessity for certificate of registration.

On and after the first day of July, 1951, no person or combination of persons shall for pay, or reward, either directly or indirectly, practice as a dispensing optician as hereinafter defined in the State of North Carolina without a certificate of registration issued pursuant to the provisions of this Article by the North Carolina State Board of Opticians hereinafter established. (1951, c. 1089, s. 1.)

§ 90-235. Definition.

Within the meaning of the provisions of this Article, the term "dispensing optician" defines one who prepares and dispenses lenses, spectacles, eyeglasses and/or appurtenances thereto to the intended wearers thereof on written prescriptions from physicians or optometrists duly licensed to practice their professions, and in accordance with such prescriptions interprets, measures, adapts, fits and adjusts such lenses, spectacles, eyeglasses and/or appurtenances thereto to the human face for the aid or correction of visual or ocular anomalies of the human eye. The services and appliances related to ophthalmic dispensing shall be dispensed, furnished or supplied to the intended wearer or user thereof only upon prescription issued by a physician or an optometrist; but duplications, replacements, reproductions or repetitions may be done without prescription, in which event any such act shall be construed to be ophthalmic dispensing, the same as if performed on the basis of a written prescription. (1951, c. 1089, s. 2.)

§ 90-236. What constitutes practicing as a dispensing optician.

Any one or combination of the following practices when done for pay or reward shall constitute practicing as a dispensing optician: Interpreting prescriptions issued by licensed physicians and/or optometrists; fitting glasses on the face; servicing glasses or spectacles; measuring of patient's face, fitting frames, compounding and fabricating lenses and frames, and any therapeutic device used or employed in the correction of vision, and alignment of frames to the face of the wearer, provided, however, that the provisions of this section shall not apply to students and apprentices. (1951, c. 1089, s. 3; 1977, c. 755, s. 1.)

§ 90-236.1. Requirements for filling contact lens prescriptions.

No person, firm or corporation licensed or registered under this Article shall fill a prescription or dispense lenses, other than spectacle lenses, unless the prescription specifically states on its face that the prescriber intends it to be for contact lenses and includes the type and specifications of the contact lenses being prescribed. No person, firm or corporation licensed under this Article shall fill a prescription beyond the expiration date stated on the face thereof.

Any person, firm or corporation that dispenses contact lenses on the prescription of a practitioner licensed under Articles 1 or 6 of this Chapter shall, at the time of delivery of the lenses, inform the recipient both orally and in writing that he return to the prescriber for insertion of the lens, instruction on lens insertion and care, and to ascertain the accuracy and suitability of the prescribed lens. The statement shall also state that if the recipient does not return to the prescriber after delivery of the lens for the purposes stated above, the prescriber shall not be responsible for any damages or injury resulting from the prescribed lens, except that this sentence does not apply if the dispenser and the prescriber are the same person.

Prescriptions filled pursuant to this section shall be kept on file by the prescriber and the person filling the prescription for at least 24 months after the prescription is filled.

Any person, firm or corporation dispensing, furnishing or supplying contact lenses in interstate commerce or at retail to recipients in this State, other than a practitioner licensed under Article 1 or Article 6 of this Chapter, is deemed a "dispensing optician" under G.S. 90-235 and is subject to the provisions of this Article. (1981, c. 600, s. 1; 1985, c. 748.)

§ 90-237. Qualifications for dispensing opticians.

In order to be issued a license as a registered licensed optician by the North Carolina State Board of Opticians, the applicant:

(1)   Shall not have violated this Article or the rules of the Board.

(2)   Shall be at least 18 years of age and a high school graduate or equivalent.

(2a)   Shall be of good moral character.

(3)   Shall have passed an examination conducted by the Board to determine his or her fitness to engage in the business of a dispensing optician.

(4)   Shall have completed a six-month internship by working full time under the supervision of a licensed optician, optometrist, or physician trained in ophthalmology, in order to demonstrate proficiency in the areas of measurement of the face, and fitting and adjusting glasses and frames to the face, lens recognition, lens design, and prescription interpretation. (1951, c. 1089, s. 4; 1977, c. 755, s. 2; 1981, c. 600, s. 2; 1997-424, s. 1.)

§ 90-238. North Carolina State Board of Opticians created; appointment and qualification of members.

The North Carolina State Board of Opticians is created. The Board's duty is to carry out the purposes and enforce the provisions of this Article. The Board shall consist of seven members appointed by the Governor as follows:

(1)   Five licensed dispensing opticians, each of whom shall serve three-year terms;

(2)   Two residents of North Carolina who are not licensed as dispensing opticians, physicians, or optometrists, who shall serve three-year terms.

Each member of the Board shall serve until the member's successor is appointed and qualifies. No person shall serve on this Board for more than two complete consecutive terms. Before beginning office, each member of the Board shall take all oaths prescribed for other State officers in the manner provided by law, which oaths shall be filed in the office of the Secretary of State. The Governor may remove any member of the Board for good cause shown, may appoint members to fill unexpired terms, and must make optician appointments from a list of three nominees for each vacancy submitted by the Board as a result of an election conducted by the Board each year and open to all licensees. In naming candidates for election, the Board must ensure that its candidates reflect the composition of the State with regards to gender, ethnic, racial, and age composition. If the Board fails to fulfill its requirements under this section, the Governor may appoint a licensed optician to fill a vacancy on the Board. (1951, c. 1089, s. 5; 1979, c. 533; 1981, c. 600, s. 3; 1997-424, s. 7; 2007-525, s. 13.)

§ 90-239. Organization, meetings and powers of Board.

Within 30 days after appointment of the Board, the Board shall hold its first regular meeting, and at said meeting and annually thereafter shall choose from among its members a chairman, vice-chairman, a secretary and a treasurer. The Board may combine the offices of secretary and treasurer. The Board shall make such rules and regulations not inconsistent with the law as may be necessary to the proper performance of its duties, may employ agents to carry out the purposes of this Article, and each member may administer oaths and take testimony concerning any matter within the jurisdiction of the Board, and a majority of the Board shall constitute a quorum. The Board shall meet at least once a year, the time and place of meeting to be designated by the chairman. Special meetings may be called by the chairman or upon request of three members. The secretary of the Board shall keep a full and complete record of its proceedings, which shall at all reasonable times be open to public inspection. (1951, c. 1089, s. 6; 1981, c. 600, ss. 4-7.)

§ 90-240. Examination.

(a) Applicants to take the examination for dispensing opticians shall be high school graduates or the equivalent who:

(1) Have successfully completed a two-year course of training in an accredited school of opticianry with a minimum of 1600 hours or

(2) Have completed three and one-half years of apprenticeship while registered with the Board under a licensed dispensing optician, with time spent in a recognized school credited as part of the apprenticeship period or

(3) Have completed three and one-half years of apprenticeship while registered with the Board under the direct supervision of an optometrist or a physician specializing in ophthalmology, provided the supervising optometrist or physician elects to operate the apprenticeship under the same requirements applicable to dispensing opticians.

(b) The examination shall be confined to such knowledge as is reasonably necessary to engage in preparation and dispensing of optical devices and shall include the following:

(1) The skills necessary for the proper analysis of prescriptions;

(2) The skills necessary for the dispensing of eyeglasses and contact lenses; and

(3) The processes by which the products offered by dispensing opticians are manufactured.

(c) The examination shall be given at least twice each year at sites and on dates that are publicly announced 60 days in advance.

(d) Each applicant shall, upon request, receive his or her examination score on each section of the examination.

(e) The Board may include as part or all of the examination, any nationally prepared and recognized examination, and will periodically review and validate any exam in use by the Board. The Board will credit an applicant with the score on any national test taken in the last three years to the extent such test may be included in the North Carolina exam.

(f) An applicant for admission on the basis of apprenticeship shall have worked full time under the supervision of a licensed dispensing optician, optometrist or physician trained in ophthalmology. An apprentice shall have obtained experience in ophthalmic fabricating and manufacturing techniques and processes for no less than six months and shall have gained experience in the other activities defined as dispensing herein. (1951, c. 1089, s. 7; 1977, c. 755, s. 3; 1981, c. 600, s. 8.)

§ 90-241. Waiver of written examination requirements.

(a) The Board shall grant a license without examination to any applicant who:

(1) Is at least 18 years of age.

(2) Is of good moral character.

(3) Holds a license in good standing as a dispensing optician in another state.

(4) Has engaged in the practice of opticianry in the other state for four years immediately preceding the application to the Board.

(5) Has not violated this Article or the rules of the Board.

(b) The Board shall grant admission to the next examination and grant license upon attainment of a passing score on the examination to a person who has worked, in a state that does not license opticians, in opticianry for four years immediately preceding the application to the Board performing tasks and taking the curriculum equivalent to the North Carolina apprenticeship, and who meets the requirements of G.S. 90-237(1) through (3).

(c) Any person desiring to secure a license under this section shall make application therefor in the manner and form prescribed by the rules of the Board and shall pay the fee prescribed in G.S. 90-246.

(d) Repealed by Session Laws 1997-424, s. 2. (1951, c. 1089, s. 8; 1977, c. 755, s. 4; 1979, c. 166, ss. 2, 3; 1981, c. 600, s. 9; 1997-424, s. 2.)

§ 90-242. Repealed by Session Laws 1981, c. 600, s. 10.

§ 90-243. Registration of places of business, apprentices.

The Board may adopt rules requiring, as a condition of dispensing, the registration of places of business where ophthalmic dispensing is engaged in, and for registration of apprentices and interns who are working under direct supervision of a licensed optician. The Board may also require that any information furnished to it as required by law or regulation be furnished under oath. (1951, c. 1089, s. 10; 1967, c. 691, s. 49; 1979, c. 166, s. 1; 1981, c. 600, s. 11.)

§ 90-244. Display, use, and renewal of license of registration.

(a) Every person to whom a license has been granted under this Article shall display the same in a conspicuous part of the office or establishment wherein he is engaged as a dispensing optician. The Board may adopt regulations concerning the display of registrations of places of business and of apprentices and interns.

(b) A license issued by the Board automatically expires on the first day of January of each year. A license shall be reinstated without penalty from January 1 through January 15 immediately following expiration. After January 15, a license shall be reinstated by payment of the renewal fee and a penalty of fifty dollars ($50.00). Licenses that remain expired two years or more shall not be reinstated. (1951, c. 1098, s. 11; 1981, c. 600, s. 12; 1997-424, s. 3.)

§ 90-245. Collection of fees.

The secretary to the Board is hereby authorized and empowered to collect in the name and on behalf of this Board the fees prescribed by this Article and shall turn over to the State Treasurer all funds collected or received under this Article, which funds shall be credited to the North Carolina State Board of Opticians, and said funds shall be held and expended under the supervision of the Director of the Budget of the State of North Carolina exclusively for the administration and enforcement of the provisions of this Article. Nothing in this Article shall be construed to authorize any expenditure in excess of the amount available from time to time in the hands of the State Treasurer derived from the fees collected under the provisions of this Article and received by the State Treasurer in the manner aforesaid. (1951, c. 1089, s. 12; 1981, c. 884, s. 9.)

§ 90-246. Fees.

In order to provide the means of administering and enforcing the provisions of this Article and the other duties of the North Carolina State Board of Opticians, the Board is hereby authorized to charge and collect fees established by its rules not to exceed the following:

(1)....... Each examination.. $200.00

(2)....... Each initial license.. $ 50.00

(3)....... Each renewal of license.. $100.00

(4)....... Each license issued to a practitioner of another

.... state to practice in this State.. $200.00

(5)....... Each registration of an optical place of business.................................. $ 50.00

(6)....... Each application for registration as an opticianry

.... apprentice or intern, and renewals thereof.. $ 25.00

(7)....... Repealed by Session Laws 1997-424, s. 4.

(8)....... Each registration of a training establishment.. $ 25.00

(9)....... Each license verification... $ 10.00.

(1951, c. 1089, s. 13; 1977, c. 755, s. 5; 1981, c. 600, s. 13; 1989, c. 673, s. 1; 1997-424, s. 4.)

§ 90-247. Repealed by Session Laws 1981, c. 600, s. 14.

§ 90-248. Compensation and expenses of Board members and secretary.

Each member of the Board shall receive for his or her services for time actually in attendance upon Board meetings and affairs of the Board only, the amount of per diem provided by G.S. 138-5 and shall be reimbursed for subsistence, mileage and necessary expenses incurred in the discharge of such duties at the same rates as set forth in G.S. 138-6 and G.S. 138-7. (1951, c. 1089, s. 15; 1953, c. 894; 1965, c. 730; 1969, c. 445, s. 6; 1981, c. 600, s. 15.)

§ 90-249. Powers of the Board.

(a) The Board shall have the power to make rules, not inconsistent with this Article and the laws of the State of North Carolina, with respect to the following areas of the business of opticianry in North Carolina:

(1) Misrepresentation to the public.

(2) Baiting or deceptive advertising.

(3) Continuing education of licensees.

(4) Location of registrants in the State.

(5) Registration of established optical places of business, but no rule restricting type or location of a business may be enacted.

(6) Requiring photographs for purposes of identification of persons subject to this Article.

(7) Content of licensure examination and reexamination.

(8) Revocation, suspension, and reinstatement of licenses, probation, and reprimands of licensees, and other penalties.

(9) Fees within the limits of G.S. 90-246.

(10) Accreditation of schools of opticianry.

(11) Registration and training of apprentices and interns.

(12) Licenses and examinations pursuant to G.S. 90-241.

(b) through (d) Repealed by Session Laws 1997-424, s. 5. (1951, c. 1089, s. 16; 1953, c. 1041, s. 19; 1973, c. 1331, s. 3; 1977, c. 755, s. 6; 1981, c. 600, s. 16; 1987, c. 827, s. 1; 1997-424, s. 5.)

§ 90-249.1. Disciplinary actions.

(a) The Board may suspend, revoke, or refuse to issue, renew, or reinstate any license for any of the following:

(1) Offering to practice or practicing as a dispensing optician without a license.

(2) Aiding or abetting an unlicensed person in offering to practice or practicing as a dispensing optician.

(3) Selling, transferring, or assigning a license.

(4) Engaging in fraud or misrepresentation to obtain or renew a license.

(5) Engaging in false or misleading advertising.

(6) Advertising in any manner that conveys or intends to convey the impression that eyes are examined by persons licensed under this Article or optical places of business registered under this Article.

(7) Engaging in malpractice, unethical conduct, fraud, deceit, gross negligence, incompetence, or gross misconduct.

(8) Being convicted of a crime involving fraud or moral turpitude.

(9) Violating any provision of this Article or the rules adopted by the Board.

(b) In addition or as an alternative to taking any of the actions permitted in subsection (a) of this section, the Board may assess a licensee a civil penalty of not more than one thousand dollars ($1,000) for the violation of any section of this Article. In any case in which the Board is authorized to take any of the actions permitted in subsection (a) of this section, the Board may instead accept an offer in compromise of the charges whereby the accused licensee shall pay to the Board a civil penalty of not more than one thousand dollars ($1,000). All civil penalties collected by the Board shall be remitted to the school fund of the county in which the violation occurred.

(c) In determining the amount of a civil penalty, the Board may consider:

(1) The degree and extent of harm caused by the violation to public health and safety or the potential for harm.

(2) The duration and gravity of the violation.

(3) Whether the violation was willful or reflects a continuing pattern.

(4) Whether the violation involved elements of fraud or deception.

(5) Prior disciplinary actions against the licensee.

(6) Whether and to what extent the licensee profited from the violation.

(d) Any person, including the Board and its staff, may file a complaint with the Board alleging that a licensee committed acts in violation of subsection (a) of this section. The Board may, without holding a hearing, dismiss the complaint as unfounded or trivial. Any hearings held pursuant to this section shall be conducted in accordance with Chapter 150B of the General Statutes. (1997-424, s. 6.)

§ 90-250. Sale of optical glasses.

No optical glass or other kindred products or instruments of vision shall be dispensed, ground or assembled in connection with a given formula prescribed by a licensed physician or optometrist except under the supervision of a licensed dispensing optician and in a registered optical establishment or office. Provided, however, that the provisions of this section shall not prohibit persons or corporations from selling completely assembled spectacles without advice or aid as to the selection thereof as merchandise from permanently located or established places of business. (1951, c. 1089, s. 17.)

§ 90-251. Licensee allowing unlicensed person to use his certificate or license.

Each licensee licensed under the provisions of this Article who shall rent, loan or allow the use of his registration certificate or license to an unlicensed person for any unlawful use shall be guilty of a Class 1 misdemeanor. (1951, c. 1089, s. 18; 1993, c. 539, s. 643; 1994, Ex. Sess., c. 24, s. 14(c).)

§ 90-252. Engaging in practice without license.

Any person, firm or corporation owning, managing or conducting a store, shop or place of business and not having in its employ and on duty, during all hours in which acts constituting the business of opticianry are carried on, a licensed dispensing optician engaged in supervision of such store, office, place of business or optical establishment, or representing to the public, by means of advertisement or otherwise or by using the words, "optician, licensed optician, optical establishment, optical office, ophthalmic dispenser," or any combination of such terms within or without such store representing that the same is a legally established optical place of business duly licensed as such and managed or conducted by persons holding a dispensing optician's license, when in fact such permit is not held by such person, firm or corporation, or by some person employed by such person, firm or corporation and on the premises and in charge of such optical business, shall be guilty of a Class 1 misdemeanor. (1951, c. 1089, s. 19; 1981, c. 600, s. 17; 1993, c. 539, s. 644; 1994, Ex. Sess., c. 24, s. 14(c).)

§ 90-253. Exemptions from Article.

Nothing in this Article shall be construed to apply to optometrists, or physicians trained in ophthalmology who are authorized to practice under the laws of this State, or to an unlicensed person working within the practice and under the direct supervision of the optometrist or physician trained in ophthalmology. An apprentice or intern registered with the Board and working under direct supervision of a licensed optician, optometrist or physician trained in ophthalmology will not be deemed to have engaged in opticianry by reason of performing acts defined as preparation and dispensing, provided the apprentice is in compliance with the rules of the Board respecting the training of apprentices.

As used in this section, "supervision" means the provision of general direction and control through immediate personal on-site inspection and evaluation of all work constituting the practice of opticianry and the provision of consultation and instruction by a licensed dispensing optician, except that on-site supervision is not required for minor adjustments or repairs to eyeglasses. (1951, c. 1089, s. 20; 1981, c. 600, s. 18.)

§ 90-254. General penalty for violation.

Any person, firm or corporation who shall violate any provision of this Article for which no other penalty has been provided shall, upon conviction, be fined not more than two hundred dollars ($200.00) or imprisoned for a period of not more than 12 months, or both, in the discretion of the court.

Whenever it appears to the Board that any person, firm or corporation is violating any of the provisions of this Article or of the rules and regulations of the Board promulgated under this Article, the Board may apply to the superior court for a restraining order and injunction to restrain the violation; and the superior courts have jurisdiction to grant the requested relief, irrespective or whether or not criminal prosecution has been instituted or administrative sanctions imposed by reasons of the violation. The venue for actions brought under this subsection shall be the superior court of any county in which such acts are alleged to have been committed or in the county where the defendants in such action reside. (1951, c. 1089, s. 21; 1981, c. 600, s. 19.)

§ 90-255. Rebates.

It shall be unlawful for any person, firm or corporation to offer or give any gift or premium or discount, directly or indirectly, or in any form or manner participate in the division, assignment, rebate or refund of fees or parts thereof with any ophthalmologist, optometrist, or wholesaler, for the purpose of diverting or influencing the freedom of choice of the consumer in the selection of an ophthalmic dispenser. (1951, c. 1089, s. 23; 1981, c. 600, s. 20.)

§ 90-255.1. Sale of flammable frames.

No person shall distribute, sell, exchange or deliver, or have in his possession with intent to distribute, sell, exchange or deliver any eyeglass frame or sunglass frame which contains any form of cellulose nitrate or other highly flammable materials. Any person violating the provisions of this section shall be guilty of a Class 2 misdemeanor. (1971, c. 239, s. 1; 1993, c. 539, s. 645; 1994, Ex. Sess., c. 24, s. 14(c).)

Article 18.

Physical Therapy.

§§ 90-256 through 90-270: Recodified as §§ 90-270.24 through 90-270.39.

Article 18A.

Psychology Practice Act.

§ 90-270.1. Title; purpose.

(a) This Article shall be known and may be cited as the "Psychology Practice Act."

(b) The practice of psychology in North Carolina is hereby declared to affect the public health, safety, and welfare, and to be subject to regulation to protect the public from the practice of psychology by unqualified persons and from unprofessional conduct by persons licensed to practice psychology. (1967, c. 910, s. 1; 1993, c. 375, s. 1.)

§ 90-270.2. Definitions.

The following definitions apply in this Article:

(1) Board. - The North Carolina Psychology Board.

(2) Examination. - Any and all examinations that are adopted by the Board and administered to applicants and licensees, including, but not limited to, the national examination, Board-developed examinations, and other examinations that assess the competency and ethics of psychologists and applicants.

(3) Jurisdiction. - Any governmental authority, including, but not limited to, a state, a territory, a commonwealth, a district of the United States, and a country or a local governmental authority thereof, that licenses, certifies, or registers psychologists.

(4) Health services. - Those activities of the practice of psychology that include the delivery of preventive, assessment, or therapeutic intervention services directly to individuals whose growth, adjustment, or functioning is actually impaired or may be at substantial risk of impairment.

(5) Institution of higher education. - A university, a college, a professional school, or another institution of higher learning that:

a. In the United States, is regionally accredited by bodies approved by the Commission on Recognition of Postsecondary Accreditation or its successor.

b. In Canada, holds a membership in the Association of Universities and Colleges of Canada.

c. In another country, is accredited by the comparable official organization having this authority.

(6) Licensed psychologist. - An individual to whom a license has been issued pursuant to the provisions of this Article, whose license is in force and

not suspended or revoked, and whose license permits him or her to engage in the practice of psychology as defined in this Article.

(7) Licensed psychological associate. - An individual to whom a license has been issued pursuant to the provisions of this Article, whose license is in force and not suspended or revoked, and whose license permits him or her to engage in the practice of psychology as defined in this Article.

(7a) Neuropsychological. - Pertaining to the study of brain-behavior relationships, including the diagnosis, including etiology and prognosis, and treatment of the emotional, behavioral, and cognitive effects of cerebral dysfunction through psychological and behavioral techniques and methods.

(8) Practice of psychology. - The observation, description, evaluation, interpretation, or modification of human behavior by the application of psychological principles, methods, and procedures for the purpose of preventing or eliminating symptomatic, maladaptive, or undesired behavior or of enhancing interpersonal relationships, work and life adjustment, personal effectiveness, behavioral health, or mental health. The practice of psychology includes, but is not limited to: psychological testing and the evaluation or assessment of personal characteristics such as intelligence, personality, abilities, interests, aptitudes, and neuropsychological functioning; counseling, psychoanalysis, psychotherapy, hypnosis, biofeedback, and behavior analysis and therapy; diagnosis, including etiology and prognosis, and treatment of mental and emotional disorder or disability, alcoholism and substance abuse, disorders of habit or conduct, as well as of the psychological and neuropsychological aspects of physical illness, accident, injury, or disability; and psychoeducational evaluation, therapy, remediation, and consultation. Psychological services may be rendered to individuals, families, groups, and the public. The practice of psychology shall be construed within the meaning of this definition without regard to whether payment is received for services rendered.

(9) Psychologist. - A person represents himself or herself to be a psychologist if that person uses any title or description of services incorporating the words "psychology", "psychological", "psychologic", or "psychologist", states that he or she possesses expert qualification in any area of psychology, or provides or offers to provide services defined as the practice of psychology in this Article. All persons licensed under this Article may present themselves as psychologists, as may those persons who are exempt by G.S. 90-270.4 and those who are qualified applicants under G.S. 90-270.5. (1967, c. 910, s. 2;

1977, c. 670, s. 1; 1979, c. 670, s. 1; 1993, c. 375, s. 1; 1993 (Reg. Sess., 1994), c. 569, s. 14; 1999-292, ss. 1, 2.)

§ 90-270.3. Practice of medicine and optometry not permitted.

Nothing in this Article shall be construed as permitting licensed psychologists or licensed psychological associates to engage in any manner in all or any of the parts of the practice of medicine or optometry licensed under Articles 1 and 6 of Chapter 90 of the General Statutes, including, among others, the diagnosis and correction of visual and muscular anomalies of the human eyes and visual apparatus, eye exercises, orthoptics, vision training, visual training and developmental vision. A licensed psychologist or licensed psychological associate shall assist his or her client or patient in obtaining professional help for all aspects of the client's or patient's problems that fall outside the boundaries of the psychologist's own competence, including provision for the diagnosis and treatment of relevant medical or optometric problems. (1967, c. 910, s. 3; 1977, c. 670, s. 2; 1979, c. 670, s. 2; 1993, c. 375, s. 1.)

§ 90-270.4. Exemptions to this Article.

(a) Nothing in this Article shall be construed to prevent the teaching of psychology, the conduct of psychological research, or the provision of psychological services or consultation to organizations or institutions, provided that such teaching, research, service, or consultation does not involve the delivery or supervision of direct psychological services to individuals or groups of individuals who are themselves, rather than a third party, the intended beneficiaries of such services, without regard to the source or extent of payment for services rendered. Nothing in this Article shall prevent the provision of expert testimony by psychologists who are otherwise exempted by this act. Persons holding an earned master's, specialist, or doctoral degree in psychology from an institution of higher education may use the title "psychologist" in activities permitted by this subsection.

(b) Nothing in this Article shall be construed as limiting the activities, services, and use of official titles on the part of any person in the regular employ of the State of North Carolina or whose employment is included under the North Carolina Human Resources Act who has served in a position of employment involving the practice of psychology as defined in this Article, provided that the person was serving in this capacity on December 31, 1979.

(c) Persons certified by the State Board of Education as school psychologists and serving as regular salaried employees of the Department of Public Instruction or local boards of education are not required to be licensed under this Article in order to perform the duties for which they serve the Department of Public Instruction or local boards of education, and nothing in this Article shall be construed as limiting their activities, services, or titles while performing those duties for which they serve the Department of Public Instruction or local boards of education. If a person certified by the State Board of Education as a school psychologist and serving as a regular salaried employee of the Department of Public Instruction or a local board of education is or becomes a licensed psychologist under this Article, he or she shall be required to comply with all conditions, requirements, and obligations imposed by statute or by Board rules upon all other licensed psychologists as a condition to retaining that license. Other provisions of this Article notwithstanding, if a person certified by the State Board of Education as a school psychologist and serving as a regular salaried employee of the Department of Public Instruction or a local board of education is or becomes a licensed psychological associate under this Article, he or she shall not be required to comply with the supervision requirements otherwise applicable to licensed psychological associates by Board rules or by this Article in the course of his or her regular salaried employment with the Department of Public Instruction or a local board of education, but he or she shall be required to comply with all other conditions, requirements, and obligations imposed by statute or a local board of education or by Board rules upon all other licensed psychological associates as a condition to retaining that license.

(d) Nothing in this Article shall be construed as limiting the activities, services, and use of title designating training status of a student, intern, fellow, or other trainee preparing for the practice of psychology under the supervision and responsibility of a qualified psychologist in an institution of higher education or service facility, provided that such activities and services constitute a part of his or her course of study as a matriculated graduate student in psychology. For individuals pursuing postdoctoral training or experience in psychology, nothing shall limit the use of a title designating training status, but the Board may develop rules defining qualified supervision, disclosure of supervisory relationships, frequency of supervision, settings to which trainees may be assigned, activities in which trainees may engage, qualifications for trainee status, nature of responsibility assumed by the supervisor, and the structure, content, and organization of postdoctoral experience.

(e) Subject to subsection (g) of this section, nothing in this Article shall be construed to prevent a qualified member of other professional groups licensed or certified under the laws of this State from rendering services within the scope of practice, as defined in the statutes regulating those professional practices, provided the person does not hold himself or herself out to the public by any title or description stating or implying that the person is a psychologist or licensed, certified, or registered to practice psychology.

(f) Nothing in this Article is to be construed as prohibiting a psychologist who is not a resident of North Carolina who holds an earned doctoral, master's, or specialist degree in psychology from an institution of higher education, and who is licensed or certified only in another jurisdiction, from engaging in the practice of psychology, including the provision of health services, in this State for up to five days in any calendar year. All such psychologists shall comply with supervision requirements established by the Board, and shall notify the Board in writing of their intent to practice in North Carolina, prior to the provision of any services in this State. The Board shall adopt rules implementing and defining this provision.

(g) Except as provided in subsection (c) of this section, if a person who is otherwise exempt from the provisions of this Article and not required to be licensed under this Article is or becomes licensed under this Article, he or she shall comply with all Board rules and statutes applicable to all other psychologists licensed under this Article. These requirements apply regardless of whether the person holds himself or herself out to the public by any title or description stating or implying that the person is a psychologist, a licensed psychological associate, or licensed to practice psychology.

(h) A licensee whose license is suspended or revoked pursuant to the provisions of G.S. 90-270.15, or an applicant who is notified that he or she has failed an examination for the second time, as specified in G.S. 90-270.5(b), or an applicant who is notified that licensure is denied pursuant to G.S. 90-270.11 or G.S. 90-270.15, or an applicant who discontinues the application process at any point must terminate the practice of psychology, in accordance with the duly adopted rules of the Board. (1967, c. 910, s. 4; 1977, c. 670, s. 3; 1979, c. 670, ss. 3, 4; c. 1005, s. 1; 1981, c. 654, ss. 1, 2; 1983, c. 82, s. 5; 1985, c. 734, ss. 1-3; 1993, c. 375, s. 1; 1995, c. 509, s. 44; 2006-175, s. 1; 2007-468, ss. 1, 2; 2013-382, s. 9.1(c).)

§ 90-270.5. Application; examination; supervision; provisional and temporary licenses.

(a) Except as otherwise exempted by G.S. 90-270.4, persons who are qualified by education to practice psychology in this State must make application for licensure to the Board within 30 days of offering to practice or undertaking the practice of psychology in North Carolina. Applications must then be completed for review by the Board within the time period stipulated in the duly adopted rules of the Board. Persons who practice or offer to practice psychology for more than 30 days without making application for licensure, who fail to complete the application process within the time period specified by the Board, or who are denied licensure pursuant to G.S. 90-270.11 or G.S. 90-270.15, may not subsequently practice or offer to practice psychology without first becoming licensed.

(b) After making application for licensure, applicants must take the first examination to which they are admitted by the Board. If applicants fail the examination, they may continue to practice psychology until they take the next examination to which they are admitted by the Board. If applicants fail the second examination, they shall cease the practice of psychology per G.S. 90-270.4(h), and may not subsequently practice or offer to practice psychology without first reapplying for and receiving a license from the Board. An applicant who does not take an examination on the date prescribed by the Board shall be deemed to have failed that examination.

(c) All individuals who have yet to apply and who are practicing or offering to practice psychology in North Carolina, and all applicants who are practicing or offering to practice psychology in North Carolina, shall at all times comply with supervision requirements established by the Board. The Board shall specify in its rules the format, setting, content, time frame, amounts of supervision, qualifications of supervisors, disclosure of supervisory relationships, the organization of the supervised experience, and the nature of the responsibility assumed by the supervisor. Individuals shall be supervised for all activities comprising the practice of psychology until they have met the following conditions:

(1) For licensed psychologist applicants, until they have passed the examination to which they have been admitted by the Board, have been notified

of the results, have completed supervision requirements specified in subsection (d) of this section, and have been informed by the Board of permanent licensure as a licensed psychologist; or

(2)   For licensed psychological associate applicants, until they have passed the examination to which they have been admitted by the Board, have been notified of the results, and have been informed by the Board of permanent licensure as a licensed psychological associate, after which time supervision is required only for those activities specified in subsection (e) of this section.

(d)   For permanent licensure as a licensed psychologist, an otherwise qualified psychologist must secure two years of acceptable and appropriate supervised experience germane to his or her training and intended area of practice as a psychologist. The Board shall permit such supervised experience to be acquired on a less than full-time basis, and shall additionally specify in its rules the format, setting, content, time frame, amounts of supervision, qualifications of supervisors, disclosure of supervisory relationships, the organization of the supervised experience, and the nature of the responsibility assumed by the supervisor. Supervision of health services must be received from qualified licensed psychologists holding health services provider certificates, or from other psychologists recognized by the Board in accordance with Board rules.

(1)   One of these years of experience shall be postdoctoral, and for this year, the Board may require, as specified in its rules, that the supervised experience be comparable to the knowledge and skills acquired during formal doctoral or postdoctoral education, in accordance with established professional standards.

(2)   One of these years may be predoctoral and the Board shall establish rules governing appropriate supervised predoctoral experience.

(3)   A psychologist who meets all other requirements of G.S. 90-270.11(a) as a licensed psychologist, except the two years of supervised experience, may be issued a provisional license as a psychologist or a license as a psychological associate, without having received a master's degree or specialist degree in psychology, by the Board for the practice of psychology.

(e)   A licensed psychological associate shall be supervised by a qualified licensed psychologist, or other qualified professionals, in accordance with Board rules specifying the format, setting, content, time frame, amounts of supervision, qualifications of supervisors, disclosure of supervisory relationships, the organization of the supervised experience, and the nature of the responsibility assumed by the supervisor. A licensed psychological associate who provides health services shall be supervised, for those activities requiring supervision, by a qualified licensed psychologist holding health services provider certification or by other qualified professionals under the overall direction of a qualified licensed psychologist holding health services provider certification, in accordance with Board rules. Except as provided below, supervision, including the supervision of health services, is required only when a licensed psychological associate engages in: assessment of personality functioning; neuropsychological evaluation; psychotherapy, counseling, and other interventions with clinical populations for the purpose of preventing or eliminating symptomatic, maladaptive, or undesired behavior; and, the use of intrusive, punitive, or experimental procedures, techniques, or measures. The Board shall adopt rules implementing and defining this provision, and as the practice of psychology evolves, may identify additional activities requiring supervision in order to maintain acceptable standards of practice.

(f)   A nonresident psychologist who is either licensed or certified by a similar Board in another jurisdiction whose standards, in the opinion of the Board, are, at the date of his or her certification or licensure, substantially equivalent to or higher than the requirements of this Article, may be issued a temporary license by the Board for the practice of psychology in this State for a period not to exceed the aggregate of 30 days in any calendar year. The Board may issue temporary health services provider certification simultaneously if the nonresident psychologist can demonstrate two years of acceptable supervised health services experience. All temporarily licensed psychologists shall comply with supervision requirements established by the Board.

(g)   An applicant for reinstatement of licensure, whose license was suspended under G.S. 90-270.15(f), may be issued a temporary license and temporary health services provider certification in accordance with the duly adopted rules of the Board. (1967, c. 910, s. 5; 1977, c. 670, s. 4; 1979, c. 670, s. 3; 1985, c. 734, s. 4; 1993, c. 375, s. 1; 2012-72, s. 1.)

§ 90-270.6. Psychology Board; appointment; term of office; composition.

For the purpose of carrying out the provisions of this Article, there is created a North Carolina Psychology Board, which shall consist of seven members appointed by the Governor. At all times three members shall be licensed psychologists, two members shall be licensed psychological associates, and two members shall be members of the public who are not licensed under this Article. The Governor shall give due consideration to the adequate representation of the various fields and areas of practice of psychology and to adequate representation from various geographic regions in the State. Terms of office shall be three years. All terms of service on the Board expire June 30 in appropriate years. As the term of a psychologist member expires, or as a vacancy of a psychologist member occurs for any other reason, the North Carolina Psychological Association, or its successor, shall, having sought the advice of the chairs of the graduate departments of psychology in the State, for each vacancy, submit to the Governor a list of the names of three eligible persons. From this list the Governor shall make the appointment for a full term, or for the remainder of the unexpired term, if any. Each Board member shall serve until his or her successor has been appointed. As the term of a member expires, or if one should become vacant for any reason, the Governor shall appoint a new member within 60 days of the vacancy's occurring. No member, either public or licensed under this Article, shall serve more than three complete consecutive terms. (1967, c. 910, s. 6; 1977, c. 670, s. 5; 1979, c. 670, s. 3; c. 1005, s. 2; 1983, c. 82, ss. 1-3; 1993, c. 375, s. 1; 2007-468, s. 3.)

§ 90-270.7. Qualifications of Board members; removal of Board members.

(a)   Each licensed psychologist and licensed psychological associate member of the Board shall have the following qualifications:

(1)   Shall be a resident of this State and a citizen of the United States;

(2)   Shall be at the time of appointment and shall have been for at least five years prior thereto, actively engaged in one or more branches of psychology or in the education and training of master's, specialist, doctoral, or postdoctoral students of psychology or in psychological research, and such activity during the two years preceding appointment shall have occurred primarily in this State.

(3)   Shall be free of conflict of interest in performing the duties of the Board.

(b)   Each public member of the Board shall have the following qualifications:

(1)   Shall be a resident of this State and a citizen of the United States;

(2) Shall be free of conflict of interest or the appearance of such conflict in performing the duties of the Board;

(3) Shall not be a psychologist, an applicant or former applicant for licensure as a psychologist, or a member of a household that includes a psychologist.

(c) A Board member shall be automatically removed from the Board if he or she:

(1) Ceases to meet the qualifications specified in this subsection;

(2) Fails to attend three successive Board meetings without just cause as determined by the remainder of the Board;

(3) Is found by the remainder of the Board to be in violation of the provisions of this Article or to have engaged in immoral, dishonorable, unprofessional, or unethical conduct, and such conduct is deemed to compromise the integrity of the Board;

(4) Is found to be guilty of a felony or an unlawful act involving moral turpitude by a court of competent jurisdiction or is found to have entered a plea of nolo contendere to a felony or an unlawful act involving moral turpitude;

(5) Is found guilty of malfeasance, misfeasance, or nonfeasance in relation to his or her Board duties by a court of competent jurisdiction; or

(6) Is incapacitated and without reasonable likelihood of resuming Board duties, as determined by the Board. (1967, c. 910, s. 7; 1977, c. 670, s. 6; 1985, c. 734, s. 5; 1993, c. 375, s. 1.)

§ 90-270.8. Compensation of members; expenses; employees.

Members of the Board shall receive no compensation for their services, but shall receive their necessary expenses incurred in the performance of duties required by this Article, as prescribed for State boards generally. The Board may employ necessary personnel for the performance of its functions, and fix the compensation therefor, within the limits of funds available to the Board;

however, the Board shall not employ any of its own members to perform inspectional or similar ministerial tasks for the Board. In no event shall the State of North Carolina be liable for expenses incurred by the Board in excess of the income derived from this Article. (1967, c. 910, s. 8.)

§ 90-270.9. Election of officers; meetings; adoption of seal and appropriate rules; powers of the Board.

The Board shall annually elect the chair and vice-chair from among its membership. The Board shall meet annually, at a time set by the Board, in the City of Raleigh, and it may hold additional meetings and conduct business at any place in the State. Four members of the Board shall constitute a quorum. The Board may empower any member to conduct any proceeding or investigation necessary to its purposes and may empower its agent or counsel to conduct any investigation necessary to its purposes, but any final action requires a quorum of the Board. The Board may order that any records concerning the practice of psychology relevant to a complaint received by the Board or an inquiry or investigation conducted by or on behalf of the Board be produced before the Board or for inspection and copying by representatives of or counsel to the Board by the custodian of such records. The Board shall adopt an official seal, which shall be affixed to all licenses issued by it. The Board shall make such rules and regulations not inconsistent with law, as may be necessary to regulate its proceedings and otherwise to implement the provisions of this Article. (1967, c. 910, s. 9; 1985, c. 734, s. 6; 1993, c. 375, s. 1.)

§ 90-270.10. Annual report.

On June 30 of each year, the Board shall submit a report to the Governor of the Board's activities since the preceding July 1, including the names of all licensed psychologists and licensed psychological associates to whom licenses have been granted under this Article, any cases heard and decisions rendered in matters before the Board, the recommendations of the Board as to future actions and policies, and a financial report. Each member of the Board shall review and sign the report before its submission to the Governor. Any Board member shall have the right to record a dissenting view. (1967, c. 910, s. 10; 1979, c. 670, s. 3; 1993, c. 375, s. 1.)

§ 90-270.11. Licensure; examination; foreign graduates.

(a) Licensed Psychologist. - The Board shall issue a permanent license to practice psychology to any applicant who pays an application fee and any applicable examination fee as specified in G.S. 90-270.18(b), who passes an examination in psychology as prescribed by the Board, and who submits evidence verified by oath and satisfactory to the Board that he or she:

(1) Is at least 18 years of age;

(2) Is of good moral character;

(3) Has received a doctoral degree based on a planned and directed program of studies in psychology from an institution of higher education. The degree program, wherever administratively housed, must be publicly identified and clearly labeled as a psychology program. The Board shall adopt rules implementing and defining these provisions, including, but not limited to, such factors as residence in the educational program, internship and related field experiences, number of course credits, course content, numbers and qualifications of faculty, and program identification and identity.

(4) Has had at least two years of acceptable and appropriate supervised experience germane to his or her training and intended area of practice as a psychologist as specified in G.S. 90-270.5(d).

(b) Licensed Psychological Associate. -

(1) The Board shall issue a permanent license to practice psychology to any applicant who pays an application fee and any applicable examination fee as specified in G.S. 90-270.18(b), who passes an examination in psychology as prescribed by the Board, and who submits evidence verified by oath and satisfactory to the Board that he or she:

a. Is at least 18 years of age;

b. Is of good moral character;

c. Has received a master's degree in psychology or a specialist degree in psychology from an institution of higher education. The degree program, wherever administratively housed, must be publicly identified and clearly labeled as a psychology program. The Board shall adopt rules implementing and defining these provisions, including, but not limited to, such factors as residence in the program, internship and related field experiences, number of course credits, course content, numbers and qualifications of faculty, and program identification and identity.

(2) Notwithstanding the provisions of this subsection, a licensed psychologist applicant who has met all requirements for licensure except passing the examination at the licensed psychologist level, may be issued a license as a licensed psychological associate without having a master's degree or specialist degree in psychology if the applicant passes the examination at the licensed psychological associate level.

(c) Foreign Graduates. - Applicants trained in institutions outside the United States, applying for licensure at either the licensed psychologist or licensed psychological associate level, must show satisfactory evidence of training and degrees substantially equivalent to those required of applicants trained within the United States, pursuant to Board rules and regulations.

(d) Prior Licensure. - A person who is licensed in good standing as a licensed practicing psychologist or psychological associate under the provisions of the Practicing Psychologist Licensing Act in effect immediately prior to the ratification of this Psychology Practice Act shall be deemed, as of October 1, 1993 to have met all requirements for licensure under this act and shall be eligible for renewal of licensure in accordance with the provisions of this act. (1967, c. 910, s. 11; 1971, c. 889, ss. 2, 3; 1975, c. 675, ss. 1, 2; 1977, c. 670, s. 7; 1979, c. 670, ss. 5, 6; 1979, 2nd Sess., c. 1176; 1981, c. 738, ss. 1, 2; 1983, c. 37, ss. 1, 2; c. 82, s. 4; 1985, c. 734, s. 7; 1987, c. 326, ss. 1, 2; c. 500, s. 1; 1989, c. 554; 1993, c. 375, s. 1; 1995, c. 509, s. 45.)

§ 90-270.12. Repealed by Session Laws 1977, c. 670, s. 8.

§ 90-270.13. Licensure of psychologists licensed or certified in other jurisdictions; licensure of diplomates of the American Board of Professional Psychology; reciprocity.

(a) Upon application and payment of the required fee, the Board shall grant permanent licensure at the appropriate level to any person who, at the time of application meets all of the following requirements:

(1) Is licensed or certified as a psychologist by a similar psychology licensing board in another jurisdiction.

(2) The license or certification is in good standing.

(3) Is a graduate of an institution of higher education.

(4) Who passes an examination prescribed by the Board.

(5) Meets the definition of a senior psychologist as that term is defined by the rules of the Board.

(a1) Upon application and payment of the required fee, the Board shall grant permanent licensure at the appropriate level to any person who, at the time of application, meets all of the following requirements:

(1) Is licensed or certified as a psychologist by a similar psychology licensing board in another jurisdiction.

(2) The license or certification is in good standing.

(3) Possesses a doctoral degree in psychology from an institution of higher education.

(4) Passes an examination prescribed by the Board.

(5) Has no unresolved complaints in any jurisdiction at the time of application in this State.

(6) Holds a current credential for psychology licensure mobility, as defined in rules adopted by the Board.

(b) The Board may establish formal written agreements of reciprocity with the psychology boards of other jurisdictions if the Board determines that the standards of the boards of the other jurisdictions are substantially equivalent to or greater than those required by this Article.

(c) The Board shall grant health services provider certification to any person licensed under the provisions of subsections (a) and (b) above when it determines that the applicant's training and experience are substantially equivalent to or greater than that specified in G.S. 90-270.20.

(d) Upon application and payment of the requisite fee, the Board shall waive the requirement of the national written examination to any person who is a diplomate in good standing of the American Board of Professional Psychology.

(e) The Board shall adopt rules implementing and defining these provisions, and, with respect to the senior psychologist, shall adopt rules including, but not limited to, such factors as educational background, professional experience, length and status of licensure, ethical conduct, and examination required.

(f) The Board may deny licensure to any person otherwise eligible for permanent licensure under this section upon documentation of conduct specified in G.S. 90-270.15. (1967, c. 910, s. 13; 1993, c. 375, s. 1; 2007-468, ss. 4-6.)

§ 90-270.14. Renewal of licenses; duplicate or replacement licenses.

(a) A license in effect on October 1, 1993, must be renewed on or before January 1, 1994. Thereafter, a license issued under this Article must be renewed biennially on or before the first day of October in each even-numbered year, the requirements for such renewal being:

(1) Each application for renewal must be made on a form prescribed by the Board and accompanied by a fee as specified in G.S. 90-270.18(b). If a license is not renewed on or before the renewal date, an additional fee shall be charged for late renewal as specified in G.S. 90-270.18(b).

(2) The Board may establish continuing education requirements as a condition for license renewal.

(b) A licensee may request the Board to issue a duplicate or replacement license for a fee as specified in G.S. 90-270.18(b). Upon receipt of the request and a showing of good cause for the issuance of a duplicate or replacement license, and the payment of the fee, the Board shall issue a duplicate or replacement license. (1967, c. 910, s. 14; 1971, c. 889, s. 1; 1975, c. 675, s. 3;

1979, c. 710; 1985, c. 734, s. 8; 1987, c. 500, s. 2; 1989 (Reg. Sess., 1990), c. 1029, s. 2; 1993, c. 375, s. 1.)

§ 90-270.15. Denial, suspension, or revocation of licenses and health services provider certification, and other disciplinary and remedial actions for violations of the Code of Conduct; relinquishing of license.

(a) Any applicant for licensure or health services provider certification and any person licensed or certified under this Article shall have behaved in conformity with the ethical and professional standards specified in this Code of Conduct and in the rules of the Board. The Board may deny, suspend, or revoke licensure and certification, and may discipline, place on probation, limit practice, and require examination, remediation, and rehabilitation, or any combination thereof, all as provided for in subsection (b) below. The Board shall act upon proof that the applicant or licensee engaged in illegal, immoral, dishonorable, unprofessional, or unethical conduct by violating any of the provisions of the Code of Conduct as follows:

(1) Has been convicted of a felony or entered a plea of guilty or nolo contendere to any felony charge;

(2) Has been convicted of or entered a plea of guilty or nolo contendere to any misdemeanor involving moral turpitude, misrepresentation or fraud in dealing with the public, or conduct otherwise relevant to fitness to practice psychology, or a misdemeanor charge reflecting the inability to practice psychology with due regard to the health and safety of clients or patients;

(3) Has engaged in fraud or deceit in securing or attempting to secure or renew a license or in securing or attempting to secure health services provider certification under this Article or has willfully concealed from the Board material information in connection with application for a license or health services provider certification, or for renewal of a license under this Article;

(4) Has practiced any fraud, deceit, or misrepresentation upon the public, the Board, or any individual in connection with the practice of psychology, the offer of psychological services, the filing of Medicare, Medicaid, or other claims to any third party payor, or in any manner otherwise relevant to fitness for the practice of psychology;

(5) Has made fraudulent, misleading, or intentionally or materially false statements pertaining to education, licensure, license renewal, certification as a health services provider, supervision, continuing education, any disciplinary actions or sanctions pending or occurring in any other jurisdiction, professional credentials, or qualifications or fitness for the practice of psychology to the public, any individual, the Board, or any other organization;

(6) Has had a license or certification for the practice of psychology in any other jurisdiction suspended or revoked, or has been disciplined by the licensing or certification board in any other jurisdiction for conduct which would subject him or her to discipline under this Article;

(7) Has violated any provision of this Article or of the duly adopted rules of the Board;

(8) Has aided or abetted the unlawful practice of psychology by any person not licensed by the Board;

(9) For a licensed psychologist, has provided health services without health services provider certification;

(10) Has been guilty of immoral, dishonorable, unprofessional, or unethical conduct as defined in this subsection, or in the then-current code of ethics of the American Psychological Association, except as the provisions of such code of ethics may be inconsistent and in conflict with the provisions of this Article, in which case, the provisions of this Article control;

(11) Has practiced psychology in such a manner as to endanger the welfare of clients or patients;

(12) Has demonstrated an inability to practice psychology with reasonable skill and safety by reason of illness, inebriation, misuse of drugs, narcotics, alcohol, chemicals, or any other substance affecting mental or physical functioning, or as a result of any mental or physical condition;

(13) Has practiced psychology or conducted research outside the boundaries of demonstrated competence or the limitations of education, training, or supervised experience;

(14) Has failed to use, administer, score, or interpret psychological assessment techniques, including interviewing and observation, in a competent

manner, or has provided findings or recommendations which do not accurately reflect the assessment data, or exceed what can reasonably be inferred, predicted, or determined from test, interview, or observational data;

(15) Has failed to provide competent diagnosis, counseling, treatment, consultation, or supervision, in keeping with standards of usual and customary practice in this State;

(16) In the absence of established standards, has failed to take all reasonable steps to ensure the competence of services;

(17) Has failed to maintain a clear and accurate case record which documents the following for each patient or client:

a. Presenting problems, diagnosis, or purpose of the evaluation, counseling, treatment, or other services provided;

b. Fees, dates of services, and itemized charges;

c. Summary content of each session of evaluation, counseling, treatment, or other services, except that summary content need not include specific information that may cause significant harm to any person if the information were released;

d. Test results or other findings, including basic test data; and

e. Copies of all reports prepared;

(18) Except when prevented from doing so by circumstances beyond the psychologist's control, has failed to retain securely and confidentially the complete case record for at least seven years from the date of the last provision of psychological services; or, except when prevented from doing so by circumstances beyond the psychologist's control, has failed to retain securely and confidentially the complete case record for three years from the date of the attainment of majority age by the patient or client or for at least seven years from the date of the last provision of psychological services, whichever is longer; or, except when prevented from doing so by circumstances beyond the psychologist's control, has failed to retain securely and confidentially the complete case record indefinitely if there are pending legal or ethical matters or if there is any other compelling circumstance;

(19) Has failed to cooperate with other psychologists or other professionals to the potential or actual detriment of clients, patients, or other recipients of service, or has behaved in ways which substantially impede or impair other psychologists' or other professionals' abilities to perform professional duties;

(20) Has exercised undue influence in such a manner as to exploit the client, patient, student, supervisee, or trainee for the financial or other personal advantage or gratification of the psychologist or a third party;

(21) Has harassed or abused, sexually or otherwise, a client, patient, student, supervisee, or trainee;

(22) Has failed to cooperate with or to respond promptly, completely, and honestly to the Board, to credentials committees, or to ethics committees of professional psychological associations, hospitals, or other health care organizations or educational institutions, when those organizations or entities have jurisdiction; or has failed to cooperate with institutional review boards or professional standards review organizations, when those organizations or entities have jurisdiction; or

(23) Has refused to appear before the Board after having been ordered to do so in writing by the Chair;

(b) Upon proof that an applicant or licensee under this Article has engaged in any of the prohibited actions specified in subsection (a) of this section, the Board may, in lieu of denial, suspension, or revocation, issue a formal reprimand or formally censure the applicant or licensee, may place the applicant or licensee upon probation with such appropriate conditions upon the continued practice as the Board may deem advisable, may require examination, remediation, or rehabilitation for the applicant or licensee, including care, counseling, or treatment by a professional or professionals designated or approved by the Board, the expense to be borne by the applicant or licensee, may require supervision for the services provided by the applicant or licensee by a licensee designated or approved by the Board, the expense to be borne by the applicant or licensee, may limit or circumscribe the practice of psychology provided by the applicant or licensee with respect to the extent, nature, or location of the services provided, as the Board deems advisable, or may discipline and impose any appropriate combination of the foregoing. In addition, the Board may impose such conditions of probation or restrictions upon continued practice at the conclusion of a period of suspension or as requirements for the restoration of a revoked or suspended license. In lieu of or in connection with any disciplinary proceedings or investigation, the Board may enter into a consent order relative to discipline, supervision, probation, remediation, rehabilitation, or practice limitation of a licensee or applicant for a license.

(c)   The Board may assess costs of disciplinary action against an applicant or licensee found to be in violation of this Article.

(d)   When considering the issue of whether or not an applicant or licensee is physically or mentally capable of practicing psychology with reasonable skill and safety with patients or clients, then, upon a showing of probable cause to the Board that the applicant or licensee is not capable of practicing psychology with reasonable skill and safety with patients or clients, the Board may petition a court of competent jurisdiction to order the applicant or licensee in question to submit to a psychological evaluation by a psychologist to determine psychological status or a physical evaluation by a physician to determine physical condition, or both. Such psychologist or physician shall be designated by the court. The expenses of such evaluations shall be borne by the Board. Where the applicant or licensee raises the issue of mental or physical competence or appeals a decision regarding mental or physical competence, the applicant or licensee shall be permitted to obtain an evaluation at the applicant's or licensee's expense. If the Board suspects the objectivity or adequacy of the evaluation, the Board may compel an evaluation by its designated practitioners at its own expense.

(e)   Except as provided otherwise in this Article, the procedure for revocation, suspension, denial, limitations of the license or health services provider certification, or other disciplinary, remedial, or rehabilitative actions, shall be in accordance with the provisions of Chapter 150B of the General Statutes. The Board is required to provide the opportunity for a hearing under Chapter 150B to any applicant whose license or health services provider certification is denied or to whom licensure or health services provider certification is offered subject to any restrictions, probation, disciplinary action, remediation, or other conditions or limitations, or to any licensee before revoking, suspending, or restricting a license or health services provider certificate or imposing any other disciplinary action or remediation. If the applicant or licensee waives the opportunity for a hearing, the Board's denial, revocation, suspension, or other proposed action becomes final without a hearing's having been conducted. Notwithstanding the foregoing, no applicant or licensee is entitled to a hearing for failure to pass an examination. In any proceeding before the Board, in any record of any hearing before the Board, in any complaint or notice of charges against any licensee or applicant for licensure, and in any decision rendered by the Board, the Board may withhold from public disclosure the identity of any clients or patients who have not consented to the public disclosure of psychological services' having been provided by the licensee or applicant. The Board may close a hearing to the public and receive in closed session evidence involving or concerning the treatment of or delivery of psychological services to a client or a patient who has not consented to the public disclosure of such treatment or services as may be necessary for the protection and rights of such patient or client of the accused applicant or licensee and the full presentation of relevant evidence. All records, papers, and other documents containing information collected and compiled by or on behalf of the Board, as a result of investigations, inquiries, or interviews conducted in connection with licensing or disciplinary matters will not be considered public records within the meaning of Chapter 132 of the General Statutes; provided, however, that any notice or statement of charges against any licensee or applicant, or any notice to any licensee or applicant of a hearing in any proceeding, or any decision rendered in connection with a hearing in any proceeding, shall be a public record within the meaning of Chapter 132 of the General Statutes, notwithstanding that it may contain information collected and compiled as a result of such investigation, inquiry, or hearing except that identifying information concerning the treatment of or delivery of services to a patient or client who has not consented to the public disclosure of such treatment or services may be deleted; and provided, further, that if any such record, paper, or other document containing information theretofore collected and compiled by or on behalf of the Board, as hereinbefore provided, is received and admitted in evidence in any hearing before the Board, it shall thereupon be a public record within the meaning of Chapter 132 of the General Statutes, subject to any deletions of identifying information concerning the treatment of or delivery of psychological services to a patient or client who has not consented to the public disclosure of such treatment or services.

(f)   A license and a health services provider certificate issued under this Article are suspended automatically by operation of law after failure to renew a license for a period of more than sixty days after the renewal date. The Board may reinstate a license and a health services provider certificate suspended under this subsection upon payment of a fee as specified in G.S. 90-270.18(b), and may require that the applicant file a new application, furnish new supervisory reports or references or otherwise update his or her credentials, or submit to examination for reinstatement. Notwithstanding any provision to the contrary, the Board retains full jurisdiction to investigate alleged violations of this Article by any person whose license is suspended under this subsection and, upon proof of any violation of this Article by any such person, the Board may take disciplinary action as authorized by this section.

(g)   A person whose license or health services provider certification has been denied or revoked may reapply to the Board for licensure or certification after the passage of one calendar year from the date of such denial or revocation.

(h)   A licensee may, with the consent of the Board, voluntarily relinquish his or her license or health services provider certificate at any time. The Board may delay or refuse the granting of its consent as it may deem necessary in order to investigate any pending complaint, allegation, or issue regarding violation of any provision of this Article by the licensee. Notwithstanding any provision to the contrary, the Board retains full jurisdiction to investigate alleged violations of this Article by any person whose license is relinquished under this subsection and, upon proof of any violation of this Article by any such person, the Board may take disciplinary action as authorized by this section.

(i)   The Board may adopt such rules as it deems reasonable and appropriate to interpret and implement the provisions of this section. (1967, c. 910, s. 15; 1973, c. 1331, s. 3; 1977, c. 670, s. 9; 1979, c. 1005, s. 4; 1985, c. 734, s. 9; 1987, c. 827, s. 1; 1991, c. 239, s. 1; c. 761, ss. 14-16; 1993, c. 375, s. 1; 1993 (Reg. Sess., 1994), c. 570, s. 7.)

§ 90-270.16. Prohibited acts.

(a)   Except as permitted in G.S. 90-270.4 and G.S. 90-270.5, it shall be a violation of this Article for any person not licensed in accordance with the provisions of this Article to represent himself or herself as a psychologist, licensed psychologist, licensed psychological associate, or health services provider in psychology.

(b)   Except as provided in G.S. 90-270.4 and G.S. 90-270.5, it shall be a violation of this Article for any person not licensed in accordance with the provisions of this Article to practice or offer to practice psychology as defined in this Article whether as an individual, firm, partnership, corporation, agency, or other entity.

(c) Except as provided in G.S. 90-270.4 and G.S. 90-270.5, it shall be a violation of this Article for any person not licensed in accordance with the provisions of this Article to use a title or description of services including the term "psychology," or any of its derivatives such as "psychologic", "psychological", or "psychologist", singly or in conjunction with modifiers such as "licensed", "practicing", "certified", or "registered". (1967, c. 910, s. 16; 1979, c. 670, s. 3; c. 1005, s. 3; 1993, c. 375, s. 1.)

§ 90-270.17. Violations and penalties.

Any person who violates G.S. 90-270.16 is guilty of a Class 2 misdemeanor. Each violation shall constitute a separate offense. (1967, c. 910, s. 17; 1993, c. 539, s. 646; 1994, Ex. Sess., c. 24, s. 14(c).)

§ 90-270.18. Disposition and schedule of fees.

(a) Except for fees paid directly to the vendor as provided in subdivision (b)(2) of this section, all fees derived from the operation of this Article shall be deposited with the State Treasurer to the credit of a revolving fund for the use of the Board in carrying out its functions. All fees derived from the operation of this Article shall be nonrefundable.

(b) Fees for activities specified by this Article are as follows:

(1) Application fees for licensed psychologists and licensed psychological associates per G.S. 90-270.11(a) and (b)(1), or G.S. 90-270.13, shall not exceed one hundred dollars ($100.00).

(2) Fees for the national written examination shall be the cost of the examination as set by the vendor plus an additional fee not to exceed fifty dollars ($50.00). The Board may require applicants to pay the fee directly to the vendor.

(3) Fees for additional examinations shall be as prescribed by the Board.

(4) Fees for the renewal of licenses, per G.S. 90-270.14(a)(1), shall not exceed two hundred fifty dollars ($250.00) per biennium. This fee may not be prorated.

(5) Late fees for license renewal, per G.S. 90-270.14(a)(1), shall be twenty-five dollars ($25.00).

(6) Fees for the reinstatement of a license, per G.S. 90-270.15(f), shall not exceed one hundred dollars ($100.00).

(7) Fees for a duplicate license, per G.S. 90-270.14(b), shall be twenty-five dollars ($25.00).

(8) Fees for a temporary license, per G.S. 90-270.5(f) and 90-270.5(g), shall be thirty-five dollars ($35.00).

(9) Application fees for a health services provider certificate, per G.S. 90-270.20, shall be fifty dollars ($50.00).

(c) The Board may specify reasonable charges for duplication services, materials, and returned bank items in its rules. (1967, c. 910, s. 19; 1993, c. 257, s. 5; c. 375, s. 1; 2003-368, s. 4.)

§ 90-270.19. Injunctive authority.

The Board may apply to the superior court for an injunction to prevent violations of this Article or of any rules enacted pursuant thereto. The court is empowered to grant such injunctions regardless of whether criminal prosecution or other action has been or may be instituted as a result of such violation. (1983, c. 82, s. 6.)

§ 90-270.20. Provision of health services; certification as health services provider.

(a) Health services, as defined in G.S. 90-270.2(4) and G.S. 90-270.2(8), may be provided by qualified licensed psychological associates, qualified licensed psychologists holding provisional, temporary, or permanent licenses, or qualified applicants. Qualified licensed psychological associates, qualified licensed psychologists holding provisional or temporary licenses, or qualified applicants may provide health services only under supervision as specified in the duly adopted rules of the Board.

(b)   After January 1, 1995, any licensed psychologist who is qualified by education, who holds permanent licensure and a doctoral degree, and who provides or offers to provide health services to the public must be certified as a health services provider psychologist (HSP-P) by the Board. The Board shall certify as health services provider psychologists those applicants who shall demonstrate at least two years of acceptable supervised health services experience, of which at least one year is postdoctoral. The Board shall specify the format, setting, content, and organization of the supervised health services experience or program. The Board may, upon verification of supervised experience and the meeting of all requirements as a licensed psychologist, issue the license and certificate simultaneously. An application fee, as specified in G.S. 90-270.18(b)(9), must be paid.

(c)   After January 1, 1995, any licensed psychological associate who is qualified by education may be granted certification as a health services provider psychological associate (HSP-PA). The Board may, upon verification of qualifications and the meeting of all requirements as a licensed psychological associate, issue the license and certificate simultaneously. An application fee, as specified in G.S. 90-270.18(b)(9), must be paid.

(d)   After January 1, 1995, any licensed psychologist holding a provisional license who is qualified by education may be granted certification as a health services provider psychologist (provisional) (HSP-PP) by the Board. The Board may, upon verification of qualifications and the meeting of all requirements for a provisional license, issue the license and certificate simultaneously. An application fee, as specified in G.S. 90-270.18(b)(9), must be paid.

(e)   Notwithstanding the provisions of subsection (b) of this section, if application is made to the Board before June 30, 1994, by a licensed psychologist who is listed in the National Register of Health Services Providers in Psychology, or who holds permanent licensure and who can demonstrate that he or she has been engaged acceptably in the provision of health services for two years or its equivalent, that licensed psychologist shall be certified as a health services provider psychologist. The applicant, in order to demonstrate two years of acceptable experience or its equivalent, must meet one of the following conditions:

(1) The applicant is a diplomate in good standing of the American Board of Professional Psychology in any of the areas of professional practice deemed appropriate by the Board;

(2) The applicant has the equivalent of two years of acceptable full-time experience, one of which was postdoctoral, at sites where health services are provided;

(3) The applicant submits evidence satisfactory to the Board demonstrating that he or she has been engaged acceptably for the equivalent of at least two years full-time in the provision of health services; or

(4) Any other conditions that the Board may deem acceptable.

(f) Notwithstanding the provisions of subsection (c) of this section, if application is made to the Board before June 30, 1994, by a licensed psychological associate who can demonstrate that he or she has been engaged acceptably in the provision of health services under supervision for two years or its equivalent, that licensed psychological associate shall be certified as a health services provider psychological associate.

(g) The Board shall have the authority to deny, revoke, or suspend the health services provider certificate issued pursuant to these subsections upon a finding that the psychologist has not behaved in conformity with the ethical and professional standards prescribed in G.S. 90-270.15. (1985, c. 734, s. 10; 1993, c. 375, s. 1; 1993 (Reg. Sess., 1994), c. 569, s. 13.)

§ 90-270.21. Ancillary services.

A psychologist licensed under this Article may employ or supervise unlicensed individuals who assist in the provision of psychological services to clients, patients, and their families. The Board may adopt rules specifying the titles used by such individuals, the numbers employed or supervised by any particular psychologist, the activities in which they may engage, the nature and extent of supervision which must be provided, the qualifications of such individuals, and the nature of the responsibility assumed by the employing or supervising psychologist. (1993, c. 375, s. 1.)

§ 90-270.22. Criminal history record checks of applicants for licensure and licensees.

(a)   The Board may request that an applicant for licensure or reinstatement of a license or that a licensed psychologist or psychological associate currently under investigation by the Board for allegedly violating this Article consent to a criminal history record check. Refusal to consent to a criminal history record check may constitute grounds for the Board to deny licensure or reinstatement of a license to an applicant or take disciplinary action against a licensee, including revocation of a license. The Board shall be responsible for providing to the North Carolina Department of Justice the fingerprints of the applicant or licensee to be checked, a form signed by the applicant or licensee consenting to the criminal record check and the use of fingerprints and other identifying information required by the State or National Repositories, and any additional information required by the Department of Justice. The Board shall keep all information obtained pursuant to this section confidential.

The Board shall collect any fees required by the Department of Justice and shall remit the fees to the Department of Justice for the cost of conducting the criminal history record check.

(b)   Limited Immunity. - The Board, its officers and employees, acting reasonably and in compliance with this section, shall be immune from civil liability for denying licensure or reinstatement of a license to an applicant or the revocation of a license or other discipline of a licensee based on information provided in the applicant's or licensee's criminal history record check. (2006-175, s. 2.)

§ 90-270.23. Reserved for future codification purposes.

Article 18B.

Physical Therapy.

§ 90-270.24. Definitions.

In this Article, unless the context otherwise requires, the following definitions shall apply:

(1)   "Board" means the North Carolina Board of Physical Therapy Examiners.

(2)   "Physical therapist" means any person who practices physical therapy in accordance with the provisions of this Article.

(3)   "Physical therapist assistant" means any person who assists in the practice of physical therapy in accordance with the provisions of this Article, and who works under the supervision of a physical therapist by performing such patient-related activities assigned by a physical therapist which are commensurate with the physical therapist assistant's education and training, but an assistant's work shall not include the interpretation and implementation of referrals from licensed medical doctors or dentists, the performance of evaluations, or the determination or major modification of treatment programs.

(4)   "Physical therapy" means the evaluation or treatment of any person by the use of physical, chemical, or other properties of heat, light, water, electricity, sound, massage, or therapeutic exercise, or other rehabilitative procedures, with or without assistive devices, for the purposes of preventing, correcting, or alleviating a physical or mental disability. Physical therapy includes the performance of specialized tests of neuromuscular function, administration of specialized therapeutic procedures, interpretation and implementation of referrals from licensed medical doctors or dentists, and establishment and modification of physical therapy programs for patients. Evaluation and treatment of patients may involve physical measures, methods, or procedures as are found commensurate with physical therapy education and training and generally or specifically authorized by regulations of the Board. Physical therapy education and training shall include study of the skeletal manifestations of systemic disease. Physical therapy does not include the application of roentgen rays or radioactive materials, surgery, manipulation of the spine unless prescribed by a physician licensed to practice medicine in North Carolina, or medical diagnosis of disease.

(5)   "Physical therapy aide" means any nonlicensed person who aids in the practice of physical therapy in accordance with the provisions of this Article, and

who at all times acts under the orders, direction, and on-site supervision of a licensed physical therapist or physical therapist assistant. An aide may perform physical therapy related activities which are assigned and are commensurate with an aide's training and abilities, but an aide's work shall not include the interpretation and implementation of referrals from licensed medical doctors or dentists, the performance of evaluations, the determination and modification of treatment programs, or any independent performance of any physical therapy procedures. (1951, c. 1131, s. 1; 1969, c. 556; 1979, c. 487; 1985, c. 701, s. 1.)

§ 90-270.25. Board of Examiners.

The North Carolina Board of Physical Therapy Examiners is hereby created. The Board shall consist of eight members, including one medical doctor licensed and residing in North Carolina, four physical therapists, two physical therapist assistants, and one public member. The public member shall be appointed by the Governor and shall be a person who is not licensed under Chapter 90 who shall represent the interest of the public at large. The medical doctor, physical therapists, and physical therapists assistants shall be appointed by the Governor from a list compiled by the North Carolina Physical Therapy Association, Inc., following the use of a nomination procedure made available to all physical therapists and physical therapist assistants licensed and residing in North Carolina. In soliciting nominations and compiling its list, the Association will give consideration to geographic distribution, practice setting (institution, independent, academic, etc.), and other factors that will promote representation of all aspects of physical therapy practice on the Board. The records of the operation of the nomination procedure shall be filed with the Board, to be available for a period of six months following nomination, for reasonable inspection by any licensed practitioner. Each physical therapist member of the Board shall be licensed and reside in this State; provided that the physical therapist shall have not less than three years' experience as a physical therapist immediately preceding appointment and shall be actively engaged in the practice of physical therapy in North Carolina during incumbency. Each physical therapist assistant member shall be licensed and reside in this State; provided that the physical therapist assistant shall have not less than three years' experience as a physical therapist assistant immediately preceding appointment and shall be actively engaged in practice as a physical therapist assistant in North Carolina during incumbency.

Members shall be appointed to serve three-year terms, or until their successors are appointed, to commence on January 1 in respective years. In the event that a member of the Board for any reason shall become ineligible to or cannot complete a term of office, another appointment shall be made by the Governor, in accordance with the procedure stated above, to fill the remainder of the term. No member may serve for more than two successive three-year terms.

The Board may immediately remove a member from the Board if the member is found by the remainder of the Board to have (i) ceased to meet the qualifications specified in this section, (ii) failed to attend three successive Board meetings without just cause, (iii) violated any of the provisions of this Article or rules adopted by the Board, or (iv) otherwise engaged in immoral, dishonorable, unprofessional, or unethical conduct. Before removing a Board member for immoral, dishonorable, unprofessional, or unethical conduct, the Board shall further find that the relevant conduct has compromised the integrity of the Board.

The Board each year shall designate one of its physical therapist members as chairman and one member as secretary-treasurer. Each member of the Board shall receive such per diem compensation and reimbursement for travel and subsistence as shall be set for licensing boards generally. (1951, c. 1131, s. 2; 1969, c. 445, s. 7; c. 556; 1979, c. 487; 1981, c. 765, s. 1; 1981 (Reg. Sess., 1982), c. 1191, s. 82; 1985, c. 701, s. 1; 2013-312, s. 1.)

§ 90-270.26. Powers of the Board.

The Board shall have the following general powers and duties:

(1) Examine and determine the qualifications and fitness of applicants for a license to practice physical therapy in this State.

(2) Issue, renew, deny, suspend, or revoke licenses to practice physical therapy in this State, or reprimand or otherwise discipline licensed physical therapists and physical therapist assistants.

(3) Conduct confidential investigations for the purpose of determining whether violations of this Article or grounds for disciplining licensed physical therapists or physical therapist assistants exist. Investigation records shall not be considered public records under Chapter 132 of the General Statutes. These

records are privileged and are not subject to discovery, subpoena, or other means of legal compulsion for release to any person other than the Board or its employees or consultants, except as provided in this section. However, any Board decisions rendered, hearing notices and statements of charges, and any material received and admitted into evidence at Board hearings shall be public records, regardless of whether the notices, statements, or materials are developed or compiled as a result of an investigation; provided that identifying information concerning the treatment or delivery of professional services to a patient who has not consented to its public disclosure may be deleted or redacted.

(3a) Establish mechanisms for assessing the continuing competence of licensed physical therapists or physical therapist assistants to engage in the practice of physical therapy, including approving rules requiring licensees to periodically, or in response to complaints or incident reports, submit to the Board: (i) evidence of continuing education experiences; (ii) evidence of minimum standard accomplishments; or (iii) evidence of compliance with other Board-approved measures, audits, or evaluations; and specify remedial actions if necessary or desirable to obtain license renewal or reinstatement.

(4) Employ such professional, clerical or special personnel necessary to carry out the provisions of this Article, and may purchase or rent necessary office space, equipment and supplies.

(5) Conduct administrative hearings in accordance with Chapter 150B of the General Statutes when a "contested case" as defined in G.S. 150B-2(2) arises under this Article.

(6) Appoint from its own membership one or more members to act as representatives of the Board at any meeting where such representation is deemed desirable.

(7) Establish reasonable fees for applications for examination, certificates of licensure and renewal, and other services provided by the Board.

(8) Adopt, amend, or repeal any rules or regulations necessary to carry out the purposes of this Article and the duties and responsibilities of the Board.

(9) Request the Department of Justice to provide criminal history record checks pursuant to G.S. 90-270.29A in connection with licensure.

(10) Issue subpoenas, on signature of the Board Chair or Executive Director, to compel the attendance of any witness or the production of any documents relative to investigations or Board proceedings. Upon written request, the Board shall revoke a subpoena if, upon a hearing, it finds that the evidence sought does not relate to a matter in issue, the subpoena does not describe with sufficient particularity the evidence sought, or for any other reason in law the subpoena is invalid.

(11) Establish or participate in programs for aiding in the recovery and rehabilitation of physical therapists and physical therapist assistants who experience chemical or alcohol addiction or abuse or mental health problems.

(12) Acquire, hold, rent, encumber, alienate, and otherwise deal with real property in the same manner as a private person or corporation, subject only to approval of the Governor and the Council of State. Collateral pledged by the Board for an encumbrance is limited to the assets, income, and revenues of the Board.

The powers and duties enumerated above are granted for the purpose of enabling the Board to safeguard the public health, safety and welfare against unqualified or incompetent practitioners of physical therapy, and are to be liberally construed to accomplish this objective. In instances where the Board makes a decision to discipline physical therapists or physical therapist assistants under powers set out by any of subsections (2) through (5) of this section, it may as part of its decision charge the reasonable costs of investigation and hearing to the person disciplined. (1979, c. 487; 1985, c. 701, s. 1; 1987, c. 827, ss. 1, 77; 2006-144, s. 1; 2013-312, s. 2.)

§ 90-270.27. Records to be kept; copies of record.

The Board shall keep a record of proceedings under this Article and a record of all persons licensed under it. The record shall show the name, last known place of business and last known place of residence, and date and number of licensure certificate as a physical therapist or physical therapist assistant, for every living licensee. Any interested person in the State is entitled to obtain a copy of that record on application to the Board and payment of such reasonable charge as may be fixed by it based on the costs involved. (1951, c. 1131, s. 12; 1969, c. 556; 1979, c. 487; 1985, c. 701, s. 1.)

§ 90-270.28. Disposition of funds.

All fees and other moneys collected and received by the Board shall be used for the purposes of implementing this Article. The financial records of the Board shall be subjected to an annual audit and paid for out of the funds of the Board. (1951, c. 1131, s. 14; 1969, c. 556; 1979, c. 487; 1985, c. 701, s. 1.)

§ 90-270.29. Qualifications of applicants for examination; application; fee.

Any person who desires to be licensed under this Article and who:

(1)   Is of good moral character;

(2)   If an applicant for physical therapy licensure, has been graduated from a physical therapy program accredited by an agency recognized by either the U.S. Office of Education or the Council on Postsecondary Accreditation; and

(3)   If an applicant for physical therapist assistant licensure, has been graduated from a physical therapist assistant educational program accredited by an agency recognized by either the U.S. Office of Education or the Council on Postsecondary Accreditation;

may make application on a form furnished by the Board for examination for licensure as a physical therapist or physical therapist assistant. At the time of making such application, the applicant shall pay to the secretary-treasurer of the Board the fee prescribed by the Board, no portion of which shall be returned. (1951, c. 1131, s. 3; 1959, c. 630; 1969, c. 556; 1979, c. 487; 1985, c. 701, s. 1.)

§ 90-270.29A. Criminal history record checks of applicants for licensure.

(a)   All applicants for licensure shall consent to a criminal history record check. Refusal to consent to a criminal history record check may constitute grounds for the Board to deny licensure to an applicant. The Board shall be responsible for providing to the North Carolina Department of Justice the fingerprints of the applicant to be checked, a form signed by the applicant consenting to the criminal history record check and the use of fingerprints and other identifying information required by the State or National Repositories, and any additional information required by the Department of Justice. The Board shall keep all information obtained pursuant to this section confidential.

(b)   The cost of the criminal history record check and the fingerprinting shall be borne by the applicant. The Board shall collect any fees required by the Department of Justice and shall remit the fees to the Department of Justice for expenses associated with conducting the criminal history record check.

(c)   If an applicant's criminal history record reveals one or more criminal convictions, the conviction shall not automatically bar licensure. The Board shall consider all of the following factors regarding the conviction:

(1)   The level of seriousness of the crime.

(2)   The date of the crime.

(3)   The age of the person at the time of the conviction.

(4)   The circumstances surrounding the commission of the crime, if known.

(5)   The nexus between the criminal conduct of the person and the job duties of the position to be filled.

(6)   The person's prison, jail, probation, parole, rehabilitation, and employment records since the date the crime was committed.

If, after reviewing the factors, the Board determines that any of the grounds set forth in the subdivisions of G.S. 90-270.36 exist, the Board may deny licensure of the applicant. The Board may disclose to the applicant information contained in the criminal history record that is relevant to the denial if disclosure of the information is permitted by applicable State and federal law. The Board shall not provide a copy of the criminal history record to the applicant. The applicant shall have the right to appear before the Board to appeal the Board's decision. However, an appearance before the full Board shall constitute an exhaustion of administrative remedies in accordance with Chapter 150B of the General Statutes.

(d) The Board, its officers, and employees, acting in good faith and in compliance with this section, shall be immune from civil liability for denying licensure to an applicant based on information provided in the applicant's criminal history record. (2013-312, s. 3.)

§ 90-270.30. Licensure of foreign-trained physical therapists.

Any person who has been trained as a physical therapist or physical therapist assistant in a foreign country and desires to be licensed under this Article and who:

(1) Is of good moral character;

(2) Holds a diploma from an educational program for physical therapists or physical therapist assistants approved by the Board;

(3) Submits documentary evidence to the Board of completion of a course of instruction substantially equivalent to that obtained by an applicant for licensure under G.S. 90-270.29; and

(4) Demonstrates satisfactory proof of proficiency in the English language; may make application on a form furnished by the Board for examination as a foreign-trained physical therapist or physical therapist assistant. At the time of making such application, the applicant shall pay to the secretary-treasurer of the Board the fee prescribed by the Board, no portion of which shall be returned. (1959, c. 630; 1969, c. 556; 1979, c. 487; 1985, c. 701, s. 1; 2013-312, s. 4.)

§ 90-270.31. Certificates of licensure.

(a) The Board shall furnish a certificate of licensure to each applicant successfully passing the examination for licensure as a physical therapist or physical therapist assistant, respectively. Upon receipt of satisfactory evidence that an applicant has graduated, within six months prior to application, from a physical therapy or physical therapy assistant program accredited as required under G.S. 90-270.29, the Board may authorize the applicant to perform as a physical therapist or physical therapist assistant in this State, but only under the immediate supervision of a physical therapist licensed in this State, until a formal decision by the Board on the application for license. If a new graduate applicant that has been authorized to perform under supervision by a licensed physical therapist fails (without due cause as determined in the Board's discretion) to take the next succeeding examination, or if the applicant fails to pass the examination, and consequently does not become licensed, the authorization for the applicant to perform under supervision shall expire. Applicants approved by the Board for performance as physical therapists or physical therapist assistants while their applications are pending under circumstances described in this subsection shall be referred to as Physical Therapist Graduate or Physical Therapist Assistant Graduate.

(b)   The Board shall furnish a certificate of licensure to any person who is a physical therapist or physical therapist assistant registered or licensed under the laws of another state or territory, if the individual's qualifications were at the date of his registration or licensure substantially equal to the requirements under this Article. When making such application, the applicant shall pay to the secretary-treasurer of the Board the fee prescribed by the Board, no portion of which shall be returned. (1951, c. 1131, ss. 4, 6; 1959, c. 630; 1969, c. 556; 1979, c. 487; 1985, c. 701, s. 1.)

§ 90-270.32. Renewal of license; lapse; revival.

(a)   Every licensed physical therapist or physical therapist assistant shall, during the month of January of every year, apply to the Board for a renewal of licensure and pay to the secretary-treasurer the prescribed fee. Licenses that are not so renewed shall automatically lapse. The Board may decline to renew licenses of physical therapists or physical therapist assistants for failure to comply with any required continuing competency measures.

(b)   The manner in which lapsed licenses shall be revived, reinstated, or extended shall be established by the Board in its discretion. (1951, c. 1131, s. 7; 1959, c. 630; 1969, c. 556; 1979, c. 487; 1985, c. 701, s. 1; 2006-144, s. 2.)

§ 90-270.33. Fees.

The Board may collect fees established by its rules, but those fees shall not exceed the following schedule for the specified items:

(1)....... Each application for licensure..
$150.00

(2)....... License renewal...
$120.00

(3)....... Transfer/verification/replace certificate...
$30.00

(4)....... Examination retake..
$60.00

(5)....... Late renewal..
$20.00

(6)....... Licensure revival (in addition to renewal)...
$30.00

(7)....... Directory..
$10.00

(8)....... Licensee lists or labels..
60.00

In all instances where the Board uses the services of a national testing service for preparation, administration, or grading of examinations, the Board may charge the applicant the actual cost of the examination services, in addition to its other fees. (1951, c. 1131, s. 2; 1969, c. 445, s. 7; c. 556; 1979, c. 487; 1985, c. 161; c. 701, s. 1; 1999-345, s. 1.)

§ 90-270.34. Exemptions from licensure; certain practices exempted.

(a) The following persons shall be permitted to practice physical therapy or assist in the practice in this State without obtaining a license under this Article upon the terms and conditions specified herein:

(1) Students enrolled in accredited physical therapist or physical therapist assistant educational programs, while engaged in completing a clinical

requirement for graduation, which must be performed under the supervision of a licensed physical therapist;

(2)   Physical therapists licensed in other jurisdictions while enrolled in graduate educational programs in this State that include the evaluation and treatment of patients as part of their experience required for credit, so long as the student is not at the same time gainfully employed in this State as a physical therapist;

(3)   Practitioners of physical therapy employed in the Armed Forces of the United States, United States Public Health Service, Veterans Administration or other federal agency, to the extent permitted under federal law, so long as the practitioner limits services to those directly relating to work with the employing government agency;

(4)   Physical therapists or physical therapist assistants licensed in other jurisdictions who are teaching or participating in special physical therapy education projects, demonstrations or courses in this State, in which their participation in the evaluation and treatment of patients is minimal;

(5)   A physical therapy aide while in the performance of those acts and practices specified in G.S. 90-270.24(5);

(6)   Persons authorized to perform as physical therapists or physical therapist assistants under the provision of G.S. 90-270.31;

(7)   Physical therapists or physical therapist assistants who are licensed in another jurisdiction of the United States or credentialed in another country, if that person by contract or employment is providing physical therapy to individuals affiliated with or employed by established athletic teams, athletic organizations, or performing arts companies temporarily practicing, competing, or performing in this State for no more than 60 days in a calendar year;

(8)   Physical therapists or physical therapist assistants licensed in another jurisdiction of the United States who enter this State to provide physical therapy during a declared local, State, or national disaster or emergency. The exemption applies no longer than the standard annual renewal time in the State. To be eligible for the exemption, the licensee shall notify the Board of the licensee's intent to practice physical therapy pursuant to this subdivision;

(9) Physical therapists or physical therapist assistants licensed in another jurisdiction of the United States who are forced to leave their residence or place of employment due to a declared local, State, or national disaster or emergency and, due to such displacement, need to practice physical therapy. The exemption applies no longer than the standard annual renewal time but may be renewed by the Board for additional periods. To be eligible for the exemption, the licensee shall notify the Board of the licensee's intent to practice physical therapy pursuant to this subdivision.

(b) Nothing in this Article shall be construed to prohibit:

(1) Any act in the lawful practice of a profession by a person duly licensed in this State;

(2) The administration of simple massages and the operation of health clubs so long as not intended to constitute or represent the practice of physical therapy. (1951, c. 1131, ss. 9, 11; 1959, c. 630; 1969, c. 556; 1979, c. 487; 1985, c. 701, s. 1; 2011-183, s. 66; 2013-312, s. 5.)

§ 90-270.35. Unlawful practice.

Except as otherwise authorized in this Article, if any person, firm, or corporation shall:

(1) Practice, attempt to practice, teach, consult, or supervise in physical therapy, or hold out any person as being able to do any of these things in this State, without first having obtained a license or authorization from the Board for the person performing services or being so held out;

(2) Use in connection with any person's name any letters, words, numerical codes, or insignia indicating or implying that the person is a physical therapist or physical therapist assistant, or applicant with "Graduate" status, unless the person is licensed or authorized in accordance with this Article;

(3) Practice or attempt to practice physical therapy with a revoked, lapsed, or suspended license;

(4) Practice physical therapy and fail to refer to a licensed medical doctor or dentist any patient whose medical condition should have, at the time of

evaluation or treatment, been determined to be beyond the scope of practice of a physical therapist;

(5)   Aid, abet, or assist any unlicensed person to practice physical therapy in violation of this Article; or

(6)   Violate any of the provisions of this Article;

said person, firm, or corporation shall be guilty of a Class 1 misdemeanor. Each act of such unlawful practice shall constitute a distinct and separate offense. (1951, c. 1131, ss. 9, 11; 1969, c. 556; 1979, c. 487; 1985, c. 701, s. 1; 1993, c. 539, s. 647; 1994, Ex. Sess., c. 24, s. 14(c).)

§ 90-270.36. Grounds for disciplinary action.

Grounds for disciplinary action shall include but not be limited to the following:

(1)   The employment of fraud, deceit or misrepresentation in obtaining or attempting to obtain a license, or the renewal thereof;

(2)   The use of drugs or intoxicating liquors to an extent which affects professional competency;

(3)   Conviction of an offense under any municipal, State, or federal narcotic or controlled substance law, until proof of rehabilitation can be established;

(4)   Conviction of a felony or other public offense involving moral turpitude, until proof of rehabilitation can be established;

(5)   An adjudication of insanity or incompetency, until proof of recovery from the condition can be established;

(6)   Engaging in any act or practice violative of any of the provisions of this Article or of any of the rules and regulations adopted by the Board, or aiding, abetting or assisting any other person in the violation of the same;

(7)   The commission of an act or acts of malpractice, gross negligence or incompetence in the practice of physical therapy;

(8) Practice as a licensed physical therapist or physical therapist assistant without a valid certificate of renewal;

(9) Engaging in conduct that could result in harm or injury to the public. (1951, c. 1131, s. 8; 1959, c. 630; 1969, c. 556; 1973, c. 1331, s. 3; 1979, c. 487; 1985, c. 701, s. 1.)

§ 90-270.37. Enjoining illegal practices.

(a) The Board may, if it finds that any person is violating any of the provisions of this Article, apply in its own name to the superior court for a temporary or permanent restraining order or injunction to restrain such person from continuing such illegal practices. The court is empowered to grant injunctive relief regardless of whether criminal prosecution or other action has been or may be instituted as a result of the violation. In the court's consideration of the issue of granting or continuing an injunction sought by the Board, a showing of conduct in violation of the terms of this Article shall be sufficient to meet any requirement of general North Carolina injunction law for irreparable damage.

(b) The venue for actions brought under this section shall be the superior court of any county in which such illegal or unlawful acts are alleged to have been committed, in the county in which the defendants in such action reside, or in the county in which the Board maintains its offices and records. (1979, c. 487; 1985, c. 701, s. 1.)

§ 90-270.38. Title.

This Article may be cited as the "Physical Therapy Practice Act". (1951, c. 1131, s. 15; 1969, c. 556; 1979, c. 487; 1985, c. 701, s. 1.)

§ 90-270.39. Osteopaths, chiropractors, and podiatrists not restricted.

Nothing in this Article shall restrict the use of physical therapy modalities by licensed osteopaths, chiropractors, or podiatrists, in the lawful practice of their professions; except that, these licensed professionals shall not be permitted to in any way hold themselves, or any employee or associate, out as practicing physical therapy or being licensed by the Board of Physical Therapy Examiners, or any other agency, to do so. (1951, c. 1131, s. 15.1; 1969, c. 556; 1979, c. 487; 1985, c. 701, s. 1.)

§§ 90-270.40 through 90-270.44. Reserved for future codification purposes.

Article 18C.

Marriage and Family Therapy Licensure.

§ 90-270.45. Title of Article.

This Article shall be known as the "Marriage and Family Therapy Licensure Act." (1979, c. 697, s. 1; 1985, c. 223, s. 1; 1993 (Reg. Sess., 1994), c. 564, s. 2.)

§ 90-270.46. Policy and purpose.

Marriage and family therapy in North Carolina is a professional practice that affects the public safety and welfare and requires appropriate licensure and control in the public interest.

It is the purpose of this Article to establish a licensure agency, a structure, and procedures that will (i) ensure that the public has a means of protecting itself from the practice of marriage and family therapy by unprofessional, unauthorized, and unqualified individuals, and (ii) protect the public from unprofessional, improper, unauthorized and unqualified use of certain titles by persons who practice marriage and family therapy. This Article shall be liberally construed to carry out these policies and purposes. (1979, c. 697, s. 1; 1985, c. 223, s. 1; 1993 (Reg. Sess., 1994), c. 564, s. 2.)

§ 90-270.47. Definitions.

As used in this Article, unless the context clearly requires a different meaning:

(1)   Renumbered.

(2)   "Board" means the North Carolina Marriage and Family Therapy Licensure Board.

(2a)   "Clinical experience" means face-to-face therapy between a therapist and a client, whether individuals, couples, families, or groups, conducted from a larger systems perspective that relates to client treatment plans, is goal-directed, and assists the client in affecting change in cognition and behavior and effect.

(2b)   "Larger systems" means any individual or group that is a part of the client's environment and that potentially impacts the client's functioning or well-being and potentially can assist in the development and implementation of a treatment plan.

(3)   "Licensed marriage and family therapist" means a person to whom a license has been issued pursuant to this Article, if the license is in force and not suspended or revoked.

(3a)   "Licensed marriage and family therapy associate" means an individual to whom a license has been issued pursuant to this Article whose license is in force and not suspended or revoked and whose license permits the individual to engage in the practice of marriage and family therapy under the supervision of an American Association for Marriage and Family Therapy (AAMFT) approved supervisor in accordance with rules adopted by the Board.

(3b)   "Marriage and family therapy" is the clinical practice, within the context of individual, couple, and marriage and family systems, of the diagnosis and treatment of psychosocial aspects of mental and emotional disorders. Marriage and family therapy involves the professional application of psychotherapeutic and family systems theories and techniques in the delivery of services to families, couples, and individuals for the purpose of treating these diagnosed mental and emotional disorders. Marriage and family therapy includes referrals to and collaboration with health care and other professionals when appropriate.

(4) "Practice of marriage and family therapy" means the rendering of professional marriage and family therapy services to individuals, couples, or families, singly or in groups, whether the services are offered directly to the general public or through organizations, either public or private, for a fee, monetary or otherwise.

(5) "Recognized educational institution" means any university, college, professional school, or other institution of higher learning that:

a. In the United States, is regionally accredited by bodies approved by the Commission on Recognition of Postsecondary Accreditation or its successor.

b. In Canada, holds a membership in the Association of Universities and Colleges of Canada.

c. In another country, is accredited by the comparable official organization having this authority and is recognized by the Board.

(6) "Related degree" means:

a. Master's or doctoral degree in clinical social work;

b. Master's or doctoral degree in psychiatric nursing;

c. Master's or doctoral degree in counseling or clinical or counseling psychology;

d. Doctor of medicine or doctor of osteopathy degree with an appropriate residency training in psychiatry; or

e. Master's or doctoral degree in any mental health field the course of study of which is equivalent to the master's degree in marriage and family therapy. (1979, c. 697, s. 1; 1985, c. 223, s. 1; 1993 (Reg. Sess., 1994), c. 564, s. 2; 2009-393, s. 1.)

§ 90-270.48. Prohibited acts.

Except as specifically provided elsewhere in this Article, it is unlawful for a person not licensed as a marriage and family therapist or as a licensed marriage and family therapy associate under this Article to practice marriage or family therapy or hold himself or herself out to the public as a person practicing marriage and family therapy. (1979, c. 697, s. 1; 1985, c. 223, s. 1; 1993 (Reg. Sess., 1994), c. 564, s. 2; 2009-393, s. 2.)

§ 90-270.48A. Exemptions.

(a) This Article does not prevent members of the clergy or licensed, certified, or registered members of professional groups recognized by the Board from advertising or performing services consistent with their own profession. Members of the clergy include, but are not limited to, persons who are ordained, consecrated, commissioned, or endorsed by a recognized denomination, church, faith group, or synagogue. Professional groups the Board shall recognize include, but are not limited to, licensed or certified social workers, licensed professional counselors, fee-based pastoral counselors, licensed practicing psychologists, psychological associates, physicians, and attorneys-at-law. However, in no event may a person use the title "Licensed Marriage and Family Therapist" or "Licensed Marriage and Family Therapy Associate," use the letters "LMFT" or "LMFTA," or in any way imply that the person is a licensed marriage and family therapist or a licensed marriage and family therapy associate unless the person is licensed as such under this Article.

(b) A person is exempt from the requirements of this Article if any of the following conditions are met:

(1) The person is (i) enrolled in a master's level program or higher in a recognized educational institution, (ii) under supervision as approved by the Board in a training institution approved by the Board, and (iii) designated by a title such as "marriage and family therapy intern."

(2) The person is practicing marriage and family therapy as an employee of a recognized educational institution, or a governmental institution or agency and the practice is included in the duties for which the person was employed by the institution or agency.

(3) Repealed by Session Laws 2009-393, s. 3, effective October 1, 2009.

(4) The person is practicing marriage and family therapy as an employee of a hospital licensed under Article 5 of Chapter 131E or Article 2 of Chapter 122C

of the General Statutes. Provided, however, no such person shall hold himself out as a licensed marriage and family therapist.

(c) No such person practicing marriage and family therapy under the exemptions provided by this section shall hold himself or herself out as a licensed marriage and family therapist or licensed marriage and family therapy associate. (1993 (Reg. Sess., 1994), c. 564, s. 2; 2001-487, s. 40(i); 2009-393, s. 3.)

§ 90-270.48B: Repealed by Session Laws 2003-117, s. 2, effective October 1, 2003, and applicable to claims for payment or reimbursement for services rendered on or after that date.

§ 90-270.49. North Carolina Marriage and Family Therapy Licensure Board.

(a) Establishment. - There is established as an agency of the State of North Carolina the North Carolina Marriage and Family Therapy Licensure Board, which shall be composed of seven Board members to be appointed as provided in G.S. 90-270.50. Board members shall be appointed for terms of four years each, except that any person chosen to fill a vacancy shall be appointed only for the unexpired term of the Board member whom the appointee shall succeed. Upon the expiration of a Board member's term of office, the Board member shall continue to serve until a successor has qualified. No person may be appointed more than once to fill an unexpired term or for more than two consecutive full terms. The Board shall elect a chair and vice-chair from its membership to serve a term of four years. No person may serve as chairperson for more than four years.

The Governor may remove any member from the Board or remove the chairperson from the position of chairperson only for neglect of duty, malfeasance, or conviction of a felony or crime of moral turpitude while in office.

No Board member shall participate in any matter before the Board in which the member has a pecuniary interest, personal bias, or other similar conflict of interest.

(b) Quorum and Principal Office. - Four of the members of the Board shall constitute a quorum of the Board. The Board shall specify the principal office of the Board within this State.

(c) Repealed by Session Laws 1993 (Reg. Sess., 1994), c. 564, s. 2. (1979, c. 697, s. 1; 1985, c. 223, s. 1; 1993 (Reg. Sess., 1994), c. 564, s. 2; 2009-393, s. 4.)

§ 90-270.50. Appointment and qualification of Board members.

(a) Nominations for Appointment. - The Governor shall appoint members of the Board only from among the candidates who meet the following qualifications:

(1) Four members shall be practicing marriage and family therapists who are licensed marriage and family therapists in the State at the time of their appointment, each of whom has been for at least five years immediately preceding appointment actively engaged as a marriage and family therapist in rendering professional services in marriage and family therapy, or in the education and training of graduate or postgraduate students of marriage and family therapy, and has spent the majority of the time devoted to this activity in this State during the two years preceding appointment.

(2) Three members shall be representatives of the general public who have no direct affiliation with the practice of marriage and family therapy.

(b) The appointment of any member of the Board shall automatically terminate 30 days after the date the member is no longer a resident of the State of North Carolina.

(c) The Governor shall fill any vacancy by appointment for the unexpired term.

(d) Each member of the Board must be a citizen of this State and must reside in a different congressional district in this State. (1979, c. 697, s. 1; 1985, c. 223, s. 1; 1993 (Reg. Sess., 1994), c. 564, s. 2.)

§ 90-270.51. Powers and duties.

(a)   The Board shall administer and enforce this Article.

(b)   Subject to the provisions of Chapter 150B of the General Statutes, the Board may adopt, amend, or repeal rules to administer and enforce this Article, including rules of professional ethics for the practice of marriage and family therapy.

(c)   The Board shall examine and pass on the qualifications of all applicants for licensure under this Article, and shall issue a license to each successful applicant.

(d)   The Board may adopt a seal which may be affixed to all licenses issued by the Board.

(e)   The Board may authorize expenditures to carry out the provisions of this Article from the fees that it collects, but expenditures may not exceed the revenues or reserves of the Board during any fiscal year.

(f)   The Board may employ, subject to the provisions of Chapter 126 of the General Statutes, attorneys, experts, and other employees as necessary to perform its duties.

(g)   Reserved for future codification purposes.

(h)   The Board may order that any records concerning the practice of marriage and family therapy and relevant to a complaint received by the Board, or an inquiry or investigation conducted by or on behalf of the Board, shall be produced by the custodian of the records to the Board or for inspection and copying by employees, representatives of or counsel to the Board. These records shall not become public records as defined by G.S. 132-1. A licensee or an agency employing a licensee shall maintain records for a minimum of five years from the date the licensee terminates services to the adult client and the client services record is closed. For minor clients the licensee or agency employing the licensee shall maintain records until the client is 22 or five years after the termination of services, whichever occurs later. A licensee shall cooperate fully and in a timely manner with the Board and its designated employees, representatives, or investigators in an inquiry or investigation conducted by or on behalf of the Board. (1979, c. 697, s. 1; 1985, c. 223, s. 1;

1987, c. 827, s. 78; 1993 (Reg. Sess., 1994), c. 564, s. 2; 2009-393, ss. 5.1, 5.2.)

§ 90-270.52. License application.

(a) Each person desiring to obtain a license under this Article shall apply to the Board upon the form and in the manner prescribed by the Board. Each applicant shall furnish evidence satisfactory to the Board that the applicant:

(1) Is of good moral character;

(2) Has not engaged or is not engaged in any practice or conduct that would be a ground for denial, revocation, or suspension of a license under G.S. 90-270.60;

(3) Is qualified for licensure pursuant to the requirements of this Article.

(b) A license obtained through fraud or by any false representation is void. (1979, c. 697, s. 1; 1985, c. 223, s. 1; 1993 (Reg. Sess., 1994), c. 564, s. 2.)

§ 90-270.53: Repealed by Session Laws 1993 (Reg. Sess., 1994), c. 564, s. 2.

§ 90-270.54. Requirements for licensure as a marriage and family therapist.

(a) Each applicant shall be issued a license by the Board to engage in the practice of marriage and family therapy as a licensed marriage and family therapist if the applicant meets the qualifications set forth in G.S. 90-270.52(a) and provides satisfactory evidence to the Board that the applicant:

(1) Meets educational and experience qualifications as follows:

a. Educational requirements: Possesses a minimum of a master's degree from a recognized educational institution in the field of marriage and family therapy, or a related degree, which degree is evidenced by the applicant's official transcripts. An applicant with a related degree may meet the educational requirements if the applicant presents satisfactory evidence of post-master's or post-doctoral training taken in the field of marriage and family therapy from a program recognized by the Board regardless whether the training was taken at a nondegree granting institution or in a nondegree program, as long as the training, by itself or in combination with any other training, is the equivalent in content and quality, as defined in the rules of the Board, of a master's or doctoral degree in marriage and family therapy;

b. Experience requirements: Has at least 1,500 hours of supervised clinical experience in the practice of marriage and family therapy, not more than 500 hours of which were obtained while the candidate was a student in a master's degree program and at least 1,000 of which were obtained after the applicant was granted a degree in the field of marriage and family therapy or a related degree (with ongoing supervision consistent with standards approved by the Board); and

(2) Passes an examination approved by the Board.

(b) Any person who is a certified marriage and family therapist on January 1, 1995, shall be deemed to be a licensed marriage and family therapist as of that date. Valid and unexpired certificates operate as licenses for the purposes of this Article until the date set for renewal of the certificate, at which time the Board shall issue the certificate holder a license in accordance with G.S. 90-270.58. (1979, c. 697, s. 1; 1981, c. 611, s. 2; 1985, c. 223, s. 1; 1993 (Reg. Sess., 1994), c. 564, s. 2; 2009-393, s. 6.)

§ 90-270.54A. Requirements for licensure as a marriage and family therapy associate.

(a) Each applicant shall be issued a license by the Board to engage in practice as a marriage and family therapy associate if the applicant meets the qualifications set forth in G.S. 90-270.52(a) and provides satisfactory evidence to the Board that the applicant:

(1) Has completed a marriage and therapy degree or related degree in accordance with G.S. 90-270.54(a)(1)a.

(2) Has shown evidence of intent to accrue the required supervised clinical experience for licensure under G.S. 90-270.54(a)(1)b.

(3) Has filed with the Board an application for licensure as a marriage and family therapy associate, which application includes evidence of the appropriate coursework and an agreement by at least one supervisor approved by the American Association of Marriage and Family Therapy to provide supervision to the applicant.

(4) Has passed the examination approved by the Board pursuant to G.S. 90-270.54(a)(2).

(b) Upon approval by the Board, a license designating the applicant as a licensed marriage and family therapy associate shall be issued. Notwithstanding G.S. 90-270.58, a license issued under this section shall be valid for three years from the date of issuance.

(c) A marriage and family therapy associate license shall not be renewed. However, if upon written petition to the Board a person licensed pursuant to this section demonstrates special circumstances and steady progress towards licensure as a marriage and family therapist, the Board may grant a one-year extension of the marriage and family therapy associate license upon receipt and approval of an application for extension and payment of the fee authorized by G.S. 90-270.57(a)(9).

(d) Nothing in this Article shall be construed to require direct third-party reimbursement under private insurance policies to a person licensed as a marriage and family therapy associate under this Article. (2009-393, s. 7.)

§ 90-270.55. Examinations.

Each applicant for licensure as a licensed marriage and family therapist shall pass an examination as determined by the Board. The Board shall set the passing score for examinations. Any request by an applicant for reasonable accommodations in taking the examination shall be submitted in writing to the Board and shall be supported by documentation as may be required by the Board in assessing the request. (1979, c. 697, s. 1; 1985, c. 223, s. 1; 1993 (Reg. Sess., 1994), c. 564, s. 2; 2009-393, s. 8.)

§ 90-270.55A: Repealed by Session Laws 2009-393, s. 9, effective October 1, 2009.

§ 90-270.56. Reciprocal licenses.

The Board may issue a license as a marriage and family therapist or a marriage and family therapy associate by reciprocity to any person who applies for the license as prescribed by the Board and who at all times during the application process:

(1)   Has been licensed for five continuous years and is currently licensed as a marriage and family therapist or marriage and family therapy associate in another state.

(2)   Has an unrestricted license in good standing in the other state.

(3)   Has no unresolved complaints in any jurisdiction.

(4)   Has passed the National Marriage and Family Therapy examination. (1979, c. 697, s. 1; 1985, c. 223, s. 1; 1993 (Reg. Sess., 1994), c. 564, s. 2; 2009-393, s. 10.)

§ 90-270.57. Fees.

(a)   In order to fund the Board's activities under this Article, the Board may charge and collect fees not exceeding the following:

(1)   Each license examination $50.00

(2)   Each license application as a marriage

and family therapist   200.00

(2a)   Each license application as a marriage and

family therapy associate   200.00

(3)　Each renewal of license
200.00

(4)　Each reciprocal license application
200.00

(5)　Each reinstatement of an expired license
200.00

(6)　Each application to return to active status
200.00

(7)　Each duplicate license
25.00

(8)　Each annual maintenance of inactive status
50.00

(9)　Each application to extend associate license
50.00.

In addition to the examination fee provided in subdivision (1) of this subsection, the Board may charge and collect from each applicant for license examination the cost of processing test results and the cost of test materials.

(b)　The Board may establish fees for the actual cost of (i) document duplication services, (ii) materials, and (iii) returned bank items as allowed by law. All fees listed in subsection (a) of this section shall be nonrefundable. (1979, c. 697, s. 1; 1985, c. 223, s. 1; 1989, c. 581, s. 1; 1993 (Reg. Sess., 1994), c. 564, s. 2; 2009-393, s. 11.)

§ 90-270.58.　Renewal of license.

All licenses for marriage and family therapists issued under this Article shall expire automatically on the first day of July of each year. The Board shall renew a license upon (i) completion of the continuing education requirements of G.S. 90-270.58C and (ii) payment of the renewal fee. (1979, c. 697, s. 1; 1985, c.

223, s. 1; 1989, c. 581, s. 2; 1993 (Reg. Sess., 1994), c. 564, s. 2; 2009-393, s. 12.)

§ 90-270.58A. Reinstatement after expiration.

A person whose license has expired may have the license reinstated as prescribed by the Board. The Board shall charge and collect a fee for reinstatement of the license. (1993 (Reg. Sess., 1994), c. 564, s. 2.)

§ 90-270.58B. Inactive status.

(a)   A person who holds a valid and unexpired license and who is not actively engaged in the practice of marriage and family therapy may apply to the Board to be placed on inactive status. A person on inactive status shall not be required to pay annual renewal fees, but shall be required to pay an annual inactive status maintenance fee. A person who is on inactive status shall not have to meet continuing education requirements.

(b)   A person on inactive status shall not practice or hold himself out as practicing marriage and family therapy or perform any other activities prohibited by this Article.

(c)   A person desiring to return to active status shall submit written application to the Board. The Board shall return the person to active status upon payment of the fee specified in G.S. 90-270.57 and upon such showing of competency to resume practice as the Board may require. (1993 (Reg. Sess., 1994), c. 564, s. 2; 2009-393, s. 13.)

§ 90-270.58C. Continuing education requirements.

The Board shall prescribe continuing education requirements for licensees. These requirements shall be designed to maintain and improve the quality of professional services in marriage and family therapy provided to the public, to keep the licensee knowledgeable of current research, techniques, and practice, and to provide other resources that will improve skill and competence in marriage and family therapy. The number of hours of continuing education shall not exceed the number of hours available that year in Board-approved courses within the State. The Board may waive these continuing education requirements for not more than 12 months, but only upon the licensee's satisfactory showing to the Board of undue hardship. The Board may waive, upon request, continuing education requirements for licensees who are on active military duty and serving overseas. (1993 (Reg. Sess., 1994), c. 564, s. 2; 2009-393, s. 14.)

§ 90-270.59. Disposition of funds.

All monies received by the Board shall be used to implement this Article. (1979, c. 697, s. 1; 1985, c. 223, s. 1; 1993 (Reg. Sess., 1994), c. 564, s. 2; 2009-393, s. 15.)

§ 90-270.60. Denial, revocation, or suspension of license; other disciplinary or remedial actions.

(a) The Board may deny, revoke, or suspend licensure, discipline, place on probation, limit practice, or require examination, remediation, or rehabilitation, or any combination of the disciplinary actions described in this subsection, of any applicant or person licensed under this Article on one or more of the following grounds:

(1) Has been convicted of a felony or entered a plea of guilty or nolo contendere to any felony charge under the laws of the United States or of any state of the United States.

(2) Has been convicted of or entered a plea of guilty or nolo contendere to any misdemeanor involving moral turpitude, misrepresentation, or fraud in dealing with the public, or conduct otherwise relevant to fitness to practice marriage and family therapy, or a misdemeanor charge reflecting the inability to practice marriage and family therapy with due regard to the health and safety of clients.

(3) Has engaged in fraud or deceit in securing or attempting to secure or renew a license under this Article or has willfully concealed from the Board material information in connection with application for a license or renewal of a license under this Article.

(4)   Has practiced any fraud, deceit, or misrepresentation upon the public, the Board, or any individual in connection with the practice of marriage and family therapy, the offer of professional marriage and family therapy services, the filing of Medicare, Medicaid, or other claims to any third-party payor, or in any manner otherwise relevant to fitness for the practice of marriage and family therapy.

(5)   Has made fraudulent, misleading, or intentionally or materially false statements pertaining to education, licensure, license renewal, supervision, continuing education, any disciplinary actions or sanctions pending or occurring in any other jurisdiction, professional credentials, or qualifications or fitness for the practice of marriage and family therapy to the public, any individual, the Board, or any other organization.

(6)   Has had a license or certification for the practice of marriage and family therapy in any other jurisdiction suspended or revoked, or has been disciplined by the licensing or certification board in any other jurisdiction for conduct which would subject the licensee to discipline under this Article.

(7)   Has violated any provision of this Article or any rules adopted by the Board.

(8)   Has aided or abetted the unlawful practice of marriage and family therapy by any person not licensed by the Board.

(9)   Has been guilty of immoral, dishonorable, unprofessional, or unethical conduct as defined in this subsection or in the current code of ethics of the American Association for Marriage and Family Therapy. However, if any provision of the code of ethics is inconsistent and in conflict with the provisions of this Article, the provisions of this Article shall control.

(10)   Has practiced marriage and family therapy in such a manner as to endanger the welfare of clients.

(11)   Has demonstrated an inability to practice marriage and family therapy with reasonable skill and safety by reason of illness, inebriation, misuse of drugs, narcotics, alcohol, chemicals, or any other substance affecting mental or physical functioning, or as a result of any mental or physical condition.

(12) Has practiced marriage and family therapy outside the boundaries of demonstrated competence or the limitations of education, training, or supervised experience.

(13) Has exercised undue influence in such a manner as to exploit the client, student, supervisee, or trainee for the financial or other personal advantage or gratification of the marriage and family therapist or a third party.

(14) Has harassed or abused, sexually or otherwise, a client, student, supervisee, or trainee.

(15) Has failed to cooperate with or to respond promptly, completely, and honestly to the Board, to credentials committees, or to ethics committees of professional associations, hospitals, or other health care organizations or educational institutions, when those organizations or entities have jurisdiction.

(16) Has refused to appear before the Board after having been ordered to do so in writing by the chair.

(b) The Board may, in lieu of denial, suspension, or revocation, take any of the following disciplinary actions:

(1) Issue a formal reprimand or formally censure the applicant or licensee.

(2) Place the applicant or licensee on probation with the appropriate conditions on the continued practice of marriage and family therapy deemed advisable by the Board.

(3) Require examination, remediation, or rehabilitation for the applicant or licensee, including care, counseling, or treatment by a professional or professionals designated or approved by the Board, the expense to be borne by the applicant or licensee.

(4) Require supervision of the marriage and family therapy services provided by the applicant or licensee by a licensee designated or approved by the Board, the expense to be borne by the applicant or licensee.

(5) Limit or circumscribe the practice of marriage and family therapy provided by the applicant or licensee with respect to the extent, nature, or location of the marriage and family therapy services provided, as deemed advisable by the Board.

(6) Discipline and impose any appropriate combination of the types of disciplinary action listed in this subsection.

In addition, the Board may impose conditions of probation or restrictions on the continued practice of marriage and family therapy at the conclusion of a period of suspension or as a requirement for the restoration of a revoked or suspended license. In lieu of or in connection with any disciplinary proceedings or investigation, the Board may enter into a consent order relative to discipline, supervision, probation, remediation, rehabilitation, or practice limitation of a licensee or applicant for a license.

(c) The Board may assess costs of disciplinary action against an applicant or licensee found to be in violation of this Article.

(d) When considering the issue of whether an applicant or licensee is physically or mentally capable of practicing marriage and family therapy with reasonable skill and safety with patients or clients, upon a showing of probable cause to the Board that the applicant or licensee is not capable of practicing professional counseling with reasonable skill and safety with patients or clients, the Board may petition a court of competent jurisdiction to order the applicant or licensee in question to submit to a psychological evaluation by a psychologist to determine psychological status or a physical evaluation by a physician to determine physical condition, or both. The psychologist or physician shall be designated by the court. The expenses of the evaluations shall be borne by the Board. Where the applicant or licensee raises the issue of mental or physical competence or appeals a decision regarding mental or physical competence, the applicant or licensee shall be permitted to obtain an evaluation at the applicant's or licensee's expense. If the Board suspects the objectivity or adequacy of the evaluation, the Board may compel an evaluation by its designated practitioners at its own expense.

(e) Except as provided otherwise in this Article, the procedure for revocation, suspension, denial, limitations of the license, or other disciplinary, remedial, or rehabilitative actions, shall be in accordance with the provisions of Chapter 150B of the General Statutes. The Board is required to provide the opportunity for a hearing under Chapter 150B of the General Statutes to any applicant whose license or health services provider certification is denied or to whom licensure or health services provider certification is offered subject to any restrictions, probation, disciplinary action, remediation, or other conditions or limitations, or to any licensee before revoking, suspending, or restricting a license or health services provider certificate or imposing any other disciplinary action or remediation. If the applicant or licensee waives the opportunity for a hearing, the Board's denial, revocation, suspension, or other proposed action becomes final without a hearing having been conducted. Notwithstanding the provisions of this subsection, no applicant or licensee is entitled to a hearing for failure to pass an examination. In any proceeding before the Board, in any record of any hearing before the Board, in any complaint or notice of charges against any licensee or applicant for licensure, and in any decision rendered by the Board, the Board may withhold from public disclosure the identity of any clients who have not consented to the public disclosure of services provided by the licensee or applicant. The Board may close a hearing to the public and receive in closed session evidence involving or concerning the treatment of or delivery of services to a client who has not consented to the public disclosure of the treatment or services as may be necessary for the protection and rights of the client of the accused applicant or licensee and the full presentation of relevant evidence.

(f)   All records, papers, and other documents containing information collected and compiled by or on behalf of the Board, as a result of investigations, inquiries, or interviews conducted in connection with licensing or disciplinary matters, shall not be considered public records within the meaning of Chapter 132 of the General Statutes. However, any notice or statement of charges against any licensee or applicant, or any notice to any licensee or applicant of a hearing in any proceeding, or any decision rendered in connection with a hearing in any proceeding, shall be a public record within the meaning of Chapter 132 of the General Statutes, though the record may contain information collected and compiled as a result of the investigation, inquiry, or hearing. Any identifying information concerning the treatment of or delivery of services to a client who has not consented to the public disclosure of the treatment or services may be redacted. If any record, paper, or other document containing information collected and compiled by or on behalf of the Board, as provided in this section, is received and admitted in evidence in any hearing before the Board, it shall be a public record within the meaning of Chapter 132 of the General Statutes, subject to any deletions of identifying information concerning the treatment of or delivery of marriage and family therapy services to a client who has not consented to the public disclosure of treatment or services.

(g)   A person whose license has been denied or revoked may reapply to the Board for licensure after one calendar year from the date of the denial or revocation.

(h) A licensee may voluntarily relinquish his or her license at anytime. Notwithstanding any provision to the contrary, the Board retains full jurisdiction to investigate alleged violations of this Article by any person whose license is relinquished under this subsection and, upon proof of any violation of this Article by the person, the Board may take disciplinary action as authorized by this section.

(i) The Board may adopt rules deemed necessary to interpret and implement this section. (1979, c. 697, s. 1; 1985, c. 223, s. 1; 1987, c. 827, s. 1; 1993 (Reg. Sess., 1994), c. 564, s. 2; 2009-393, s. 16.)

§ 90-270.61. Penalties.

Any person not licensed as a marriage and family therapist under this Article who engages in the practice of marriage and family therapy, or holds himself or herself out to be a marriage or family therapist or engaged in marriage and family therapy in violation of this Article is guilty of a Class 2 misdemeanor. (1979, c. 697, s. 1; 1985, c. 223, ss. 1, 1.1; 1993 (Reg. Sess., 1994), c. 564, s. 2.)

§ 90-270.62. Injunction.

As an additional remedy, the Board may proceed in a superior court to enjoin and restrain any person without a valid license from violating the prohibitions of this Article. The Board shall not be required to post bond to such proceeding. (1979, c. 697, s. 1; 1985, c. 223, s. 1; 1993 (Reg. Sess., 1994), c. 564, s. 2.)

§ 90-270.63. Criminal history record checks of applicants for licensure as a marriage and family therapist and a marriage and family therapy associate.

(a) Definitions. - The following definitions shall apply in this section:

(1) Applicant. - A person applying for licensure as a licensed marriage and family therapy associate pursuant to G.S. 90-270.54A or licensed marriage and family therapist pursuant to G.S. 90-270.54.

(2) Criminal history. - A history of conviction of a State or federal crime, whether a misdemeanor or felony, that bears on an applicant's fitness for licensure to practice marriage and family therapy. The crimes include the criminal offenses set forth in any of the following Articles of Chapter 14 of the General Statutes: Article 5, Counterfeiting and Issuing Monetary Substitutes; Article 5A, Endangering Executive and Legislative Officers; Article 6, Homicide; Article 7A, Rape and Other Sex Offenses; Article 8, Assaults; Article 10, Kidnapping and Abduction; Article 13, Malicious Injury or Damage by Use of Explosive or Incendiary Device or Material; Article 14, Burglary and Other Housebreakings; Article 15, Arson and Other Burnings; Article 16, Larceny; Article 17, Robbery; Article 18, Embezzlement; Article 19, False Pretenses and Cheats; Article 19A, Obtaining Property or Services by False or Fraudulent Use of Credit Device or Other Means; Article 19B, Financial Transaction Card Crime Act; Article 20, Frauds; Article 21, Forgery; Article 26, Offenses Against Public Morality and Decency; Article 26A, Adult Establishments; Article 27, Prostitution; Article 28, Perjury; Article 29, Bribery; Article 31, Misconduct in Public Office; Article 35, Offenses Against the Public Peace; Article 36A, Riots, Civil Disorders, and Emergencies; Article 39, Protection of Minors; Article 40, Protection of the Family; Article 59, Public Intoxication; and Article 60, Computer-Related Crime. The crimes also include possession or sale of drugs in violation of the North Carolina Controlled Substances Act in Article 5 of Chapter 90 of the General Statutes and alcohol-related offenses, including sale to underage persons in violation of G.S. 18B-302 or driving while impaired in violation of G.S. 20-138.1 through G.S. 20-138.5. In addition to the North Carolina crimes listed in this subdivision, such crimes also include similar crimes under federal law or under the laws of other states.

(b) The Board may request that an applicant for licensure, an applicant seeking reinstatement of a license, or a licensee under investigation by the Board for alleged criminal offenses in violation of this Article consent to a criminal history record check. Refusal to consent to a criminal history record check may constitute grounds for the Board to deny licensure to an applicant, deny reinstatement of a license to an applicant, or revoke the license of a licensee. The Board shall ensure that the State and national criminal history of an applicant is checked. The Board shall be responsible for providing to the North Carolina Department of Justice the fingerprints of the applicant or licensee to be checked, a form signed by the applicant or licensee consenting to the criminal history record check and the use of fingerprints and other identifying information required by the State or National Repositories of Criminal Histories, and any additional information required by the Department of Justice in accordance with G.S. 114-19.27. The Board shall keep all information obtained pursuant to this section confidential. The Board shall collect any fees required by the Department of Justice and shall remit the fees to the Department of Justice for expenses associated with conducting the criminal history record check.

(c) If an applicant's or licensee's criminal history record check reveals one or more convictions listed under subdivision (a)(2) of this section, the conviction shall not automatically bar licensure. The Board shall consider all of the following factors regarding the conviction:

(1) The level of seriousness of the crime.

(2) The date of the crime.

(3) The age of the person at the time of the conviction.

(4) The circumstances surrounding the commission of the crime, if known.

(5) The nexus between the criminal conduct of the person and the duties and responsibilities of a licensee.

(6) The person's prison, jail, probation, parole, rehabilitation, and employment records since the date the crime was committed.

(7) The subsequent commission by the person of a crime listed in subdivision (a)(2) of this section.

If, after reviewing these factors, the Board determines that the applicant's or licensee's criminal history disqualifies the applicant or licensee for licensure, the Board may deny licensure or reinstatement of the license of the applicant or revoke the license of the licensee. The Board may disclose to the applicant or licensee information contained in the criminal history record check that is relevant to the denial. The Board shall not provide a copy of the criminal history record check to the applicant or licensee. The applicant or licensee shall have the right to appear before the Board to appeal the Board's decision. However, an appearance before the full Board shall constitute an exhaustion of administrative remedies in accordance with Chapter 150B of the General Statutes.

(d) The Board, its officers, and employees, acting in good faith and in compliance with this section, shall be immune from civil liability for denying licensure or reinstatement of a license to an applicant or revoking a licensee's license based on information provided in the applicant's or licensee's criminal history record check. (2009-393, s. 17; 2012-12, s. 2(jj).)

§ 90-270.64. Reserved for future codification purposes.

Article 18D.

Occupational Therapy.

§ 90-270.65. Title.

This Article shall be known as the "North Carolina Occupational Therapy Practice Act." (1983 (Reg. Sess., 1984), c. 1073, s. 1.)

§ 90-270.66. Declaration of purpose.

The North Carolina Occupational Therapy Practice Act is enacted to safeguard the public health, safety and welfare, to protect the public from being harmed by unqualified persons, to assure the highest degree of professional services and conduct on the part of occupational therapists and occupational therapy assistants, to provide for the establishment of licensure requirements, and to insure the availability of occupational therapy services of high quality to persons in need of such services. It is the purpose of this Article to provide for the regulation of persons offering occupational therapy services to the public. (1983 (Reg. Sess., 1984), c. 1073, s. 1; 2005-432, s. 1.)

§ 90-270.67. Definitions.

As used in this Article, unless the context clearly requires a different meaning:

(1) Accrediting body. - The Accrediting Council for Occupational Therapy Education.

(1a) Board. - The North Carolina Board of Occupational Therapy.

(1b) Examining body. - The National Board for Certification in Occupational Therapy.

(2) Occupational therapist. - An individual licensed in good standing to practice occupational therapy as defined in this Article.

(3) Occupational therapy assistant. - An individual licensed in good standing to assist in the practice of occupational therapy under this Article, who performs activities commensurate with his or her education and training under the supervision of a licensed occupational therapist.

(4) Occupational therapy. - A health care profession providing evaluation, treatment and consultation to help individuals achieve a maximum level of independence by developing skills and abilities interfered with by disease, emotional disorder, physical injury, the aging process, or impaired development. Occupational therapists use purposeful activities and specially designed orthotic and prosthetic devices to reduce specific impairments and to help individuals achieve independence at home and in the work place.

(5) Person. - Any individual, partnership, unincorporated organization, or corporate body, except that only an individual may be licensed under this Article. (1983 Reg. Sess., 1984), c. 1073, s. 1; 1989, c. 256, s. 1; c. 770, s. 46; 2005-432, s. 2; 2006-226, s. 18.)

§ 90-270.68. Establishment of Board, terms, vacancies, removal, meetings, compensation.

(a) Establishment of Board. - The North Carolina Board of Occupational Therapy is created. The Board shall consist of seven members who are appointed by the Governor and are residents of this State at the time of and during their appointment, as follows:

(1) Three members shall be occupational therapists and one member shall be an occupational therapy assistant. Each of these members shall be licensed to practice in North Carolina and have practiced, taught, or engaged in research in occupational therapy for at least three of the five years immediately preceding appointment to the Board.

(2) One member shall be a physician in good standing with the North Carolina Medical Board and licensed by and registered with the North Carolina Medical Board to practice medicine in this State.

(3) One member shall represent the public at large and shall be a person who is not a health care provider licensed under this Chapter or the spouse of a licensed health care provider.

(4) One member shall be a counselor, educator, or school-based professional certified or licensed under North Carolina law who is employed in the North Carolina public school system and is not an occupational therapist or an occupational therapy assistant.

The occupational therapist members and the occupational therapy assistant member shall be nominated by the North Carolina Occupational Therapy Association, Inc., following the use of a procedure made available to all occupational therapists and occupational therapy assistants licensed and residing in North Carolina. In soliciting nominations and compiling its list, the Association shall give consideration to geographic distribution, clinical specialty, and other factors that will promote representation of all aspects of occupational therapy practice. The records of the nomination procedures shall be filed with the Board and made available for a period of six months following nomination for reasonable inspection by any licensed practitioner of occupational therapy.

The physician member shall be nominated by the North Carolina Occupational Therapy Association, Inc., after consultation with the North Carolina Medical Society. The counselor, educator, or school-based professional member shall be nominated by the North Carolina Occupational Therapy Association, Inc., after consultation with the North Carolina School Counselors Association.

(b) Terms. - Members of the Board shall serve four-year staggered terms. No member shall serve more than two consecutive four-year terms, unless a member is appointed to fill a vacancy for an unexpired term, then that member may complete the unexpired term and serve one additional four-year term.

(c) Vacancies. - In the event a member of the Board cannot complete a term of office, the vacancy shall be filled by appointment by the Governor, in accordance with the procedures set forth in this section, for the remainder of the unexpired term. Vacancies shall be filled by the Governor within 45 days of receipt of the nominations from the North Carolina Occupational Therapy Association, Inc., or, in the case of public members, within 45 days of the receipt of notice of vacancy.

(d) Removal. - The Board may remove any of its members for neglect of duty, incompetence, or unprofessional conduct. A member subject to disciplinary proceedings shall be disqualified from participating in Board business until the charges are resolved.

(e) Meetings. - Each year the Board shall meet and designate a chairperson, a vice-chairperson, and a secretary-treasurer from among its members. The Board may hold additional meetings upon call of the chairperson or any two board members. A majority of the Board membership shall constitute a quorum.

(f) Compensation. - Members of the Board shall receive no compensation for their services, but shall be entitled to travel, per diem, and other expenses authorized by G.S. 93B-5. (1983 (Reg. Sess., 1984), c. 1073, s. 1; 1989, c. 256, s. 2; 2005-432, s. 3.)

§ 90-270.69. Powers and duties of the Board.

The Board shall have the following powers and duties:

(1) Establish and determine the qualifications and fitness of applicants for licensure to practice occupational therapy in this State.

(2) Conduct investigations, subpoena individuals and records, and do all other things necessary and proper to discipline persons licensed under this Article and to enforce this Article.

(2a) Communicate disciplinary actions to relevant State and federal authorities and to other state occupational therapy licensing authorities.

(3) Issue and renew, and deny, suspend, revoke or refuse to issue or renew any license under this Article.

(4) Adopt, amend, or repeal any reasonable rules or regulations necessary to carry out the purposes of this Article, including but not limited to rules establishing ethical standards of practice.

(5) Employ professional, clerical, investigative or special personnel necessary to carry out the provisions of this Article, and purchase or rent office space, equipment and supplies.

(6) Adopt a seal by which it shall authenticate its proceedings, official records, and licenses.

(7) Conduct administrative hearings in accordance with Chapter 150B of the General Statutes when a "contested case" as defined in G.S. 150B-2(2) arises under this Article.

(8) Establish reasonable fees for applications, initial and renewal licenses, and other services provided by the Board.

(9) Submit an annual report to the Governor and General Assembly of all its official actions during the preceding year, together with any recommendations and findings regarding improvement of the profession of occupational therapy.

(10) Publish and make available upon request the licensure standards prescribed under this Article and all rules and regulations established by the Board.

(11) Conduct a training program as needed for new Board members designed to familiarize new members with their duties. (1983 (Reg. Sess., 1984), c. 1073, s. 1; 1987, c. 827, ss. 1, 77; 2005-432, s. 4; 2008-187, s. 40(a).)

§ 90-270.70. Requirements for licensure.

(a) Any individual who desires to be licensed as an occupational therapist or occupational therapy assistant shall file a written application with the Board on forms provided by the Board, showing to the satisfaction of the Board that the applicant:

(1)   Is of good moral character; and

(2)   Has passed an examination approved by the Board as provided in this Article.

Applicants for licensure as an occupational therapist must also have successfully completed an accredited occupational therapy educational curriculum and the required supervised fieldwork as determined by the Board. Applicants for licensure as an occupational therapy assistant must also have successfully completed an accredited occupational therapy assistant educational curriculum and the required supervised fieldwork as determined by the Board.

(b)   Occupational therapists who are trained outside of the United States and its territories shall satisfy the examination and educational requirements as stated in subsection (a) of this section. The Board shall require these applicants to meet examination eligibility requirements as established by the credentialing body recognized by the Board before taking the examination. (1983 (Reg. Sess., 1984), c. 1073, s. 1; 2005-432, s. 5.)

§ 90-270.71: Repealed by Session Laws 2005-432, s. 6, effective September 22, 2005.

§ 90-270.72. Exemption from requirements.

The Board may exempt an applicant from certain licensure requirements if the applicant presents proof satisfactory to the Board of current licensure as an occupational therapist or occupational therapy assistant in another state or the District of Columbia, Puerto Rico, or Guam, provided the other jurisdiction's licensure standards are considered by the Board to be substantially equivalent to or higher than those prescribed in this Article. (1983 (Reg. Sess., 1984), c. 1073, s. 1; 2005-432, s. 7.)

§ 90-270.73. Issuance of license.

(a) The Board shall issue a license to any individual who meets the requirements of this Article upon payment of the license fee prescribed in G.S. 90-270.77.

(b) Any individual licensed as an occupational therapist under this Article may use the words "occupational therapist" and may use the letters "O.T." or "O.T./L." in connection with his or her name or place of business.

(c) Any individual licensed as an occupational therapy assistant under this Article may use the words "occupational therapy assistant" and may use the letters "O.T.A." or "O.T.A./L." in connection with his or her name or place of business.

(d) Repealed by Session Laws 2008-187, s. 40(b), effective August 7, 2008. (1983 (Reg. Sess., 1984), c. 1073, s. 1; 2005-432, s. 8; 2008-187, s. 40(b).)

§ 90-270.74: Expired.

§ 90-270.75. Renewal of license.

(a) Licenses issued under this Article shall be subject to annual renewal upon completion of continuing education and competency requirements as may be required by the Board, upon the payment of a renewal fee specified under G.S. 90-270.77 and in compliance with this Article, and shall expire unless renewed in the manner prescribed by the Board. The Board may provide for the late renewal of a license upon the payment of a late fee in accordance with G.S. 90-270.77, but no such late renewal may be granted more than five years after a license expires.

(b) A suspended license is subject to expiration and may be renewed as provided in this section, but such renewal shall not entitle the licensee to engage in the licensed activity or in any other conduct or activity in violation of the order or judgment by which the license was suspended until the license is reinstated. If a license revoked on disciplinary grounds is reinstated, the licensee shall pay the renewal fee and any late fee that may be applicable. (1983 (Reg. Sess., 1984), c. 1073, s. 1; 1989, c. 256, s. 3; 2005-432, s. 10.)

§ 90-270.76. Suspension, revocation and refusal to renew license.

(a)   The Board may deny or refuse to renew a license, may suspend or revoke a license, or may impose probationary conditions on a license if the licensee or applicant for licensure has engaged in any of the following conduct:

(1)   Obtaining a license by means of fraud, misrepresentation, or concealment of material facts.

(2)   Engaging in unprofessional conduct pursuant to rules established by the Board or violating the Code of Ethics adopted and published by the Board.

(3)   Having been convicted of or pleaded guilty or nolo contendere to a crime involving moral turpitude or any crime which indicates that the occupational therapist or occupational therapy assistant is unfit or incompetent to practice occupational therapy or that the occupational therapist or occupational therapy assistant has deceived or defrauded the public.

(4)   Engaging in any act or practice violative of any of the provisions of this Article or any rule or regulation adopted by the Board or aiding, abetting or assisting any person in such a violation.

(5)   Committing an act or acts of malpractice, gross negligence or incompetence in the practice of occupational therapy.

(6)   Practicing as a licensed occupational therapist or occupational therapy assistant without a current license.

(7)   Engaging in conduct that could result in harm or injury to the public.

(8)   Having an occupational therapy license revoked or suspended or other disciplinary action taken whether in this State or another jurisdiction.

(9)   Being unfit or incompetent to practice occupational therapy by reason of deliberate or negligent acts or omissions regardless of whether actual injury to a patient is established.

(b) The denial, refusal to renew, suspension, revocation or imposition of probationary conditions upon a license may be ordered by the Board after a hearing held in accordance with G.S. Chapter 150B and rules adopted by the Board. An application may be made to the Board for reinstatement of a revoked license if the revocation has been in effect for at least one year. (1983 (Reg. Sess., 1984), c. 1073, s. 1; 1987, c. 827, s. 1; 2005-432, s. 11.)

§ 90-270.77. Fees.

The Board shall adopt and publish, in the manner established by its rules and regulations, fees reasonably necessary to cover the cost of services rendered for the following purposes:

(1) For an initial application, a fee not to exceed ten dollars ($10.00).

(2) For issuance of an initial license, a fee not to exceed one hundred dollars ($100.00).

(3) For the renewal of a license, a fee not to exceed fifty dollars ($50.00).

(4) For the late renewal of a license, a fee not to exceed fifty dollars ($50.00).

(5) Expired.

(6) For copies of Board rules and licensure standards, charges not to exceed the actual cost of printing and mailing. (1983 (Reg. Sess., 1984), c. 1073, s. 1; 2005-432, s. 12.)

§ 90-270.78. False representation of license prohibited.

(a) It is unlawful for any person who is not licensed in accordance with this Article or whose license has been suspended, revoked or not renewed by the Board to:

(1) Engage in the practice of occupational therapy.

(2) Orally, in writing, in print or by sign, or in any other manner, directly or by implication, represent that he or she is engaging in occupational therapy.

(3) Use in connection with his or her name or place of business the words "occupational therapist" or "occupational therapy assistant", or the letters "O.T.", "O.T./L.", "O.T.A.", or "O.T.A./L.", or any other words, letters, abbreviations or insignia indicating or implying that the person is an occupational therapist, or occupational therapy assistant.

(b) Any person who resides in another state or foreign country and who, by use of electronic or other medium, performs any of the acts described as the practice of occupational therapy pursuant to this Article, but is not licensed pursuant to this Article, shall be regarded as practicing occupational therapy without a North Carolina license and is subject to the provisions of this Article and appropriate regulation by the Board. (1983 (Reg. Sess., 1984), c. 1073, s. 1; 2005-432, s. 13; 2008-187, s. 40(c); 2009-570, s. 11.)

§ 90-270.79. Violation a misdemeanor.

Any person who violates any provision of this Article shall be guilty of a Class 1 misdemeanor. Each act of such unlawful practice shall constitute a distinct and separate offense. (1983 (Reg. Sess., 1984), c. 1073, s. 1; 1993, c. 539, s. 648; 1994, Ex. Sess., c. 24, s. 14(c).)

§ 90-270.80. Injunctions.

The Board may make application to any appropriate court for an order enjoining violations of this Article, and upon a showing by the Board that any person has violated or is about to violate this Article, the court may grant an injunction, restraining order, or take other appropriate action. (1983 (Reg. Sess., 1984), c. 1073, s. 1.)

§ 90-270.80A. Civil penalties, disciplinary costs.

(a) Authority to Assess Civil Penalties. - The Board may assess a civil penalty not in excess of one thousand dollars ($1,000) for the violation of any section of this Article or the violation of any rules adopted by the Board. The clear proceeds of any civil penalty assessed under this section shall be remitted to the Civil Penalty and Forfeiture Fund in accordance with G.S. 115C-457.2.

(b) Consideration Factors. - Before imposing and assessing a civil penalty, the Board shall consider the following factors:

(1) The nature, gravity, and persistence of the particular violation.

(2) The appropriateness of the imposition of a civil penalty when considered alone or in combination with other punishment.

(3) Whether the violation was willful and malicious.

(4) Any other factors that would tend to mitigate or aggravate the violations found to exist.

(c) Schedule of Civil Penalties. - The Board shall establish a schedule of civil penalties for violations of this Article and rules adopted by the Board.

(d) Costs. - The Board may assess the costs of disciplinary actions against any person found to be in violation of this Article or rules adopted by the Board. (2005-432, s. 14.)

§ 90-270.81. Persons and practices not affected.

Nothing in this Article shall be construed to prevent or restrict:

(1) Any person registered, certified, credentialed, or licensed to engage in another profession or occupation or any person working under the supervision of a person registered, certified, credentialed, or licensed to engage in another profession or occupation in this State from performing work incidental to the practice of that profession or occupation as long as the person does not represent himself or herself as an occupational therapist or occupational therapy assistant.

(2) Any person employed as an occupational therapist or occupational therapy assistant by the government of the United States, if he or she provides occupational therapy solely under the direction or control of the organization by which he or she is employed.

(3) Any person pursuing a course of study leading to a degree or certificate in occupational therapy at an accredited or approved educational program if the activities and services constitute a part of a supervised course of study and if the person is designated by a title which clearly indicates his or her status as a student or trainee.

(4) Any person fulfilling the supervised fieldwork experience required for licensure under this Article if the person is designated by a title, which clearly indicates his or her status as a student or trainee.

(5) Occupational therapists or occupational therapy assistants licensed in other jurisdictions who are consulting, teaching, or participating in special occupational therapy education projects, demonstrations or courses in this State, provided their evaluation and treatment of patients is minimal.

(6) The practice of occupational therapy by an occupational therapist or occupational therapy assistant licensed in another jurisdiction who comes into this State, whether in person or by use of any electronic or other medium, on an irregular basis, to consult with a North Carolina licensed occupational therapist or occupational therapy assistant or to consult with faculty at an academic facility about education and training. This shall not apply to occupational therapists or occupational therapy assistants residing in a neighboring state and regularly practicing in this State. (1983 (Reg. Sess., 1984), c. 1073, s. 1; 2005-432, s. 15.)

Article 19.

Sterilization Operations.

§ 90-271. Operation lawful upon request of married person or person over 18.

It shall be lawful for any physician or surgeon licensed by this State when so requested by any person 18 years of age or over, or less than 18 years of age if legally married, to perform upon such person a surgical interruption of vas deferens or Fallopian tubes, as the case may be, provided a request in writing is made by such person prior to the performance of such surgical operation, and provided, further, that prior to or at the time of such request a full and reasonable medical explanation is given by such physician or surgeon to such person as to the meaning and consequences of such operation; and provided, further, that the surgical interruption of Fallopian tubes is performed in a hospital or ambulatory surgical facility licensed by the Department of Health and Human Services. (1963, c. 600; 1965, cc. 108, 941; 1971, c. 1231, s. 1; 1973, c. 476, s. 152; c. 998, s. 1; 1977, c. 7; 1979, c. 728; 1997-443, s. 11A.118(a).)

§ 90-272. Operation on unmarried minor.

Any such physician or surgeon may perform a surgical interruption of vas deferens or Fallopian tubes upon any unmarried person under the age of 18 years when so requested in writing by such minor and in accordance with the conditions and requirements set forth in G.S. 90-271, provided that the juvenile court of the county wherein such minor resides, upon petition of the parent or parents, if they be living, or the guardian or next friend of such minor, shall determine that the operation is in the best interest of such minor and shall enter an order authorizing the physician or surgeon to perform such operation. (1963, c. 600; 1971, c. 1231, s. 1.)

§ 90-273. Repealed by Session Laws 1973, c. 998, s. 2.

§ 90-274. No liability for nonnegligent performance of operation.

Subject to the rules of law applicable generally to negligence, no physician or surgeon licensed by this State shall be liable either civilly or criminally by reason of having performed a surgical interruption of vas deferens or Fallopian tubes authorized by the provisions of this Article upon any person in this State. (1963, c. 600.)

§ 90-275. Article does not affect duty of guardian to obtain order permitting guardian to consent to sterilization of a mentally ill or mentally retarded ward.

Nothing in this Article shall be deemed to affect the provisions of G.S. 35A-1245. (1963, c. 600; 2003-13, s. 6.)

Article 20.

Nursing Home Administrator Act.

§ 90-275.1. Title.

This Article shall be known and may be cited as the "Nursing Home Administrator Act." (1969, c. 843, s. 1.)

§ 90-276. Definitions.

For the purposes of this Article and as used herein:

(1) "Administrator-in-training" means an individual registered with the Board who serves a training period under the supervision of a preceptor.

(2) "Board" means the North Carolina State Board of Examiners for Nursing Home Administrators.

(3) "Nursing home" means any institution or facility defined as such for licensing purposes under G.S. 131E-101(6), whether proprietary or nonprofit, including but not limited to nursing homes owned or administered by the federal or State government or any agency or political subdivision thereof and nursing homes operated in combination with a home for the aged or any other facility.

(4) "Nursing home administrator" means a person who administers, manages, supervises, or is in general administrative charge of a nursing home, whether such individual has an ownership interest in such home and whether his functions and duties are shared with one or more individuals.

(5) "Preceptor" means a person who is a licensed and registered nursing home administrator and meets the requirements of the Board to supervise administrators-in-training during the training period. (1969, c. 843, s. 1; 1981, c. 722, s. 3; 1981 (Reg. Sess., 1982), c. 1234, s. 1; 2001-153, s. 1.)

§ 90-277. Composition of Board.

There is created the State Board of Examiners for Nursing Home Administrators. The Board shall consist of seven members. The seven members shall be voting members and shall meet the following criteria:

(1) All shall be individuals representative of the professions and institutions concerned with the care and treatment of chronically ill or infirm elderly patients.

(2) Less than a majority of the Board members shall be representative of a single profession or institutional category.

(3) Three of the Board members shall be licensed nursing home administrators, at least one of whom shall be employed by a for-profit nursing home and at least one of whom shall be employed by a nonprofit nursing home. These three Board members shall be considered as representatives of institutions in construing this section.

(4) Four of the Board members shall be public, noninstitutional members, with no direct financial interest in nursing homes.

(5) The terms of the Board members shall be limited to two consecutive terms.

Effective July 1, 1973, the Governor shall appoint three members, one of whom shall be a licensed nursing home administrator, for terms of three years, and four members, two of whom shall be licensed nursing home administrators, for terms of two years. Thereafter, all terms shall be three years. However, no member shall serve more than two consecutive full terms. Any vacancy occurring in the position of an appointive member shall be filled by the Governor for the unexpired term in the same manner as for new appointments. Appointive members may be removed by the Governor for cause after due notice and hearing.

Any member of the Board shall be automatically removed from the Board upon certification by the Board to the Governor that the member no longer satisfies the criteria set forth in subdivisions (1) through (4) of this section for appointment to the Board. (1969, c. 843, s. 1; 1973, c. 728; 1981, c. 722, s. 4; 1995, c. 86, s. 1.)

§ 90-278. Qualifications for licensure.

The Board shall have authority to issue licenses to qualified persons as nursing home administrators, and shall establish qualification criteria for such nursing home administrators.

(1)   A license as a nursing home administrator shall be issued to any person upon the Board's determination that the person:

a.   Is at least 18 years of age, of good moral character and of sound physical and mental health; and

b.   Has successfully completed the equivalent of two years of college level study (60 semester hours or 96 quarter hours) from an accredited community college, college or university prior to application for licensure;

or

has completed a combination of education and experience, acceptable under rules promulgated by the Board, prior to application for licensure. Under this provision, two years of supervisory experience in a nursing home shall be equated to one year of college study;

c.   Has satisfactorily completed a course prescribed by the Board, which course contains instruction on the services provided by nursing homes, laws governing nursing homes, protection of patient interests and nursing home administration; and

d.   Has successfully completed the training period as an administrator-in-training as prescribed by the Board. If a person has served at least 12 weeks as a hospital administrator or assistant administrator of a hospital-based long-term care nursing unit or hospital-based swing beds licensed under Article 5 of Chapter 131E or Article 2 of Chapter 122C, the Board shall consider this experience comparable to the initial on-the-job portion of the administrator-in-training program only; and

e. Has passed the national and State examinations designed to test for competence in the subject matters referred to in sub-subdivision c. of this subdivision within one year from the date of completion of the administrator-in-training program.

(2) Repealed by Session Laws 1981, c. 722, s. 6.

(3) A temporary license may be issued under requirements and conditions prescribed by the Board to any person to act or serve as administrator of a nursing home without meeting the requirements for full licensure, but only when there are unusual circumstances preventing compliance with the procedures for licensing elsewhere provided by this Article. The temporary license shall be issued by the chairman only for the period prior to the next meeting of the Board, at which time the Board may renew such temporary license for a further period only up to one year. (1969, c. 843, s. 1; 1973, c. 476, s. 128; 1981, c. 722, ss. 5-7; 1981 (Reg. Sess., 1982), c. 1234, s. 2; 1983, c. 737; 1987, c. 492, s. 1; 1991, c. 710, s. 1; 2013-346, s. 1.)

§ 90-279. Licensing function.

The Board shall license nursing home administrators in accordance with rules and regulations issued and from time to time revised by it. A nursing home administrator's license shall not be transferable and shall be valid until expiration or until suspended or revoked for violation of this Article or of the standards established by the Board pursuant to this Article. Denial of issuance or renewal, suspension or revocation by the Board shall be subject to the provisions of Chapter 150B of the General Statutes. (1969, c. 843, s. 1; 1973, c. 1331, s. 3; 1987, c. 827, s. 1.)

§ 90-280. Fees; display of license; duplicate license; inactive list.

(a) Each applicant for an examination administered by the Board and each applicant for an administrator-in-training program and reciprocity endorsement shall pay a processing fee set by the Board not to exceed five hundred dollars ($500.00) plus the actual cost of the exam.

(b)   Each person licensed as a nursing home administrator shall be required to pay a license fee in an amount set by the Board not to exceed one thousand dollars ($1,000). A license shall expire on the thirtieth day of September of the second year following its issuance and shall be renewable biennially upon payment of a renewal fee set by the Board not to exceed one thousand dollars ($1,000).

(c)   Each person licensed as a nursing home administrator shall display his or her license certificate, along with the current certificate of renewal, in a conspicuous place in his or her place of employment.

(d)   Any person licensed as a nursing home administrator may receive a duplicate license or verification of license by payment of a fee set by the Board not to exceed one hundred dollars ($100.00).

(e)   Any person licensed as a nursing home administrator who is not acting, serving, or holding himself or herself out to be a nursing home administrator may have his or her name placed on an inactive list for such period of time not to exceed four years upon payment of a fee set by the Board not to exceed two hundred dollars ($200.00) per year. Each year during that four-year period, upon request and payment of the fee, the person's name may remain on an inactive list for one additional year.

(f)   Any person having a temporary license issued pursuant to G.S. 90-278(3) shall pay a fee in an amount set by the Board not to exceed five hundred dollars ($500.00). If the Board renews the temporary license, no further fee shall be required.

(g)   The Board may set fees not to exceed one thousand dollars ($1,000) for conducting and administering initial training and continuing education courses, and may set a fee not to exceed one hundred dollars ($100.00) per hour for certifying a course submitted for review by another individual or agency wishing to offer such courses or may set an annual fee not to exceed four thousand dollars ($4,000) for certifying a course provider in lieu of certifying each course offered by the provider. (1969, c. 843, s. 1; 1977, c. 652; 1979, 2nd Sess., c. 1282; 1981 (Reg. Sess., 1982), c. 1234, s. 4; 1983, c. 215; 1995 (Reg. Sess., 1996), c. 645, s. 1; 1999-217, s. 1; 2013-346, s. 2.)

§ 90-281. Collection of funds.

All fees and other moneys collected and received by the Board shall be handled as provided by law and as prescribed by the State Treasurer. Such funds shall be used and expended by the Board to pay the compensation and travel expenses of members and employees of the Board and other expenses necessary for the Board to administer and carry out the provisions of this Article. (1969, c. 843, s. 1; 1983, c. 913, s. 10.)

§ 90-282. Repealed by Session Laws 1981, c. 722, s. 8, effective July 1, 1981.

§ 90-283. Organization of Board; compensation; employees and services.

The Board shall elect from its membership a chairman, vice-chairman and secretary, and shall adopt rules and regulations to govern its proceedings. Board members shall be entitled to receive only such compensation and reimbursement as is prescribed by Chapter 93B of the General Statutes for State boards generally. At any meeting a majority of the voting members shall constitute a quorum. The Board shall have the power to employ or retain professional personnel, including legal counsel subject to G.S. 114-2.3, and clerical or other special personnel deemed necessary to carry out the provisions of this Article. (1969, c. 843, s. 1; 1981, c. 722, s. 9; 2001-153, s. 2; 2013-346, s. 3.)

§ 90-284. Exclusive jurisdiction of Board.

The Board shall have exclusive authority to determine the qualifications, skill and fitness of any person to serve as an administrator of a nursing home under the provisions of this Article, and the holder of a license under the provisions of this Article shall be deemed qualified to serve as the administrator of a nursing home for all purposes. (1969, c. 843, s. 1.)

§ 90-285. Functions and duties of the Board.

The Board shall meet at least once annually in Raleigh or any other location designated by the chairman and shall have the following functions and duties:

(1)   Develop, impose and enforce rules and regulations setting out standards which must be met by individuals in order to receive and hold a license as a nursing home administrator, which standards shall be designed to insure that nursing home administrators shall be individuals who are of good character and who are otherwise suitable, by education, training and experience in the field of institutional administration, to serve as nursing home administrators.

(2)   Develop and apply appropriate methods and procedures, including examination and investigations, for determining whether individuals meet such standards, and administer an examination at least twice each year at such times and places as the Board shall designate.

(3)   Issue licenses to qualified individuals consistent with G.S. 90-278 and G.S. 90-287 and any rules adopted by the Board implementing those provisions.

(4)   Establish and implement procedures designed to insure that individuals licensed as nursing home administrators will, during any period that they serve as such, comply with the requirements of such standards.

(5)   Receive, investigate, and take appropriate action with respect to any charge or complaint filed with the Board to the effect that any individual licensed as a nursing home administrator has failed to comply with the requirements of such standards.

(6)   Conduct a continuing study and investigation of nursing homes and nursing home administrators within the State in order to make improvements in the standards imposed for the licensing of administrators and of procedures and methods for the enforcement of such standards, and to raise the quality of nursing home administration in such other ways as may be effective.

(7)   Conduct, or cause to be conducted by contract or otherwise, one or more courses of instruction and training sufficient to meet the requirements of this Article, and make provisions for the conduct of such courses and their accessibility to residents of this State, unless it finds that there are sufficient

courses conducted by others within this State. In lieu thereof the Board may approve courses conducted within and without this State as sufficient to meet the education and training requirements of this Article.

(8) Make rules and regulations, not inconsistent with law, as may be necessary for the proper performance of its duties, and to take such other actions as may be necessary to enable the State to meet the requirements set forth in section 1908 of the Social Security Act, the federal rules and regulations promulgated thereunder, and other pertinent federal authority.

(9) Receive and disburse any funds appropriated or given to the Board, including any federal funds, to carry out the purposes of this Article.

(10) Maintain a register of all applications for licensing and registration of nursing home administrators, which register shall show: the place or residence, name and age of each applicant; the name and address of employer or business connection of each applicant; the date of application; information of educational and experience qualifications; the action taken by the Board and the dates; the serial number of the license issued to the applicant; and such other pertinent information as may be deemed necessary.

(11) Develop an administrator-in-training program to insure that nursing home administrators have adequate training and experience prior to licensure. (1969, c. 843, s. 1; 1981, c. 722, ss. 10, 11; 1981 (Reg. Sess., 1982), c. 1234, s. 3; 2013-346, s. 4.)

§ 90-285.1. Suspension, revocation or refusal to issue a license.

The Board may suspend, revoke, or refuse to issue a license or may reprimand or otherwise discipline a licensee after due notice and an opportunity to be heard at a formal hearing, upon substantial evidence that a licensee:

(1) Has violated the provisions of this Article or the rules adopted by the Board;

(2) Has violated the provisions of Part 2 of Article 6 of Chapter 131E of the General Statutes and rules promulgated thereunder;

(3)   Has been convicted of, or has tendered and has had accepted a plea of no contest to, a criminal offense showing professional unfitness;

(4)   Has practiced fraud, deceit, or misrepresentation in securing or procuring a nursing home administrator license;

(5)   Is incompetent to engage in the practice of nursing home administration or to act as a nursing home administrator;

(6)   Has practiced fraud, deceit, or misrepresentation in his or her capacity as a nursing home administrator;

(7)   Has committed acts of misconduct in the operation of a nursing home under his jurisdiction;

(8)   Repealed by Session Laws 2013-346, s. 5, effective July 23, 2013.

(9)   Is addicted or dependent upon the use of alcohol or any controlled substance, including morphine, opium, cocaine, or other drugs recognized as resulting in abnormal behavior;

(10)   Has practiced without being registered biennially;

(11)   Has transferred or surrendered possession of, either temporarily or permanently, his or her license or certificate to any other person;

(12)   Has paid, given, has caused to be paid or given or offered to pay or to give to any person a commission or other valuable consideration for the solicitation or procurement, either directly or indirectly, of nursing home patronage;

(13)   Has been guilty of fraudulent, misleading, or deceptive advertising;

(14)   Has falsely impersonated another licensee;

(15)   Has failed to exercise regard for the safety, health or life of the patient;

(16)   Has permitted unauthorized disclosure of information relating to a patient or his or her records; or

(17) Has discriminated among patients, employees, or staff on account of race, gender, religion, color, national origin, mental or physical disability, or any other class protected by State or federal law. (1981, c. 722, s. 12; 2001-153, s. 3; 2008-187, s. 41; 2013-346, s. 5.)

§ 90-286. Renewal of license.

Every holder of a nursing home administrator's license shall renew it biennially by application to the Board. The Board shall grant renewals when the applicant has paid the fee required by this Article and has satisfactorily completed continuing education courses as may be prescribed by the Board, unless the Board finds that the applicant has acted or failed to act in such a manner as would constitute grounds for suspension, revocation or denial of a license as provided by this Article. The Board shall adopt rules defining the content of continuing education courses approved or required by it under this section and shall make a copy of these rules available to each licensee. The Board shall not require any licensee to successfully complete more than 30 hours of continuing education courses every two years. The Board shall certify and administer continuing education courses for nursing home administrators and shall keep a record of the courses successfully completed by each licensee. (1969, c. 843, s. 1; 1981, c. 722, s. 13; 1983, c. 72.)

§ 90-287. Reciprocity with other states.

The Board may issue a nursing home administrator's license to any person who holds a current license as a nursing home administrator from another jurisdiction, provided that the Board finds that the standards for licensure in such other jurisdiction are at least the substantial equivalent of those prevailing in this State and that the applicant has passed the national and the State examinations administered by the Board and is otherwise qualified. (1969, c. 843, s. 1; 2013-346, s. 6.)

§ 90-288. Misdemeanor.

It shall be unlawful and constitute a Class 1 misdemeanor,

(1) For any person to act or serve in the capacity as, or hold himself out to be, a nursing home administrator, or use any title, sign, or other indication that he is a nursing home administrator, unless he is the holder of a valid license as a nursing home administrator, issued in accordance with the provisions of this Article, and

(2) For any person to violate any of the provisions of this Article or any rules and regulations issued pursuant thereto. (1969, c. 843, s. 1; 1993, c. 539, s. 649; 1994, Ex. Sess., c. 24, s. 14(c).)

§ 90-288.01. Criminal history record checks of applicants for licensure.

(a) The following definitions apply in this section:

(1) Applicant. - A person applying for initial licensure pursuant to either G.S. 90-278 or G.S. 90-287 or applying for renewal of licensure pursuant to G.S. 90-286.

(2) Criminal history. - A history of conviction of a state or federal crime, whether a misdemeanor or felony, that bears on an applicant's fitness for licensure as a nursing home administrator. The crimes include the criminal offenses set forth in any of the following Articles of Chapter 14 of the General Statutes: Article 5, Counterfeiting and Issuing Monetary Substitutes; Article 5A, Endangering Executive, Legislative, and Court Officers; Article 6, Homicide; Article 7A, Rape and Other Sex Offenses; Article 8, Assaults; Article 10, Kidnapping and Abduction; Article 13, Malicious Injury or Damage by Use of Explosive or Incendiary Device or Material; Article 14, Burglary and Other Housebreakings; Article 15, Arson and Other Burnings; Article 16, Larceny; Article 17, Robbery; Article 18, Embezzlement; Article 19, False Pretenses and Cheats; Article 19A, Obtaining Property or Services by False or Fraudulent Use of Credit Device or Other Means; Article 19B, Financial Transaction Card Crime Act; Article 20, Frauds; Article 21, Forgery; Article 26, Offenses Against Public Morality and Decency; Article 26A, Adult Establishments; Article 27, Prostitution; Article 28, Perjury; Article 29, Bribery; Article 31, Misconduct in Public Office; Article 35, Offenses Against the Public Peace; Article 36A, Riots, Civil Disorders, and Emergencies; Article 39, Protection of Minors; Article 40, Protection of the Family; Article 59, Public Intoxication; and Article 60, Computer-Related Crime. The crimes also include possession or sale of drugs

in violation of the North Carolina Controlled Substances Act, Article 5 of Chapter 90 of the General Statutes, and alcohol-related offenses, including sale to underage persons in violation of G.S. 18B-302 or driving while impaired in violation of G.S. 20-138.1 through G.S. 20-138.5.

(b) Criminal History Record Check. - The Board shall require a criminal history record check of all applicants for initial licensure and temporary licensure. The Board, in its discretion, may require a criminal history record check of an applicant for license renewal. Refusal to consent to a criminal history record check may constitute grounds for the Board to deny licensure to an applicant. The Board shall provide to the North Carolina Department of Justice the fingerprints of the applicant to be checked, a form signed by the applicant consenting to the criminal history record check and the use of fingerprints and other identifying information required by the State or National Repositories, and any additional information required by the Department of Justice. The Board shall keep all information obtained pursuant to this section confidential. The Board shall collect any fees required by the Department of Justice and shall remit the fees to the Department of Justice for expenses associated with conducting the criminal history record check.

(c) Convictions. - If the applicant's criminal history record check reveals one or more convictions listed under subdivision (2) of subsection (a) of this section, the conviction shall not automatically bar licensure. The Board shall consider all of the following factors regarding the conviction:

(1) The level of seriousness of the crime.

(2) The date of the crime.

(3) The age of the applicant at the time of the conviction.

(4) The circumstances surrounding the commission of the crime, if known.

(5) The nexus between the criminal conduct of the applicant and the job duties of the position to be filled.

(6) The applicant's prison, jail, probation, parole, rehabilitation, and employment records since the date the crime was committed.

(7) The subsequent commission by the applicant of a crime listed in subsection (a) of this section.

(d) Denial of Licensure. - Except as otherwise provided by law, if the Board refuses to issue or renew a license based on information obtained in a criminal history record check, the Board shall not provide a copy of the criminal history record check to the applicant. An applicant has the right to appear before the Board to appeal the Board's decision. An appearance before the Board shall constitute an exhaustion of administrative remedies in accordance with Chapter 150B of the General Statutes.

(e) Limited Immunity. - The Board, its officers and employees, acting in good faith and in compliance with this section, shall be immune from civil liability for its actions based on information provided in an applicant's criminal history record check. (2008-183, s. 1; 2012-12, s. 2(kk); 2013-346, s. 7.)

§ 90-288.02. Confidentiality of investigative records.

Records, papers, and other documents containing information collected and compiled by or on behalf of the Board as a result of an investigation, inquiry, or interview conducted in connection with certification, licensure, or a disciplinary matter shall not be considered public records within the meaning of Chapter 132 of the General Statutes. Any notice or statement of charges, notice of hearing, or decision rendered in connection with a hearing shall be a public record. Information that identifies a resident who has not consented to the public disclosure of services rendered to him or her by a person certified or licensed under this Chapter shall be deleted from the public record. All other records, papers, and documents containing information collected and compiled by or on behalf of the Board shall be public records, but any information that identifies a resident who has not consented to the public disclosure of services rendered to him or her shall be deleted. (2013-346, s. 8.)

§ 90-288.03. Reserved for future codification purposes.

§ 90-288.04. Reserved for future codification purposes.

§ 90-288.05. Reserved for future codification purposes.

§ 90-288.06. Reserved for future codification purposes.

§ 90-288.07. Reserved for future codification purposes.

§ 90-288.08. Reserved for future codification purposes.

§ 90-288.09. Reserved for future codification purposes.

Article 20A.

Assisted Living Administrator Act.

§ 90-288.10. Title.

This Article shall be known as the Assisted Living Administrator Act. (1999-443, s. 1.)

§ 90-288.11. Purpose.

The administrators of assisted living residences are responsible for the residents who require daily care to attend to their physical, mental, and emotional needs. Therefore, the certification of assisted living administrators is necessary to ensure adequate levels of care across the State and to protect public health, safety, and welfare. (1999-443, s. 1.)

§ 90-288.12. Certification required; exemptions.

(a) No person shall perform or offer to perform services as an assisted living administrator unless the person has been certified under the provisions of this Article. A certificate granted under this Article shall be valid throughout the State.

(b) The provisions of this Article shall not apply to:

(1) Combination homes as defined in G.S. 131E-101 and hospitals that contain adult care beds.

(2) Family care homes as defined in G.S. 131D-2.1(9).

(3) Continuing care facilities, as defined in Article 64 of Chapter 58 of the General Statutes, if adult care beds are housed in the same facility as nursing home beds. (1999-443, s. 1; 2009-462, s. 4(b).)

§ 90-288.13. Definitions.

The following definitions apply in this Article:

(1) Administrator-in-training. - An individual who serves a training period under the supervision of an approved preceptor.

(2) Assisted living administrator. - An individual certified to operate, administer, manage, and supervise an assisted living residence or to share in the performance of these duties with another person who has been so certified.

(3) Assisted living residence. - A facility defined in G.S. 131D-2.1(5), whether proprietary or nonprofit. The term also includes institutions or facilities that are owned or administered by the federal or State government or any agency or political subdivision of the State government.

(4) Department. - The Department of Health and Human Services.

(5) Preceptor. - An individual who is certified by the Department as an assisted living administrator and who meets the requirements established by the Department to serve as a supervisor of administrators-in-training. (1999-443, s. 1; 2009-462, s. 4(c).)

§ 90-288.14. Assisted living administrator certification.

An applicant shall be certified by the Department as an assisted living administrator if the applicant meets all of the following qualifications:

(1) Is at least 21 years old.

(2) Provides a satisfactory criminal background report from the State Repository of Criminal Histories, which shall be provided by the State Bureau of Investigation upon its receiving fingerprints from the applicant. If the applicant has been a resident of this State for less than five years, the applicant shall provide a satisfactory criminal background report from both the State and National Repositories of Criminal Histories.

(3) Successfully completes the equivalent of two years of coursework at an accredited college or university or has a combination of education and experience as approved by the Department.

(4) Successfully completes a Department approved administrator-in-training program of at least 120 hours of study in courses relating to assisted living residences.

(5) Successfully completes a written examination administered by the Department. (1999-443, s. 1.)

§ 90-288.15. Issuance, renewal, and replacement of certificates.

(a) The Department shall issue a certificate to any applicant who has satisfactorily met the requirements of this Article. The certificate shall show the full name of the person and an identification number and shall be signed by the Secretary of the Department. A certificate may not be transferred or assigned.

(b) All certificates shall expire on December 31 of the second year following issuance. All applications for renewal shall be filed with the Department and shall be accompanied by documentation of the certificate holder's completion of the annual continuing education requirements established by the Department regarding the management and operation of an assisted living residence.

(c) The Department shall replace any certificate that is lost, destroyed, or mutilated subject to rules established by the Department. (1999-443, s. 1.)

§ 90-288.15A. Fees.

The Department may impose fees not to exceed the following amounts:

(1) Assisted Living Administrator

| Examination Fee | $50.00 |

(2) Assisted Living Administrator Certificate

| Renewal Fee | $30.00 |

every two years.

(2010-31, s. 10.36A(b).)

§ 90-288.16. Certification by reciprocity.

The Department may grant, upon application, a certificate to a person who holds a valid certificate as an assisted living community administrator issued by another state if, in the Department's determination, the standards of competency for the certificate are substantially equivalent to those in this State. (1999-443, s. 1.)

Vision Books Order Form

Fax Orders:	1-980-299-5965
Phone Orders:	1-704-898-0770
E-mail Orders:	www.visionbooks.org
Mail Orders:	Vision Books, LLC P.O. Box 42406 Charlotte, NC 28215

Shipp To:
Name_____
Address_____
City_____State_____Zip_____
Phone_____Fax_____
Email_____@_____

Bill To: We can bill a third party on your behalf.
Name_____
Address_____
City_____State_____Zip_____
Phone____(_____)_____Fax_____
Email_____@_____

Pamphlet Number ($15.00 Each)	Qty	Total Cost
_____	_____	_____
_____	_____	_____
_____	_____	_____
_____	_____	_____
_____	_____	_____
_____	_____	_____
_____	_____	_____
_____	_____	_____
Full Volume Set 1-92	**92 Pamphlets**	**1,380.00**

Free Shipping Shipping & Handling on Full Volume Orders
Add $1.00 Shipping & Handling per pamphlet $_____

Total Cost $_____

Thank you for your support. Management!

DID YOU ENJOY THIS BOOK?

Vision Books, LLC would like to hear from you! If you or someone you know has been fasely imprisoned, we would like to hear your story. If the 'North Carolina Criminal Law and Procedure' has had an effect in your life or if you have suggestions, we would like to hear from you. Send your letters to:

Vision Books, LLC
Attn: Staff Writers
P.O. Box 42406
Charlotte, NC 28215
Email: staff@visionbooks.org

Order Additional Copies:

Fax Orders:	1-980-299-5965
Phone Orders:	1-704-898-0770
E-mail Orders:	www.visionbooks.org
Mail Orders:	Vision Books, LLC P.O. Box 42406 Charlotte, NC 28215

www.ingramcontent.com/pod-product-compliance
Lightning Source LLC
Chambersburg PA
CBHW051628170526
45167CB00001B/99